THE RETURN OF KING ARTHUR

THE RETURN OF
KING ARTHUR

_Completing the Quest
for Wholeness, Inner Strength,
and Self-Knowledge_

DIANA DURHAM

Jeremy P. Tarcher/Penguin
a member of Penguin Group (USA) Inc. New York

Most Tarcher/Penguin books are available at special quantity discounts for bulk purchase for sales promotions, premiums, fund-raising, and educational needs. Special books or book excerpts also can be created to fit specific needs. For details, write Penguin Group (USA) Inc. Special Markets, 375 Hudson Street, New York, NY 10014.

Jeremy P. Tarcher/Penguin
a member of
Penguin Group (USA) Inc.
375 Hudson Street
New York, NY 10014
www.penguin.com

Library of Congress Cataloging-in-Publication Data

Durham, Diana.
The return of King Arthur : completing the quest for wholeness, inner strength, and self-knowledge / by Diana Durham.
p.   cm.
Includes bibliographical references.
ISBN 1-58542-297-5
1. Self-actualization (Psychology).   2. Jungian psychology.
3. Arthurian romances—History and criticism.   4. Grail—Legends—History and criticism.   I. Title.
BF637.S4D88   2004   2003060393
158.1—dc22

Printed in the United States of America
1   3   5   7   9   10   8   6   4   2

This book is printed on acid-free paper. ∞

Book design by Kate Nichols

For Jonathan, Raphael and Aidyn—

and for the One
we all are and serve

Let not your heart be troubled,
neither let it be afraid.

CONTENTS

FOREWORD

The Western world lost one of its great treasures by relegating Myth to the level of children's stories. Before that disastrous move (about the time of the French enlightenment) we were deeply nourished by the teachings of mythology. Young or old, educated or not, extroverted or introverted—the profound truths of the inner world were easily available to us.

Myths have a sublime power to transcend time and speak in a language that bridges the chasms in our world that threaten to annihilate us. The Grail Myth is probably the last great offering of the collective unconscious and is the most pertinent of all its treasures. We are in the midst of this great story, all of us agonizing from the fisher king wound, driven to find the Grail Castle, tugging at the sword maddeningly stuck in the stone. To find the modern relevance of this story is to set one instantly on his own intimate search.

Diana Durham does masterful work in bringing this jewel of the Western world into just such relevance; she makes it possible to begin one's own grail quest in terms understandable for our present mentality. Not the least of Ms. Durham's skills is to bring the place of women out of obscurity and thus provide focal points essential to understanding this great Myth.

—Robert A. Johnson, D.Hum.
Author of *He; She; Inner Work; We;*
Owning Your Own Shadow

INTRODUCTION

HAVE YOU EVER HAD a dream that leapt out at you? A flow of image and emotion so vivid that instead of dissolving almost instantly when you wake up, it stays with you long enough for its meaning to be pondered consciously. Parts of the dream may seem nonsensical, parts realistic. Sometimes I have been able to have a conversation or dialogue between a dream of mine and events and issues in my life, between subconscious and conscious understanding. Real life appears to be rational and ordered, but in a sense it has no meaning or order until we can create or perceive it. The dream may seem irrational, but it contains symbols that encode meaning. The two can help illumine each other so that a synthesis of understanding arises out of the interaction between the one and the other that may lead to a deeper understanding of our waking experience.

Myths are like these vivid dreams. They are not always easy to understand, and their symbolism can at times appear illogical, but an interplay between the myth and our experience can also open up healing insight into our lives. Jungian analysts frequently use myth to help penetrate the problems and phobias of their patients. But myths do not float up out of one individual's subconscious mind; they emerge out of the collective subconscious and are held in the collective memory. This means that they can illuminate and give meaning not only to the individual life but also to the life of a whole society.

In this book I share the insights that I have gained from over 15 years of dialogue and reflection between the myths of King Arthur and the quest for the Grail and what has been essentially the spiritual journey—or quest—of my life.

The two entwined tales of King Arthur and the Quest for the Grail are deeply embedded in Western culture, emerging as they appear to have done simultaneously in Britain, parts of Europe, and Ireland. And they have been told and retold in countless ways through countless centuries. Arthur, who has been brought up in obscurity and with the magician Merlin as his teacher, draws the sword Excalibur from the stone and as a result becomes king. He unites the kingdom of Britain for the first time and establishes the Knights of the Round Table. During his reign the quest for the Grail is embarked on. The story of the Grail quest features a naive and impulsive young man called Perceval, who, after being knighted by King Arthur sets off on the quest for the Grail. He comes upon the Grail Castle, the place where the Grail chalice (or cup) is kept. It is also home to a strange figure called the Wounded Fisher King, who presides over a wasteland kingdom, which is a reflection of his wound. This wound will not be healed or the wasteland restored until Perceval asks whom the Grail serves. On this first visit to the Grail Castle, Perceval fails to ask about the Grail, and the rest of the story is about finding his way back there, and asking the question.

I have found it a fascinating and pleasurable process to unlock bit by bit the complex and rich symbolism of these tales, and I hope that the reader of this book will share that fascination and pleasure. But my aim in writing it all down is that the insights the myths reveal will be helpful to others in understanding the dynamics of the spiritual quest that I believe in one way or another underlie each individual's life.

However, as I have said, myths elucidate much more than just the individual life—whether that be mine or anyone else's. Myths belong to the collective unconscious and throw light on the collective life. This is certainly the case with the stories of King Arthur and the Grail quest. Therefore, this book also offers a perspective on what can appear to be the confusing nature of the times we are living in, when old structures are breaking down and the new have not yet formed clearly enough for us to see, again based on the meaning of the symbolism of these two interconnected legends.

Both strands of these stories derive from many sources. There are numerous early writings, particularly Welsh, recorded in the twelfth century—when the oral tradition began to break down—but dating from the sixth, eighth, and ninth centuries, which mention Arthur in passing. From the twelfth to the fifteenth centuries there was an outpouring of pseudohistories, romances, and Grail texts, some of the best known of which are Geoffrey of Monmouth's "History of the Kings of Britain," Thomas Malory's "Morte D'Arthur," and Chrétien de Troyes' "Perceval."

These sources divide roughly into the Arthur stories and the Grail stories. The content of the Arthur stories may derive in part from an actual historical leader of the fifth or sixth century who fought off Saxon invaders, and from Celtic folklore. In fact both strands contain echoes of Celtic legend, and in the Grail stories there is also symbolism that appears to be rooted in ancient fertility cults and eastern Mediterranean mystery religions.

Out of all of this complexity of derivation, the symbolism of these stories bobs up and speaks to us like a dream that has surfaced out of our collective subconscious mind, and it is their meaning and relevance to us now that I am concerned with in this book, not their genealogy, or whether they are historically accurate.

The Grail stories are set within the backdrop of the King Arthur tales. Perceval sets off on his quest after Arthur has drawn the sword from the stone and founded Camelot. This nestling of one story within the other is itself significant, because it is my belief that the quest for the Grail symbolizes essentially the inner spiritual journey toward the source of being *that can only happen as it is undertaken individually.* In other words, the quest for the Grail is the story of the individual growth toward wholeness, while the story of King Arthur and the Round Table pertains more to the outer world in which we find ourselves. (That said, there are some symbols and events within the Grail stories that pertain to society as a whole, just as there are symbols within the Arthur stories that can be interpreted on the basis of the individual experience.) The main point anyway is that the individual journey is set within the backdrop of the larger life and outworking of society.

For most of us that larger, outer world will usually have at least two major components: an immediate, community setting such as our family, or neighborhood, college, or workplace; and the wider community still of the global society. In my case the more immediate context that has been significant is a network of intentional spiritual communities and connected friends. My individual life and process has been set against the backdrop of this collective life for over 25 years. I have lived both communally and conventionally but always in association with the larger network. Witnessing—and participating in—the story of this network is what has helped afford me insight into the meaning of the King Arthur strand of these stories; that is, the strand that relates to the collective story.

I first began thinking about the Arthur and Grail legends 20 years ago while living in one of these communities. We were about 50 people, with a network of several hundred others associated through events, a mailing list, and personal friendships. Central to all of this activity was a coherent system of leadership. The founder of the network and others who had responsibility for the different communities took on the role—in theory only temporarily—of spiritual "God"-parent to those living in or associating with the communities. This figure of spiritual mentor or God-parent is symbolized in the myths by King Arthur. If the trust and the connection went deep enough, this spiritual parenting could create a safe space that allowed old insecurities and inadequacies to surface and be healed. The intent was always that the individual would be "weaned" from this parent/child or leader/follower relationship on to his or her own experience of wholeness. The aim of both the leadership and the community network itself was to "grow" spiritual maturity in as many as were drawn to participate, the bottom-line belief being that changing or healing one's own consciousness is the most effective way to make a difference in the world one lives in.

From my own experience, I can attest to the fact that when this God-parenting process worked, it *really* worked. It was amazingly healing and empowering, going far beyond the reach of traditional therapies. However, learning to live in this openness together could also be extremely uncomfortable because the forces released within one's own subconscious when in the presence of someone truly able to offer blessing and healing can at times be almost overwhelming in their intensity and depth. My reflections on the stories of Arthur and the Grail took shape as I moved through this territory and observed others moving through it, experiencing both its marvels and its terrors. I thought of it as the surreal terrain of the quest: full of dark woods, strange portents, black knights; and of dreadful adventures: being unhorsed, fighting with giants, marooned in the Perilous Chapel. I saw how on the one hand it is a troublous and frightening landscape; and how on the other, when something suddenly clears in consciousness, and innocence shines out like the naked children sitting in the tree who guide Perceval on his way, one is instantly transported to the Grail Castle with its numinous gift of blessing.

The more I thought about my individual and our collective experiences, the more they shed light on the meaning of the Arthur and Grail myths, and the more I thought about these myths, the more they shed light on our experience. To begin with, it was the Grail quest stories and symbolism that caught my attention, elucidating, as I believe they do, the topography of the inner landscape one has to travel through *as an individual* in order to achieve some degree of spiritual maturity. But as the collective story of our network started to apparently unravel after the death of its founder, it was the story of the dissolution of the Round Table that I focused on, particularly the very end of Arthur's story when he commands Sir Bedivere to throw the sword Excalibur into the lake.

There is nothing unusual about a movement or a community—even a corporation—starting to founder when the person who initiated and led it is no longer around. It is almost predictable that this will happen. And so it was with us. People left, some of the communities had to be sold, there were financial problems, and there was a sense of betrayal in many who had dedicated their lives to the "cause" and now found themselves in a sense out of a job, or—for those who had lived communally for many years—with little or no income and poor employment prospects. For about a decade, all was confusion, and attempts to reconfigure in new ways could not seem to make headway.

Had the sword gone into the lake, had everything been lost? And what about the Grail? Had I or my peers and friends become emotionally whole and matured into a fully grounded expression of spiritual identity and source? Had the Grail been found, and if so, why couldn't it help the situation—after all, the Grail is supposed to be able to restore the wound and the wasteland. If our troubles were multiplying, what implication did this have for the success—or not—of our spiritual mission?

Puzzling over these questions and pondering back and forth between the King Arthur and Grail legends and what was happening to our network, I found the insights that gradually emerged to be the most exciting of all. When the sword is thrown into the lake, it marks the end of the time when we located authority in someone else. And so it also marks the end of our dependency on those leaders who wielded that sword on our behalf, who played the role of spiritual mentor for us. But more than this, I believe it also marks the transition from leadership being held by one lone patriarch to a time when leadership is held collectively.

In the end no one person organized our network back into coherence. It happened, and is still happening, spontaneously, as bit by bit, almost one by one, different individuals have emerged out of the waters of chaos and confusion, having sufficiently completed the internal, individual work that the spiritual quest entails. The leadership of the network has been reconfigured collectively so that a small grouping share the leadership. Moreover, the nature of that leadership is no longer that of spiritual parent to child but of peer to peer. And we find ourselves forming not so much a physical community anymore but what might be called a field of oneness, an experience, still new, of functioning as different aspects of the one consciousness.

The Grail is found in the legends, and finding the Grail symbolizes not only the individual experience of open-hearted connection to spiritual source in *oneself* but also the emergence of the possibility of collective leadership. When Arthur throws that sword into the lake, a woman's hand reaches up to take it. A new opportunity has been fertilized: a new union between masculine and feminine, and the emergence of an era of collective sovereignty. When we talk about the rise of the feminine we are describing a crucial aspect of this new era. Obviously this new possibility has been emerging for some time in the form of the suffragettes and the women's movement. Closely allied with the struggle for equal rights for women was the civil rights movement in the United States. Leadership has been rising up from the grassroots, bringing immense changes and balancing out some of the injustices of society's myopic structures. Collective leadership implies both the roundness of the chalice cup—without hierarchy, containing all—the feminine; and the absoluteness of the sword, the element of individual responsibility required for true leadership: the masculine.

Very often the emotional echo of those vivid dreams that we are able to recall even on waking haunts us long after their imagery has faded, suffused as they are by a longing, sometimes even a tasting—of what? It's difficult to put into words: something to do with the life lived in us, the power of it, the love, desire, and beauty of it released and fused together and *embodied* in a way we know in the dream is deeply natural to us, and yet that, upon waking, we remember also is only too fleeting.

So it is with the legends of King Arthur and the Grail quest. When we hear these stories, whether in their entirety or in snatches here and there, in children's storybooks, or in a film like John Boorman's *Excalibur,* long after we have forgotten the details of what happened, the emotional memory of them remains. For these stories touch deep places of longing within us—for potency, for brotherhood. I believe the sensing of a different way to live that both our dreams and the myths evoke in us has something to do with our hearts being imprisoned, not fully available for our expression. We are hemmed in, trapped. Imagine for a moment that the Grail chalice, a cup made of the purest gold and embedded with priceless gems, represents our heart realm. It is to find this precious Grail cup that Perceval embarks on the quest. He comes upon it in the Grail Castle, which is the home of a strange wounded king.

Our heart has been in the charge of a wound. The myth is about how to heal this wound and how to free the heart.

Therefore, the era of the collective Grail, of collective leadership, is also the era of the healing of the heart realm. I believe this quest for healing the heart has been the core motivation—and is the true legacy— of my generation, the baby boomer generation. We were brought up in the aftermath of World War II, and the images of Auschwitz and Dachau broke in on our consciousness when we were still quite young. The mushroom clouds of first the A-bomb, dropped on Hiroshima and Nagasaki, and then the H-bomb, which fueled the Cold War nuclear proliferation, arose like giant question marks over our growing up and young adulthood. How could these things have happened? What were the changes needed in us as human beings to put an end to the madness?

These questions spurred first a rebellion against the old order, then, as the youth movements of the 1960s and 1970s matured and differentiated, protest led to self-exploration and the manifold developments in what have been termed the New Age and alternative fields, all exploring essentially the spiritual/healing/emotional dimensions of being. The path to the heart is the spiritual path. The heart cannot be healed until identity is made whole and is rooted in the spiritual source of oneself.

As this change gradually takes place, authority returns to the individual and begins to seep away from its traditional depositories. I see the same transition from singular to collective leadership that happened in our spiritual network paralleled in the larger world. Companies are changing their structure from one unwieldy chain of command, with all the power pushed up to the top, to a collection of smaller, "team-based" units. When the allied forces brought together by George Bush Senior wished to undertake military action within Iraq, they sought the authority to do so from the United Nations in a series of resolutions: the war was fought as a collective action—America and its allies, and with the sanction of leadership collectively configured in the form of the UN.

The dynamics of collective leadership are new and still revealing themselves. In my experience, they emerge as the healing in the heart is filled out, because when we know something of this healing in the heart, we also immediately know that our heart realm is the medium of connection with everyone else we come into contact with. We feel a greater sense of oneness with others. We can see that we are all parts of one whole. Sometimes those vivid dreams contain an experience of a union with another person or persons that is so deep there is no differentiation between the emotional/sexual/spiritual components of the experience, a kind of connection that goes way beyond what we are normally able to share. While I am not in any way saying that we are supposed to feel this way about everyone we meet, I do believe there is an emotional truth to these dreams; I think they are telling us about the inherent oneness that exists between us. We cannot really participate in the collective nature of our times until we know this oneness. And we cannot know the oneness until our own hearts are freed.

The wasteland presided over by the wounded king was a reflection of his wound and would only be restored when the wound was healed. The wound produces a wasteland. A fragmented identity, one that does not know oneness, leads to abuse, conflict, and ultimately war. The death camps of Treblinka and Sobibor have passed into history, along with the millions who were gassed to death in them, but in the 1990s we saw "ethnic cleansing" in the Balkans. The Cold War may be over now, but many smaller wars are being waged around the world, and nuclear weapons still abound; and since September 11, 2001, in particular, we have the threat of large-scale terrorist acts and reactive, so-called preemptive military action, such as the Iraqi war of 2003. Moreover, today we find ourselves living in what is fast becoming an ecological wasteland, as pollution and overdevelopment wreak havoc in the Earth's natural resources and its flora and fauna. This literal wasteland also stems from the wound, because the sense of partial identity caused by the wound has deluded us into believing that the *spiritual* hunger caused by the wound can be assuaged by consuming more and more *material* goods. And this accelerating habit of consumption is given further impetus by the way the wound of fragmented identity will often disguise itself as the so-called rationalist and materialist approach to life. This approach says in effect that as we are after all mere machine products of chance evolution, we have a mandate, a perfect right, to use up what are also viewed as the merely material resources at our disposal. If we do not heal the wound, we will not be able to restore the wasteland, because we will not be dealing with its root cause. Much, therefore, rests upon the healing of the heart—upon the emergence of the Grail. It is not just a matter of individual fulfillment, but of participating in a collective consciousness that can bring about a sea change in our global society. In this way, the multiple individual paths come to determine the nature of the collective destiny. In the end, the two entwined stories of King Arthur and the Grail, of the larger world and our personal lives, must become one story. One heart, one way.

—Diana Durham
October 2001

THE *DRAMATIS PERSONAE*, PLACES, AND SYMBOLS OF THE LEGEND

DRAMATIS PERSONAE

MERLIN: The magician who mentors Arthur's growing up and advises his kingship. He sees into the future. Like Arthur, Merlin does not die but ends up trapped in a crystal cave underground. There is also the promise of his return linked to that of Arthur. Merlin represents the "magical" resurrective power that lies trapped in one's own subconscious mind, gripped by the rigid structures of fear and shame.

KING ARTHUR: The fabled leader who draws the sword out of the stone, unites the kingdom of Britain for the first time, presides over the glittering court of Camelot, forms the Round Table of knights, and helps initiate their quest for the Holy Grail. He represents enlightened leadership, particularly the spiritual mentor who blesses, creatively challenges, and empowers his "subjects."

GUINEVERE: Arthur's wife, who falls in love with Lancelot, Arthur's best knight. She represents the feminine wisdom that brings the gift of the future, in the shape of the Round Table. This is also the compulsion that often flies in the face of what is socially acceptable and can therefore bring fresh direction and insight. She is also the passionate desire of the heart that can act without regard to context and timing.

LANCELOT: The son of King Ban and Queen Elayne of Benwick in France, Lancelot is orphaned as a baby and looked after by the Lady of the Lake. When he joins the fellowship of the Round Table he wins renown as the best knight in the world, and he is Arthur's greatest support. He also falls in love with Guinevere and has eyes for no one else. Despite his great prowess, Lancelot fails on the quest for the grail. He represents the heroic part of ourselves that must transfer its attention from achieving greatness to the inner work of transformation in order to become whole.

MORGANA: Arthur's half-sister; she has magical powers. Before he marries Guinevere, Arthur falls for Morgana, not recognizing her, as he was brought up in a separate household. They sleep together, and Morgana conceives a son, Mordred, from their semi-incestuous union. Morgana is deeply resentful of Arthur and, among other spiteful actions, steals his scabbard and casts it into a lake so that it is lost. Morgana represents the less socially acceptable face of the feminine: power, sexuality. She is also the aspect of the feminine that has responsibility for context and timing.

ARTHUR, LANCELOT, GUINEVERE, AND MORGANA: between them constitute four aspects of our own consciousness, or of consciousness as it configures one-to-one and in the collective. Arthur and Lancelot represent two different aspects of the mind, and Guinevere and Morgana represent two different aspects of the heart. Their interrelationships in the stories can be understood as the way consciousness can malfunction if the connection to the deeper levels of being—symbolized by finding the Grail—is not in place.

MORDRED: Arthur's bastard son by his half-sister Morgana. He initiates the final battle that ends Arthur's kingdom. Mordred's name means "fear of death"; thus he represents the destructive controls in the sub-conscious mind that must be overcome on the quest.

THE GRAIL KING: An old man with white hair who lives in an inner room of the Grail Castle and is served by the Grail. He represents a higher and greater authority than any earthly power. His could be an-other name for God.

THE WOUNDED FISHER KING: The king who also lives inside the Grail Castle and is guardian of the Grail. He suffers continuously from a mysterious wound, and his only solace is fishing. His wound will not be healed until an "innocent fool" comes to the Grail Castle and asks what the purpose of the Grail is. His wound is essentially the partial identity caused by the sense of separation from our inner source of being. It is both an individual condition and a controlling consciousness within society. The Wounded Fisher King also represents a flawed temporal leader, one who undermines or corrupts those in his power.

PERCEVAL: An unsophisticated young man who, raised in obscurity, nevertheless finds his way to Arthur's court, is knighted, and sets off to find the Grail. He represents the individual experience of all those who are willing to undergo transformation.

BLANCHEFLEUR: Perceval's sweetheart. She represents the emotional realm that must work in harmony with the mind to achieve the Grail quest.

THE HAG: An old woman who visits Perceval at Arthur's court during a banquet in his honor; she lists all his faults, chief among them his failure to ask the question when in the Grail Castle and thus relieve the king and land from suffering. She is the truth-telling aspect of the deep feminine, and can also be said to represent here withered Mother Earth herself.

YOU, THE READER: You are the hero or heroine who must undergo the perils of the quest and return to reconfigure the Round Table of the new collective paradigm in which we are now living.

PLACES

KING ARTHUR'S COURT/CAMELOT: Represents the model of community or fellowship of noble purpose that inspires us and sets the conditions for the individual work of the quest. It also represents the temporal, everyday world—the world of process and application.

THE GRAIL CASTLE: Represents our house of being, with its inner core of radiance, outer consciousness, and subconscious. It also represents the spiritual world, the world of epiphany and revelation.

THE WASTELAND: The kingdom of the Wounded Fisher King, which lies waste because it reflects his wound. It can represent the inner wasteland of alienated, individual consciousness; the wasteland of abuse, terrorism, war, and genocide—all "man's inhumanity to man"; as well as the literal wasteland caused by ecological breakdown and the extinction of species. It can also mean the poisoned atmosphere and regime that grow up around a Wounded Fisher King leader.

THE REALM OF THE QUEST: The fantastic and uncharted terrain of woods, magical castles, deserts, lakes, graveyards, stone chapels, and so on through which Perceval travels. It represents the subconscious mind and heart and specifically their wounded, damaged layers.

SYMBOLS

THE QUEST: The journey through magical realms and encounters with various knights, friendly and hostile, maidens in distress, monsters, and so on. It symbolizes the process of clarification of the subconscious.

THE GRAIL: A cup or chalice (*chalice* is derived from a Latin word for cup and is a more poetic/old-fashioned term) that is kept in the Grail Castle and serves the Grail King. (The word *grail* is derived from older words in Middle English and old French that mean "dish.") It represents the open heart, and the state of union with God, symbolized by the phrase from the Psalm 23 "my cup runneth over." The Grail represents the feminine principle, and the body, or "golden bowl," that is a container for God's love. It also therefore symbolizes love.

THE SWORD: There is the sword Arthur removes from the stone; also the sword or lance that wounds the fisher king and the sword that is given to Perceval on his first visit to the Grail Castle. The sword represents one's power, which has been given away to others and must be taken back. As the Grail is the heart, the sword is the conscious mind that is aligned with God, the masculine principle, and a symbol of truth.

THE QUESTION: What Perceval must ask about the Grail, along the lines of "Whom does the Grail serve?" The asking of it is crucial to the healing of both the wounded king and the wasteland. The asking represents our own turning from orientation in the material realm to centering in the inner, spiritual realm; also our being weaned from dependency on temporal leaders into our own strength and our own direct connection to God—to the divine in us.

THE PROPHECY OF RETURN: King Arthur is known as the "once and future king"; the Latin phrase *Quondam rexque futurus* is inscribed on his grave. This prophecy symbolizes the return of those who have been on the quest and achieved a grounded spirituality. It is the spirit of Arthur that returns, embodied in many individuals in a condition of collective sovereignty.

THE ROUND TABLE: Made by Merlin and kept by King Leodogrance of Wales, Guinevere's father, it is her wedding gift to Arthur. Arthur institutes the Knights of the Round Table, where he and his knights sit as peers, all with equal access to the center, symbolizing God. Our collective return from the private, inner realms of the quest is the reconfiguring of the Round Table, which is transformed from community to the consciousness of oneness; and the roundness of which then echoes the Grail itself in its aspect of our circle of oneness, the wholeness of life, the Earth itself.

1

KING ARTHUR AND
THE GRAIL KING

*All that is visible must grow beyond itself, extend into the realm
of the invisible. Thereby it receives its true consecration and clarity
and takes firm root in the cosmic order. (The Cauldron)*
  —I CHING, TRANSLATED BY RICHARD WILHELM AND CARY F. BAYNES

*The source of man's being is positive. The human being should
be negative or responsive to that positive expression of the source
of his being.*   —MARTIN EXETER, "THE ONE LAW"

THE LEGENDS OF KING ARTHUR and the Grail Quest
begin with Merlin. Merlin is no ordinary mortal; he is a
magician who has mysterious powers and can see into the
future. Thus it could be said that these stories begin in the realm
of magic. Merlin and his magical realm represent the mysterious
workings of the subconscious mind. He "resides" in those unfathomable layers of wisdom where exist the powers that regulate
the heartbeat, form the living child in the womb, and cause us to
know events before they happen. Merlin can do things ordinary
mortals cannot. The subconscious mind has powers that our conscious mind does not. Has anyone caused the fertilized egg to develop from fetus to baby just by thinking about it? Nevertheless,
the subconscious mind needs the cooperation of the conscious
mind, and in these tales Merlin needs the cooperation of ordinary
mortals in order to fulfill his mission. Merlin is seeking to bring
about a new era in the battle-torn land of Britain. He knows that
somehow this raggle-taggle collection of barbarous warring fief-

doms has got to be united and transformed into a great kingdom, be-cause he can foresee that this kingdom will in turn give birth to some-thing crucial to the destiny of all humankind. But even though Merlin has magical powers he cannot bring about this new era on his own. He has to work *through* ordinary mortals. When we first meet Merlin in the tales, he is faced with the problem of the current king, Uther Pen-dragon. Uther is a hardworking warhorse who has won many battles and holds together a fragile alliance. Unfortunately Uther is also rough-mannered, aggressive, and ruled by his passions, and Merlin knows only too well that Uther will never have what it takes to unite the kingdom.

Uther has arranged for a reconciliatory meeting with one of his greatest enemies, Gorlois, the Duke of Cornwall. He invites Gorlois and his wife Ygraine to visit with him, but he falls in love with the beautiful Ygraine. This leads to further enmities between the two camps, and while Ygraine is kept locked up in Cornwall's (or Gorlois's) castle of Tintagel, her husband takes up in another castle where Uther and his men lay siege to him. Uther is fainting from sheer anger and desire when Merlin's help is sought. Seeing through the mists of the future, Merlin, instead of trying to dissuade Uther, makes a deal with him. He will change Uther into the likeness of Gorlois, and have him come to Ygraine in Tintagel at night while the real Gorlois is still away fighting. The condition is that Uther will hand over to Merlin's keeping the baby that will be born from their union that night. All goes as planned, but Gorlois is slain in battle some hours before Uther's visit, so that later Ygraine realizes it wasn't her husband she lay with. Eventually, Uther marries Ygraine anyway, but the deal has been made, and when the baby boy is born he is duly handed over to Merlin. Merlin places the baby Arthur in the care of a trusted knight, Sir Hector, who lives in a remote part of the kingdom, to be brought up as his own son.

So Merlin is working to bring about a new era through the birth of a king. But not just any old king. It must be someone who is king not only because of his bloodline but because of another quality as well. What is this quality? Arthur is the son of the earthly (and earthy) King Uther, but because of the magical circumstances surrounding his birth and his upbringing under Merlin's direction, he is also the son of the magical realm and the inheritor of a transcendent spirit.

After Uther Pendragon dies there is a time of instability when several lords vie with one another for the kingship. Merlin instructs the archbishop of Canterbury to send for all the lords of the realm and gentlemen-at-arms to come to London at Christmastime in order to show by some miracle who should rightly be king. So the peers of the realm, including Sir Hector with his newly knighted, real son, Kay, and Arthur, gather together and come first to a great church to pray, and after matins and the first mass, there appears in the churchyard, against the high altar, a large stone, with an anvil set on top of it and a sword stuck point down in the anvil. Golden letters inscribed around the sword declare that whoever can draw the sword out is king of all England. After more prayers, some of the knights attempt to pull out the sword but without success. While everyone waits to see what is going to happen, jousts and tournaments are organized to keep the company occupied and together. On the way to the jousts Kay finds he has left his sword at their lodgings, and asks Arthur to fetch it for him. Arthur speeds off but finds the lodgings locked up. So he decides to go to the churchyard and fetch the sword from the stone for Kay. He pulls it out easily and gives it to Kay. At first Kay tries to pretend that he has pulled the sword out, but his father does not believe him, and takes them both back to the stone and anvil. He tells Arthur to put the sword back in and then both Sir Hector and Kay try to pull it out, again without success. Sir Hector asks Arthur to try pulling it out again, he does so, and thus, to his own astonishment, Arthur is declared king.

The symbolism here is also underlining the special quality of Arthur's kingship. Merlin works with the archbishop of Canterbury to bring about Arthur's accession. The sword in the stone appears in the churchyard right next to the high altar and after mass and first matins. Here are magic and Christianity woven together. The old feminine mysteries and the new masculine religion—both mother and father God. Arthur is king not just because of his bloodline but because he is sanctioned by these higher powers. A spiritual lineage as well as a bloodline is invoked. He is king because he is representing the realm of sacred as well as temporal power.

Arthur goes on to unite the kingdom of England for the first time. He marries Guinevere, whose wedding present to him is a round table.

Thus together they initiate the order of the Knights of the Round Table, and the great court of Camelot comes into being.

The sword comes out of the stone at Arthur's touch because it belongs to him. Merlin's magic, the stirrings of the subconscious mind, have brought about the circumstances that will allow for the birth of the king, the one who is able to draw the sword out of the crystallized, rigid structure of metal and stone; the one who releases the truth from memory and tradition and turns it back into a living presence; the leader who exudes a sense of authentic power and who leads through inspiration, not by adherence to the rule book, to precedent, or to what is customary. Here in the figure of King Arthur is represented in a sense the true, lone, great patriarch, the hero who brings about a renewal of the world—who saves it in times of peril. This figure could be Jesus, Buddha, Mohammed, or some other avatar, or a great political leader—a Churchill who rallies a country, or a whole world, at its time of gravest darkness.

This is the leader who provides the context in which the individual path toward wholeness can take shape. The individual path to wholeness is symbolized by the story of the quest for the Grail. The Grail stories are set within the backdrop of the King Arthur story. Perceval sets off on his adventures in the quest after Arthur has drawn the sword from the stone and founded Camelot. Merlin could foresee that Arthur needed to be born, become king, and unite the kingdom. But why? Because he also foresaw that all this great outworking would in its turn give birth to something even more important. Something crucial to the destiny of humankind. And what was that? The quest for the Grail. Not so much the seeking for but the finding of the Grail.

The role of the leader who can draw the sword from the stone is twofold. First, he brings about those conditions of peace and order that will allow the spiritual quest to be embarked on. Second, and more important, he represents to us that quickening energy of spiritual source—that which gave him the ability to draw out the sword in the first place. In the figure of King Arthur both roles are symbolized. He establishes peace in the land, and it is during his reign that the quest for the Grail is embarked on. However, in the "real" world, these two roles are not always so clearly combined in one leader. We might say that the first role, that of bringing about a new era through a great struggle, is usually more the domain of the great military or political leaders. I already mentioned Winston Churchill. In more recent times Nelson Mandela stands out as a political leader of huge stature who by his selflessness and integrity has prevailed over enormous hardships and therefore has not only led but has also inspired a nation and a world. Nevertheless, even though he is, and Churchill was, an example, an inspiration, and a true hero, we would stop short of conferring on these great men the title of spiritual leader or mentor. This role was clearly the domain of Jesus and the other avatars I mentioned—Buddha, Mohammed—as well as many others I have not mentioned. This is the leader whose role it is to represent to us that quickening energy of spiritual source because he or she is consciously aware of his or her own connection to the higher, sacred power. This is the role primarily of the spiritual mentor, and it is this aspect of the King Arthur leader that I am most concerned with in this book. Because when we come into the presence of this quickening energy, it catalyzes a process of inner growth and clarification within us *that is what constitutes the quest*. Thus we move along the path toward finding the Grail, which symbolizes our own experience of union with spiritual source.

The individual path to wholeness is symbolized, as I have said, by the story of the quest for the Grail, the best known of which is Chrétien de Troyes's "Perceval." Perceval was brought up in Wales, which denoted a wild and remote part of the world. He was given no schooling and wore simple canvas clothes. The remote and primitive conditions of Perceval's upbringing signify what are often the preconditions of the spiritual quest: a combination of innocence and unworldliness. One day, after he has reached adolescence, Perceval is out in the woods when he sees five knights go riding by. Perceval is stunned by the apparition of the knights. He has no idea who or what they are, but the fineness of their mien and apparel dazzle him. Adolescence here can mean that a cycle of development has worked out invisibly in us to the point where new insight can be catalyzed. Just as the story of Arthur begins with Merlin—begins in the realm of the subconscious mind—so do our individual stories. Something begins to percolate deep inside us, an unconscious drive to bring about a new era. As I have said, Merlin had to work through ordinary mortals in the everyday world, he could not bring about the changes on his own; likewise, the powers and insights of one's own subconscious do not find fulfillment unless they break surface into one's conscious mind, and can thus become actualized in the ordinary, here-and-now world.

Before Perceval sees the knights, he has been a simple country bumpkin, unaware that anything exists outside of his forest home. But now he has something different to measure his world and himself by. He finds out from his mother that they are knights from the court of King Arthur and resolves to follow them to Arthur's court and become a knight himself.

So in ourselves the stirring of the subconscious mind remains a process beyond conscious awareness until one day a catalytic event occurs—we meet someone or catch sight of something—that causes this process to break surface. Then, like Perceval, whose world changes forever after he catches sight of the two shining outriders of Arthur's court, we become aware for the first time that there might be a different way to live, that there exist kingdoms and conditions beyond what we currently know. We get a perspective on ourselves and our lives and realize that there is more.

In these early stages of spiritual awakening, something must appear to inspire us, but there must also be something in us that can be inspired, something that can respond to an emissary of the king. After all, probably lots of other people caught sight of the knights that day, riding through the forest, but their presence did not have the same impact it had on Perceval. There must first be the presence of Merlin in one's subconscious, stirring the longing for the king and his new era.

What in the myth appears to be a singular event or symbol is in our experience often depicting a whole process, one that repeats over a cycle of time and may even recur in different ways throughout our lives. Perceval catches sight of the knights and more or less immediately sets off for—and finds—King Arthur's court. In my own experience, the appearance of outriders took place many times, over a number of years, and there were several "visitations." None of them were individually as dramatic in their impact as in Perceval's case but cumulatively they were. The first "outriders" for me were writers. Some of literature's "greats": E. M. Forster, Virginia Woolf, D. H. Lawrence, T. S. Eliot. I valued these writers for the transcendent dimension of the human experience they wrote about as much as for the skill with which they wrote. Then a very unlikely-seeming outrider came along—a long-lost, in fact never known about, cousin visiting from her home in Canada. At the time she stayed a couple of nights with us, she was in her midtwenties and I was a withdrawn and unhappy 17-year-old, living in emotional isolation from my parents. My brother had left home, and we had moved away from the town where I had grown up, so my culture of friends was gone too. My general state of mind and my "Englishness" prejudiced me against my cousin's "New World" friendliness, and I was cold and disdainful toward her, dismissing her as a "nicey nice," oversugary "American," vaguely lumping both countries together. Nevertheless, she came into my room at night on the pretext of borrowing a nighty, and somehow she managed to penetrate my frostiness and really connect with me. I began to see that there was something very purposeful and strong behind her open and easy exterior, and that impressed me. She told me about the spiritual community she was involved in, and she spoke about the nature of who we truly are. I replied that I didn't know who I was, and I remember as I said the words how the enormity of their meaning rang out for me. It was a relief to say them, even though I had never thought in these terms before; it felt as if just to have spoken them was the beginning of something important. At the same time I realized I wasn't just talking about me, I was talking about the whole context in which I was growing up. *No one* knew who they were! This realization also reverberated in the room, opening up as it did such vast implications—implications that ultimately led the way into my future.

That late-night interlude stayed with me, like a seed. It was the first time a human being had spoken deeply and meaningfully to me.

About a year later that seed began to germinate. My cousin had written to me once or twice and urged me to come and visit her. I had finished high school, and the summer loomed before me like a great emptiness. I decided to take up her offer.

Now Merlin had been at work to make this trip possible, because for several years beforehand I had worked part-time and saved all the money I earned for another trip—or so I had imagined. My best friend from my former town and I had planned that when we left school we would buy a convertible Morris Minor—these cars were for some reason cult objects for us—and drive across Europe to Greece. This projected trip was elaborated in our imaginations into a fantasy about growing up. Images of ourselves in white sundresses, duly suntanned, blurred into images of white-robed goddesses poised against marble statuary and eternal blue skies. Dazzled by a sense of impending apotheosis, we felt vaguely that there amid the gleaming pillars of the Parthenon and the purple blue depths of the Aegean we would be transported into another state. However, in reality my friend bought a minivan when she passed her driving test, not a Morris Minor, and when she left school, a year ahead of me, I had already moved away, and she went and got married. But the money was still in my account. So instead of driving eastward to the blue and white vistas of Greece, I found myself flying west toward the completely unknown land of Canada and my cousin.

Very often a sign that something has impacted us deeply is that we don't acknowledge this fully to ourselves. My cousin had told me she was living on a spiritual commune up in the Caribou region of British Columbia, and even though what she and I had shared together was ultimately what was drawing me there and must obviously have derived from her association with this community, I did not admit this to myself, nor was I at all attracted by the notion of a spiritual commune. I pictured hippies, plaid shirts, and odd and perhaps uncomfortable communal habits like praying together or singing round the campfire. My attitude was that I was off to have an adventure, a holiday, and make the best of whatever odd circumstances I might have to fit that around. I was in fact reluctant to seek out the "court" from which this outrider had come, yet that is what I was doing.

I reasoned that if things got too uncomfortable up in the Caribou, I could always return to the normal comfortable suburban existence of my aunt and uncle in Vancouver. So it was a shock, after I landed in that city and was met by my cousin's brother-in-law, to learn that his father and mother-in-law also lived up in this remote community! It meant I had no choice but to stay there, and it dispelled my (at least recognizable) images of a hippy community, because my aunt and uncle were of the same generation as my parents, and to my mind people of my parents' age definitely did not belong in hippie communes of the 1970s, even "spiritual" ones. Nevertheless, another part of me was excited, and the journey up to the Caribou region was as astonishing as I could have hoped for. A small, three-coach train took the best part of a day to climb the 3,000 or so feet up from sea level through the Coast Mountains to the Fraser Plateau. The train wobbled on wooden trestle bridges over ravines where green rapids fell in boiling silver masses over boulders, past lake after serene lake and through forests full of silver rivers, and clung to the sides of dusty mountains hundreds of feet above the Thompson River canyon. I had for the first and most vivid time in my life the very satisfying feeling that I was on an adventure, headed through scenery that was utterly different from suburban England, for the complete unknown.

In part this sense of adventure came from the Wild West scenery, so unlike anything I had ever experienced before; in part it came from the fact that I was on the trail of the "outrider," my cousin, who had shown me something new about who I was. Consciously or unconsciously, I was being drawn to the court of the king, seeking initiation into the mysteries of knighthood and spiritual growth.

The community and its setting certainly did not look anything like Camelot. It was composed of an odd collection of log cabins and small homes or apartment buildings, clustered in a valley with open ranching country on one side and a small, almost frontierlike town on the other, strung along the main highway heading north, which had originally been hammered out by those seeking their fortunes in one of the late nineteenth-century gold rushes. One or two larger buildings were part of the community complex, including a communal dining room and a chapel and meeting room complex. Although I was welcomed warmly by my cousin and aunt and uncle, I was not, to my surprise, made quite as much a fuss of as I had expected. Over the next few days, while the 80 or so other residents (some of whom were long-haired and young, others middle-aged or elderly and "ordinary" looking) were extremely kind and friendly to me, I could also sense that there was no emotional investment in "winning me over," in whether I liked what was going on or not. If I wanted to join in, that was fine; if I didn't, that was also fine. After about five weeks of my stay there, I still didn't understand what it was all about—they spoke about "being in the moment," and "it's not what you do that's important, but who you are." They told me not to try to understand it with my mind. All I really knew was that something rang true about these people; they were genuine, more vibrant and alive than most people I had met before, and I wanted to become like them.

In fact the impact of the knights on Perceval is twofold. First, seeing them, he wants to become like them; second, because of seeing them, he becomes aware of the court of the king, of something beyond them again. He sets off for King Arthur's court because he knows that in order to become a knight like them, he has to find the king. Only the king can initiate him into knighthood. Why is this? Because only the king has the authority to do this. Where does this authority come from? From a higher authority again—from that higher power that sanctioned Arthur, symbolized by his ability to draw the sword from the stone. Arthur is king because he represents a higher order of energy still. Just as the outriders whom Perceval sees represented Arthur, so Arthur represents a level of authority beyond himself— represents the heavenly king. It is this energy that lights Arthur up with radiance and draws Perceval into his presence.

For me, the community was the court of King Arthur to which I was drawn because I caught sight of its outriders, and eventually I met the man who was the point of inspiration for this community—and in one sense the source of its atmosphere—and who most of all came to play the role of the King Arthur leader for me. He was a man of formidable presence. When I first met him, I knew instantly that I was not just bumping into another human personality, with a finite sense of self. Nor was I meeting an inflated human ego with a false sense of self-importance. Nothing could have been further from the truth. He had that feel about him that was like a blade, cutting everything down to size without even saying anything. His authority lay in the sense one had of his being invested elsewhere, invested not so much in the out-working of events and people but in their *cause*. Yet far from making him appear remote or distracted, this condition of investment in cause or source meant on the contrary that he was present right on the razor's edge of the moment. The radiance of his presence was almost tangible. One knew unmistakably that one was in the presence of love. He happened to be an Englishman, of aristocratic descent, and as such evinced some characteristics typical of well-bred Britishness: he was generally understated, he was not emotionally effusive, he had a well-developed and dry sense of humor, he was not physically demonstrative, and he did not attempt to make you feel comfortable. Nevertheless, he embodied in the most powerful way that I have ever known the presence of love. Not niceness, not emotional empathy, not sympathy, not well-meaning charity—not any of these minor offshoots of love but love itself: something amazingly strong, expansive, flexible, joyful, kind, silvery, golden. Something that riveted you to the spot and filled you with happiness and assurance—because in recognizing that presence in him, one knew instinctively that it was also present in oneself.

Love is as good a name as any for the heavenly king. We often say God is love, and the phrase "Love God" works as much as a definition as a commandment. So here I was, meeting my spiritual mentor, myself, and the presence of God—or love—all at the same time. Even though he was very unlike me—a man in his seventies, and from another era and background—yet he was a man; he was not anything essentially different from me. What he was, I was; what he exemplified, I could also come to exemplify. If I walked in his footsteps, I would sooner or later begin to strike out and make my own footsteps. This was the beginning of entrainment into the radiant presence of the spiritual mentor, which was ultimately the entrainment into the presence of God within myself.

God is not usually cast as a character in a story—for obvious reasons. Milton once tried it in his poem "Paradise Lost." Attempting to create a nonhuman, "transparent" effect, Milton had God speak in stately, abstract language, with no coloration of simile or metaphor, much less colloquialism. As a result, God ended up sounding rather stiff and uninteresting. This is what Alastair Fowler in his introduction to "Paradise Lost" says about the criticisms of Milton: "Critics often call the portrayal of God in *Paradise Lost* a failure, without adequately considering how ludicrous it would be to call any such portrayal a complete success, or even a good likeness." Any portrayal of God is unlikely to be a "success, or even a good likeness," because what is meant by the word *God* is a focalization or frequency of energy and consciousness (we can say *love*) that cannot really be defined or known *about* by the human mind but can only be known as it is differentiated in our experience. When one meets someone whose presence is a differentiation of this energy, that person's presence can catalyze in one a process of inner clarification that leads to one's own, direct experience of the differentiation of love. This process of clarification is what constitutes the quest. The quest for the Grail is the quest to achieve one's own direct connection to the energy of the heavenly king, because the Grail, as I will show, symbolizes the condition of union between that higher energy and one's own being.

Two of the best known versions of the quest stories are Chrétien de Troyes's "Perceval" and Wolfram von Eschenbach's "Parzival." Both these authors get around the difficulty of characterizing God by having him represented by the mysterious presence of a king whom we catch only glimpses of and about whom we learn mainly from other characters.

I will have to jump ahead a little in the story in order to talk about this king. At a certain point on Perceval's quest journey, he comes upon a castle that appears to be the home of another king, the Wounded Fisher King. This wounded king hosts Perceval for the night, and during the evening's banquet, the Grail chalice appears, along with several other precious objects. The Grail and other treasures are carried by a number of young men and women, who emerge from one inner room of the castle, proceed through the banqueting hall where Perceval and the wounded king are sitting, and disappear into another inner room. The room into which they disappear is where this other mysterious king lives. So now we have three kings: King Arthur, the Wounded Fisher King, and the mysterious king of the inner room. For clarity's sake, I am going to call this latter king the Grail King (and the castle in which he resides the Grail Castle). The Grail King represents the presence of God.

In Chrétien de Troyes's poem Perceval does not know that the Grail King is living in that inner room. He only learns about him later on in the tale when he meets a hermit who gives him absolution toward the end of his quest. The hermit explains that it is this king who is served from the Grail, and that he is related to Perceval:

> The person served from it [i.e. the Grail] is my brother: your mother was my sister and his. And the Rich Fisher man, believe me, is the son of that king who has himself served from the grail. But don't imagine he has pike, lamprey or salmon: he's served with a single consecrated wafer brought to him in that grail—that supports his life in full vigor, so holy a thing is the grail. And he, whose life is so spiritual that all it needs is the host that comes in the grail, has been there for twelve years like that, without leaving the room which you saw the grail enter.

This genealogy makes the Grail King grandfather to Perceval and father to the fisher king. This fatherly nature, plus his extreme spirituality—he exists in vigorous life on just a single wafer from the Grail—are symbolic of his divine nature. Later I will show why his relationship with the Grail is also indication of his divinity. In Wolfram von Eschenbach's "Parzival," we catch only a glimpse of the Grail King when Parzival sees through an open door "the most beautiful old man he had ever beheld," with hair as white as snow. Here it is the beauty of the man, and the white hair, symbolizing purity, as well as his proximity to the Grail, that form the clues to the transcendent nature of the Grail King.

The inner room of the Grail Castle where the Grail King lives could symbolize the holy of holies within the temple of old, the inner sanctum of ourselves where the wellspring of spirit rises. This is where we want to get to, but we cannot just barge in. We have to find the way to *become* that room and to be fed by the invisible wellspring. There is a paradox here. We want to find the holy of holies where the Grail King lives, but we cannot find it outside of ourselves: we only know it as it becomes an inner reality. Yet to begin with, we only know it as this reality is portrayed to us in the form of the spiritual mentor—who is outside of ourselves. We have to be entrained into the feel of that wellspring as it emerges through the radiant presence of the spiritual mentor.

The mentor is able to represent this heavenly energy to us only if there exists an openness to the presence of the heavenly king in himself or herself. Robert Bly writes about this relationship in his book *Iron John,* which explores the importance of mentorship. Bly calls the King Arthur leader/spiritual mentor the "political king"; the heavenly king he calls the "upper Sacred King": "The political king is a part of a three-tiered world; and he derives his energy and authority from his ability to be transparent or receptive to the king above him." When the mentor himself has a connection to the higher energy, he can act as a conduit for others, an open connection to the divine by means of which his "subjects" can gain their own relationship to the heavenly king. In this way, we as individuals can prime the pump of our individualized source of divinity, the "inner king" within ourselves, and thus *become weaned from dependence on the leader into a sense of our own authority.* In fact, the ability to mentor, to mirror the presence of the divine, is *the* defining characteristic of leadership. Bly recognizes the important role this "political king" plays in the maturing process of others:

> Many men of the generation now forty-five or so projected their undeveloped inner King on Jack Kennedy, who spoke openly of Camelot, and on Martin Luther King, and on Bobby Kennedy. When forces in the United States opposed to any spiritual kingship killed the Kennedys and King in mid-career, it was a catastrophe for the men of that generation. Some men have told me in tears that they lost something then, and have never regained it; they have never gotten back on track.
>
> Leaders, then, need to be strong enough so that the young men can let them carry their inner King for a while, and then to live long enough so that the young men can take it back, still undamaged, and let the King live inside them.

In other words, the process of being weaned from the mentor figure onto one's own connection with the upper sacred king, which then brings to life one's "inner king," was not able to be completed because the "political" king, in this case Kennedy, was no longer present to play that role for these men.

The term *godparent* may be a remnant of the understanding that to ignite the relationship with the heavenly king energy this presence must be represented by a real, flesh-and-blood person to whom the child or teenager or young adult can relate. In an ideal world, this role might even be held by the parents themselves. Certainly most religious and spiritual practices have recognized the importance of a fleshly intermediary between man and God; hence we have the role of priest, guru, shaman, and so on. However, within the structure of Christianity, which has dominated Western spiritual thought for two millennia, the concept of original sin has kept God and man apart, holding that humankind is fundamentally flawed and therefore separate from God. This has meant that the priest figure stops short of taking on the mantle of God's representative and thereby, for the most part, closes the channel instead of opening it. Closing the channel to God in this way also means that people remain dependent on the priest for a sense of connection to the divine instead of achieving their own connection.

The Buddhist tradition takes a different view. Here the spiritual master is allowed to take on the presence of Buddha himself and thus become a gateway for the disciple to cross through and be weaned onto his or her own relationship with the divine. In *The Tibetan Book of Living and Dying* Sogyal Rinpoche emphasizes the need to cultivate deliberately the view that the master—or in my terms the spiritual mentor—is the Buddha himself in order to achieve the desired enlightenment:

> The Tibetans know that if you relate to your teacher as a buddha, you will receive the blessings of a buddha, but if you relate to your master as a human being, you will only get the blessings of a human being.

The primary role then, of the temporal leader, as Rinpoche understands very well, is to provide a connection to the heavenly king and, in the process, to wean the disciple or follower from worship of the mentor onto an awareness of his or her own inner king or "buddha nature":

When your mind and heart are fully open in joy and wonder and recognition and gratitude to the mystery of the living presence of enlightenment in the master, then slowly, over many years, transmission from the master's wisdom mind and heart to yours can take place, revealing to you the full splendor of your own buddha nature, and with it the perfect splendor of the universe itself.

Essentially the process that has begun when one meets the spiritual mentor is the process of realigning one's polarity. If there is one central characteristic all the mystical traditions and some religions share in common, it is a discipline that can enable us to gradually transfer our energy response from the outer world to the inner, to reverse our polarity so that we are magnetized inwardly to the spiritual source within us instead of outwardly to the world around us. This principle is basic to all magic or yogic powers. The Western Mystery tradition, for instance, derived from the Kabbala, is a complex system of inward meditation on the symbol of the Tree of Life in order to master certain differentiations of inner power. Many systems of Eastern meditation seek the same inner mastery. One could summarize the aims of these approaches as the attempt to allow their adherents to become, using electrical terms, "negative," or responsive to God—to spirit that lives within us—rather than "positive," or resistant to the inner source, due to a habitual "addiction" to (this is in fact the root cause of all addictions) or a negative response to the outer world. (I am using the terms *positive* and *negative* in their neutral, electrical sense. I am not wishing to draw upon their more New Age connotations of "good" and "bad.")

Again, using the analogy of electricity, two positives repel, as do two negatives. There cannot be union between them, nor can the current flow. The Grail King or heavenly king is radiant; he is a positive current. If the temporal king becomes negative to the higher king, that power from the higher king can flow through the temporal leader into the kingdom. There is, literally, no resistance.

In ancient times, the king was thought to rule by means of such an energy flow. In Cuzco, Peru, and in the Forbidden City in China, the king and emperor sat at the center of a network of roadways that radiated out from the central hub of the kingdom and were thought to literally carry the energy of the king like the rays of light from the sun. *Ruler* means both one who rules and a straight measuring stick, reinforcing this idea that it was the flow of energy down the straight roads that "ruled" the kingdom. The Polynesians called this energy *mana* and conceived of it as flowing from high to low:

> And, since mana flowed from high to low, an unguarded contact between chief and a commoner was therefore an evil thing: the chief suffered a loss of mana, which he should preserve for the good of the people, and the commoner, with his limited capacity for mana, might be blown out like a fuse.

It is this energy that gives the king his gift of blessing. King Arthur is the leader who knows how to bless; he has a largesse about him as a result of his connection to the higher king. Is it literally an "energy" that moves up and down or that gets blocked, as the ancients thought of it? It is difficult to say what is really involved here. Certainly anyone who has been blessed by someone who has the power to bless feels it—not physically but in the depths of his or her being. Do we feel love? We do—again, we don't feel it physically, not like a literal wind that blows over us, but we feel the power of it warming and nourishing us, body and soul. The electrical analogy is appropriate in another way here, because although modern civilization knows how to harness and use electricity, we don't understand what it *is*. Similarly, we don't know what the force, the mana, is that flows between people, and, unlike electricity, we are not very skilled in how to use it constructively.

The tales of Arthur's birth, upbringing, and accession demonstrate this connection to the realms of higher energy. As I already related, Arthur was conceived with the aid of Merlin's magic when Merlin changed Uther Pendragon into the likeness of Gorlois, the duke of Cornwall, so that he could sleep with Gorlois's wife, Ygraine. When Arthur is old enough, Merlin aids in his education, using his magical arts. In the children's story *The Sword in the Stone,* T. H. White has Merlin transform Arthur into a bird and a fish so that he learns about both the sky and underwater worlds. There are echoes here of the shamanic art of trance descent and "flight" in which the shaman descends to the

underworld or flies up into the overworld to learn the secrets of creation and to bring back wisdom and guidance for his tribe. Mercea Eliade writes that "the shaman specializes in a trance during which his
soul is believed to leave his body and ascend to the sky or descend to
the underworld." Merlin, with his magical, shape-changing arts, is of
course aligned with the shaman, and in his guidance of Arthur, he
trains the future king in the shamanic arts as well.

This shamanic connection has a significant bearing on the *spiritual*
lineage of Arthur. Back in the mists of time, the shamans were often
the first leaders of the tribe. Author Paul Devereux writes: "A shaman
was . . . an active interloper of the spirit world." The central importance of the shaman was his or her ability to connect with the spiritual
realm. It was the connection to the spirit realms that gave the shaman
his or her authority. In other words, a *spiritual,* not a *physical* heritage
qualified him or her as a leader of the tribe. Here we have a parallel
with the magical traditions, which sought to entrain the initiate to the
inner, spiritual worlds. The American anthropologist Michael Harner
defines a shaman as "a man or woman who is in direct contact with the
spirit world through a trance state." There is a fascinating linking of
meaning between the words *trance, en-trance,* and *en-chant.* The shaman
often used *chanting* as one of the techniques to induce *trance.* So *en-tranced,*
the technique of the shaman, became *enchanted,* the magical rites of the
magician/wizard figure of Merlin. Both serve as *en-trances*—gateways—
to magical or spiritual realms.

Over time, as societies changed and developed, there was a gradual
shift from shaman to priest to king and a concomitant development
away from the spirit world to the world of *form,* away from the inner to
the outer world. However, the notion that authority derived from the
spiritual realm remained in the idea of the "divine king." Vestiges of
these shamanic roots still cling to the traditions of the British monarchy. In 1919, Harold Bailey wrote that the "notion of Imperial divinity is not yet dead . . . though the spirit may now have fled, its traces
still remain in our regal ceremonial." In fact, the spiritual connection
fled a long time ago, causing an almost neurotic concern over the question of what constituted the king's authority throughout the history of
the British monarchy. During the Wars of the Roses, the right of each

contender for the throne was as hotly contested in words as it was in battle. It was very important to justify winning the battle. The way authority was claimed, however, was based purely on establishing a clear bloodline from whoever was deemed to be the "true" previous king. Thus the physical lineage came to be emphasized at the expense of the spiritual. The king's family tree was more important than his character or ability to govern—was more important than his connection to the Grail King, or to God. This emphasis degenerated further into all the physical trappings of kingship, land ownership in particular. Instead of being attuned to heaven, the king had to own the earth, even forcibly take it in battle, and then parcel it out to various dukes and lords as rewards for financing his wars. Thus became established the aristocracy, the "*landed* gentry," characterized by property ownership, their own bloodlines, tradition, and the stockpiling of art treasures. In other words, by *form*. English law today is still based on the ownership of land and property.

What we have encoded in the stories of Merlin and Arthur is a recognition that *true authority comes from a connection to the spiritual realm,* the realm where the Grail King resides, and *not from a bloodline or the physical ownership of land.* This is underscored again when Arthur's kingship is established not by Merlin announcing his parentage but by Arthur's pulling the sword out of the stone. Arthur is king not by reason of a bloodline or adherence to the structures of tradition and culture but by reason of his presence. But there is another layering of meaning here. Arthur was not seeking to become king, whereas all the other knights who tried to pull the sword out *wanted* to be king. They were seeking something outside of themselves—a role, a title, a *form*—that would confer authority upon them. They were polarized, in other words, in the material, outer world and were looking to it for power. Arthur, on the other hand, *was* the king. He was not seeking validity, he already had it—and therefore the sword came to him and with it the kingdom. Here is the "electrical" negative and positive principle at work. Arthur's guileless attitude—that is, not wanting power for his own sake—and his ability to pull the sword out is telling us that Arthur is "transparent to" the higher king, the Grail King. Arthur is "negative" to the spiritual or inner realm, making him automatically "positive" to—having authority over—the outer world, which can therefore, being "negative" itself, come to him, "join" with him. This positivity is the very opposite of domination. It is the act of blessing. King Arthur blesses the kingdom: he unites it for the first time, and a time of peace and prosperity ensues.

The king's blessing is like the elixir of life to us when we first feel its impact, and it may seem as if we are home and dry when we find a mentor or role model, but the opposite is true. We are probably more vulnerable at this stage than if we had never left our obscure forest homes. The reason for this is that at the same time we become aware of the king we also become aware of our need for him. We become aware of how weak and incomplete we are. It is very important that this happen, because unless we become aware of this "wound" of incompleteness, we can never heal it; nevertheless, the discovery puts us in a potentially dangerous situation.

What we long for initially is a spiritual parent, who will love and bless us and make us whole in a way that we know deep down has never happened because our parents themselves were in need of emotional healing and so were unable to provide this kind of spiritual centering for us.

Our need for spiritual parenting is often transferred to our other relationships. We look to partners, lovers, even children to nourish us at deep levels where we feel incomplete. However, seeking to fulfill this need through these other relationships, albeit unconsciously, is always a fruitless attempt and can also be destabilizing to these relationships. Children are not meant to have the lifeblood sucked out of them by our need or to have their child egos overinflated by our need's indulgence. Some women like to mother men, but in the end they usually grow tired of it and end up feeling bitter and let down. Likewise, a man will often "look after" a girllike woman, but such an arrangement is dissatisfying in the long run. The child-woman never exercises her own strength, and the parent-husband never has love and nourishment returned on an equal footing and is always hungry for that support. Such relationships cannot develop but can only deteriorate into complicit and structured patterns of role and response; or they take the form of emotional cannibalism, where people feed on one another to gain strength. Much has been written about the phenomenon of codependency, in which an addictive personality is looked after by someone who appears to be the stronger partner but who is in fact addicted to being needed. Sometimes the relationship of minister or priest to his or her congregation has similar dynamics. The parishioners want to be comforted and made to feel that their lives are meaningful without having to make any real changes, and the minister wants to feel needed by them.

As adults, we develop a veneer of competence and sophistication, even "toughness," that helps us forget how vulnerable we are deep down. It is difficult, sometimes even for those who have children of their own, to remember the awe-ful potency of a child's love for his or her parents, how tender and fierce it is, and how completely devastating it is for the child when this love is betrayed in some way, which it so often is, whether through outright cruelty, neglect, insensitivity, or simply by not being valued. These are the feelings—the longing and the fear of rejection that accompanies the longing because of the former experience of rejection—that resurface in us in the presence of an authentic spiritual parent. In some ways these feelings reemerge even more strongly because we have lost the openhearted innocence of childhood and are burdened with self-consciousness, inhibition, and often self-dislike. We should never underestimate just how potentially traumatic this reawakening is—or how ripe it is for redoing right the second time, so that the wound can be healed over and the person made whole.

Obviously, having a loving partner in one's life can go a long way to healing and nurturing one's wounds of incompleteness, but one will never step into one's own core fire, one's own strength and essence, until one meets God in the flesh and *then becomes weaned from him.* This is the essence of leadership: the empowerment of others. This empowerment is in two parts: first, we have to be fully received in love, just as we are, and *blessed;* and then, we have to be *challenged,* sent off on the quest for personal fulfillment, independently of anyone.

In the initial stages of relating to a King Arthur leader, however, there is a phase of openhearted submission to him. Anyone who has experienced this knows that it is an intoxicatingly joyful experience—like falling in love. It is a very important part of the process of healing and growth. We are learning what it means to feel deeply again, to love absolutely, to let a current of passion move through our souls that will rearrange the very molecules of our being. I see this as a cleansing fire, which clears out the heart and exercises spiritual muscles that have atrophied. This kind of fiery love for the leader pulls around one's polarity in the outer world and realigns one, first in the figure of the leader, and then in the presence of God, and then in one's own connection with God and one's own divinity and power.

So at first the "subject" is joyfully fulfilled in *serving* King Arthur. When, during my own process of being spiritually parented, the man who played this role for me stayed over for a few days in a friend's apartment, I remember feeling surprised at how utterly contented I was just to look after his physical needs. Cooking, cleaning, and running errands were all charged with magical intensity and gave marvelous opportunities for snatches of conversation. No one observing this situation objectively, without insight into the inner dynamics, could possibly have understood the magic and potency this time held for me.

So ecstatic, in fact, is this stage of being in love with the leader that some individuals are tempted to prolong it beyond what is appropriate to the cycle of maturing. A Peter Pan mentality can creep in, whereby we never want to grow up. It is so safe and nourishing to remain in the benign penumbra of King Arthur. What's more, while one stays there, one never has to take responsibility for the direction of one's own life; one can just go on serving his life. In this way we become dependent on the spiritual mentor or, in Bly's terms, the temporal king for our connection to the Grail King, so that our experience remains vicarious, and we fail to achieve our own direct connection to the higher energy. In its worst form, a dependent "subject" can become a parasite on the leader, leaching energy from him but giving little in return except abject and mindless adoration.

Therefore, paradoxically, although at first King Arthur's presence is empowering, after a while he can have an inhibiting effect on those around him who grow dependent on him. Very subtly we can start to find excuses for not growing up. King Arthur seems untouchable, his achievements unmatchable. He will do it all; we don't have to do anything. Sometimes, it seems that the king has to die, or step down, so that we can grow up. While reminiscing about the man who had played the King Arthur role for him, a friend once remarked to me: "I'd have walked off a cliff if X had asked me to do it." At the time, I felt rather than reasoned that something was not right and quipped, "It's just as well he never asked you." The leader who had inspired this devotion had died, unexpectedly, of a heart attack, and many people were left feeling shipwrecked and directionless upon his death. This was, however, the only way that many of them got to move on to the next stage of spiritual maturity. Jesus himself encouraged his disciples to grow beyond the servant stage: "Henceforth I call you not servants; for the servant knoweth not what his Lord doeth; but I have called you friends" (John 15:15). Being a friend instead of being a servant implies that you will know of the responsibilities of the leader and shoulder your share of them. This sharing of responsibility is partly what the roundness of King Arthur's table signifies: teamwork rather than hierarchy. In my own experience, I was always encouraged to grow from being "servant" or "follower" to friend. But I'm afraid it took a long time and the passage of a lot of water under the bridge before I—and many others— came to really understand what this meant.

2

THE SPIRAL QUEST

My fiftieth year had come and gone.
I sat, a solitary man,
In a crowded London shop,
An open book and empty cup
On the marble table top.

While on the shop and street I gazed
My body for a moment blazed,
And twenty minutes, more or less,
It seemed so great my happiness,
That I was blessed, and could bless.
—WILLIAM BUTLER YEATS, "VACILLATION"

PERCEVAL ARRIVES at King Arthur's court and is duly knighted by the king. Only the presence of the spiritual mentor, of the king, can catalyze the recognition in us of our own spiritual birthright. This was what happened to me when I met the founder of the spiritual community I visited: I recognized in him the promise of my own radiance and power. This recognition could be called an initiation into knighthood. Initiation means a beginning: the beginning of a new awareness. A squire of old would become a knight by kneeling while the king touched him lightly on both shoulders with his sword. The newly initiated knight would then swear oaths of loyalty to the king. When we feel the impact of the spiritual mentor's presence, we have been anointed by the sword—by the power—of the king, and our oath of allegiance is the deliberate decision to align with the radiant energy that we have recognized in the spiritual mentor.

While for me the King Arthur figure was exemplified by one particular man, very often the energy of the spiritual mentor does not constellate so neatly in our lives. As I have noted, the myth can condense into just one symbol an experience that in reality plays out in a more convoluted way. Instead of one person, there may be several individuals—a role model, a therapist or healer, an insightful relative—who collectively help initiate us into self-awareness.

We may have aligned ourselves with the radiant mentor energy, but there is still the need to prove out our newfound sense of identity, to *actualize* our potential. To do this we will have to undertake the inner work of the quest.

The impact of the King Arthur energy on us is twofold. First, we feel blessed and received by him just the way we are. Second, we are challenged by him. This is not a deliberate challenge, it is simply the effect on our psyche of this creative, catalyst energy. The challenge takes the form of stirring the pot of our emotional and mental makeup. It is as if a shaping tone starts to rearrange the invisible blueprint of our being. This process of invisible reshaping is the path toward wholeness, is the quest itself. But to begin with, we are unaware of all this. At first it seems to us as if the initiation into knighthood is the end and aim of our seeking. We've become aware of our spiritual birthright; we've become a knight. We've made it.

This initial flush of confidence is represented for us in the myth by Perceval dashing off after Arthur has knighted him to find the Red Knight, whom he duly vanquishes. Then, donning the Red Knight's armor, Perceval sets off again into the forest, not with any thought of being on a quest but in search of his mother! I think this symbolizes rather well that quotation from Goethe: "Everybody wants to be somebody, but nobody wants to grow." We would like to believe that the realization is the deed. No one willingly or consciously sets off on the process of change that the initiation into knighthood is going to require. We think we can just be knighted and then return to our familiar worlds. But it doesn't work that way.

Perceval never finds his mother again. Instead, later on in the story, he learns that she has died. Once the process of the quest has begun, we will never find our familiar worlds again, for the simple reason that our own sense of self, and therefore the world created by that sense of self, will have changed.

In fact, as the challenging energy of the mentor begins to take effect, it is not only the familiar that is lost to us, it is also the king's court. Perceval charges out of Arthur's castle, and he never really returns. For strangely enough, the actualization process begins by leading us far away from where we thought we had arrived. It is not the golden inner halls of Arthur's court that we find ourselves entering but a dark and forbidding forest. It is as if our heads are turned looking in one direction, but we find our feet taking us in another. In my own experience there came a time when instead of that wonderful, overarching sense of empowerment and love, I started to feel insignificant and resentful. Rather than finding Arthur's presence assuring and uplifting, I found him daunting and uncomfortable. What was happening? The shaping energy was stirring up the shadow in me. His radiance had started to highlight those unloved, malformed parts of myself that I thought I had hidden. Almost without my realizing it, I had started out on the quest, had begun the exploration into the shadowy and fearful realm of my own subconscious.

The landscape of the quest in all versions of the story is surreal and dreamlike. It is full of dark forests, wild moors, barren deserts, and enchanted castles and is peopled by monsters and prodigies, fearsome knights and beautiful damsels. A place both frightening and fantastic, it symbolizes well the terrain of the subconscious. This subconscious terrain is the terrain of the quest, and the journey of the quest is the process of purification and healing of this realm.

One of the interesting things about Chrétien de Troyes's version of the story is that Perceval never declares that he is undertaking the quest. He simply finds himself on the quest when he comes across the Wounded Fisher King and the Grail Castle. We are just like Perceval; we do not make a conscious decision to go off on a quest—we simply find ourselves embarked on it. We can never get away from the terrain of the quest, because it is the terrain of our subconscious. It is with us all the time. Whether we realize it or not—or like it or not—we are seeking, questing, to understand this realm.

Now, I need to clarify something about the nature of the subconscious, because I have already said that Merlin the magician represents the subconscious, and Merlin denotes wisdom and magic and certainly not a condition of confusion and fear that is in need of clarification. What I want to suggest, very simply, is that Merlin "resides" in the deeper layers of the subconscious mind. The quest is not concerned with this deep level of the subconscious mind but with the layers that lie just beneath the surface of the conscious mind.

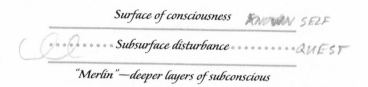

Surface of consciousness   KNOWN SELF

Subsurface disturbance   QUEST

"Merlin"—deeper layers of subconscious

It is in this subsurface level that the memories of wounding, pain, and fear are imprinted, and it is this level that requires purification and healing through undertaking the quest. If we connect with the quickening energy of the spiritual mentor, the process of purification and clarification can start to work more purposefully, because of the resonance set up between the king's energy and the wisdom of Merlin—of the deep subconscious. These two are in agreement, and our lives are set spinning into coherence between the two poles of these archetypal energies. This coherence is the new era that Merlin seeks to bring about with the birth of the king energy in ourselves.

The commencement of our quest is a delicate time, for it is when our shadow parts first begin to be revealed. As these shadow parts start to rise, we may find ourselves disliking or resisting whoever is representing the King Arthur energy to us. We project our own shadow parts onto him to justify our dislike and avoid staring too deeply into the painful jadestone of ourselves. This is a crucial phase in which we must deliberately choose to remember our knighthood vows and not become "forsworn" by giving in to the feelings that emerge. If we do give in to them, we will break the alignment with the radiant energy and will not progress much further but will be repelled from Arthur's presence and out of the process of change and growth. If we can desist from reacting to the negative feelings, we find that soon Arthur's court lies far behind us. We are no longer shadowboxing but fully embarked on the quest. Moving on further into the shadowy territory of ourselves, we are now far enough advanced on our journey that it is too late to turn back. We are in a no–man's–land: the old world has been left behind, but we have not yet entered the new. We may still live in the ordinary world, but we find we are no longer a part of it. We are in it but not of it, even though at times we might like to be. We cannot go back because we know too much.

Much of my twenties was spent in this kind of limbo. Although the busy, teeming world of London poured past all around me, it seemed somehow distant and not relevant. I lived and worked in this world but did not belong to it. Dazzled by the prospect of genuine spiritual presence, I kept myself aloof. The ordinary run of pleasures and motivations did not entice me anymore. I had lost my taste for them, and they had lost their meaning for me. I had no relationships, pursued no coherent career, developed no (conventional) skills. My life revolved around the meetings and routines of the small nucleus of my community's spiritual network and the communal house we lived in. The most I got to interact with the glittering city was having the occasional cup of coffee and slice of cheesecake in a nearby cafe. This was not a comfortable way to be, nor was it something I set out deliberately to do. Sometimes I felt uneasy at my floating, apparently directionless state and would attempt to act in a more rational way: go back and study for my M.A. in American literature; but no, the grant that had once been awarded me was no longer available in the new Thatcher's Britain; and the job as editorial assistant on a small medical newspaper disappeared when the paper was bought by a larger competitor. It was as if my attempts to act more purposefully could not gainsay the deeper currents of direction that were pursuing something much more difficult to define. In my late twenties I gave up what had become a dead-end and excruciatingly confined job as editorial assistant on an obscure legal magazine and moved to the countryside, where a sister community to the one in Canada had now been established.

Perhaps the most difficult part of no-man's-land is the sense of incoherence. I hardly knew who I was anymore: my personality, my opinions, my carefully constructed self-image were all molten and in flux. After the early sureness at Arthur's court, the clarity of my life's purpose—the certainty of what knighthood was about—now everything seemed merely confusing. There was a loss of momentum, and worse, I started to feel enmired again in my sordidly familiar messiness: thorny problems with family members, leftover resentments, a sense of failure, self-dislike, self-doubt, futility, regret. This wilderness experience, the classic rite of passage for all who pledge themselves to spiritual growth, is so uncomfortable that many do not want to set out on it. It feels like everything has gone, has been taken away; but what is really happening is that the foundations are being cleared and then re-laid for the new growth. Even though it is difficult to understand when in the midst of these feelings, the discomfort is a sign that something is really happening. If we just went on feeling euphoric, it would be a fairly sure indication that no fundamental change was occurring in us. The lid would still be firmly on, and we would remain "whited sepulchres": clean and shiny on the outside but inside full of decay—partially processed experience and confused understanding. The real and the whole cannot be built on the flawed and the partial. This is the meaning of being willing to lay down one's life in order to find it.

Paradoxically, this huge upwelling of discomfort is not caused by the King Arthur leader pointing out what is wrong with us. On the contrary, the flushing out of the rotting flesh and decaying bones of our emotional memory is catalyzed by being blessed. King Arthur's energy resonates with and focuses on what is right with us, that is, our core identity. This is his blessing. To focus on what is wrong with us gets nowhere: it is darkness breeding more darkness, the blind leading the blind. To focus on what is right means there is light present, light that naturally shows up the darkness, or causes shadows to be cast. It is not the light's intention to do this, it is simply a by-product of the shining of the spiritual light. This light then gives one the basis for handling the darkness without being overwhelmed by it.

One of the greatest principles of spiritual development is to start with what is right—in oneself, in another, in a situation—and build on that. This does not mean suppression or censorship of what may be considered wrong. Far from it. This will give us a basis on which to allow what is wrong or incomplete to be changed, made whole. Bringing up children is a good example of this. Most people know that if a child is constantly scolded, told he or she is wrong, that child then starts to become more and more "wrong," and the relationship between child and parent grows more tenuous and confrontational. If the relationship of trust is emphasized and encouragement given rather than criticism, the situation opens up very differently. Often what seems wrong is simply incomplete: a childish attempt to do something on one's own that one is not quite capable of bringing off but does not want to ask about in case one is told off or told "No."

The same applies to everyone. We only have the strength to face our "dark side" if we have once seen or intimated our radiance. This may be why the results of psychoanalysis can be disappointing or meager, despite in some cases years of analysis. I remember a fellow student who lived in the same corridor as me in my university hall of residence. She had been under analysis for many years, and this process, with all the detailed ins and outs of the peculiarities of her psyche, absorbed her completely. She rarely left her room, and when I entered it and had a conversation with her it was like being drawn into a Kafkaesque hall of mirrors. Images of herself and her problems echoed and reflected in a miniature infinity, hopelessly entangled and baffling. She was enmeshed in this claustrophobic state, fascinated by her own fascination, and one felt a desire to grab her by the shoulders and shake her loose from it all. Years of attention to what was "wrong" had reinforced rather than resolved the malfunctioning patterns of her neurosis.

There are many versions of the Grail quest stories, and they all manage to be confusingly different and similar at the same time—just as our many individual stories do. All of the different versions are rambling and fantastical, rather like the labyrinthine complexities of my fellow student's world inside her little room, and they make for arduous reading. The events that I outline here are drawn from several of these different versions. Perceval, Gawain, Lancelot, and the other knights travel sometimes in groups or in pairs but for the most part alone. Between them they rescue many other knights and even more damsels in distress and overcome literally hundreds of hostile knights, many of whom are sent packing to Arthur's court. In particular there is the Red Knight, whose armor Perceval takes after killing him. Later on a black knight on a black horse appears and is swallowed up in a tomb. Great storms rage through the skies. They come upon various enchanted castles and also a mysterious, deserted chapel. The heroes also meet and engage in combat with a huge gray man, an immense black man with one eye (the other was lost in a fight with a magic serpent), and a giant.

The rescuing of knights and damsels is a metaphor for freeing those parts of ourselves that have been subject to false conditioning. The encounters with hostile knights and monsters represent the "monster" patterns of emotional control that rise up out of the subsurface levels of the subconscious and seek to reexert their influence over us as they have in the past. These emotional controls relate primarily to feelings of fear, and its close companions shame and guilt.

The Black Knight, who is swallowed up in a tomb, and the Perilous Chapel, in which a giant black hand appears and extinguishes the candle flickering on the altar, have to do specifically with the fear of death. The color black symbolizes death; in addition, some scholars suggest that echoed in these strange encounters are ancient initiation rites, in which the initiate has to face his or her own mortality. The only way the fear of death can be overcome is by experiencing the fact that our primary identity is rooted in spirit and not in flesh. As I will show, this question of identity is key to the completion of the quest and to the whole meaning of the myth.

The storms are emotional storms, and we all know what storms do: they break up the tension, release pent-up emotion, and cause rain—the water of truth—to pour down on parched earth. So the storms indicate a process of emotional release and renewal.

One of the strangest adventures is in the Castle of Wonders, also called the Castle of Maidens. Here Gawain, or in some versions Perceval, lies down in full armor on an enchanted bed, whereupon crossbar bolts and arrows fly in at him through the windows, after which a giant lion leaps on him. He survives the bolts and arrows and overcomes the lion, cutting off its head and feet. He is then told that he has freed all the (mainly female) inhabitants of the castle, who are now ready to serve him. The Celtic name for the otherworld, which can be said to represent the magical subconscious realm, is the "Island of Women," and the presence of many women, both young and old, in the Castle of Wonders or Maidens therefore correlates this castle with the other-world and hence with the subconscious realm. Gawain's ability to survive both arrows and lion while on the bed demonstrates the attainment of a liberated relationship with the feminine of the subconscious and in particular with the "animal," merely instinctual feminine of sexuality. So here we see that the process of "purification" of the subconscious does not mean the attempt to somehow purge oneself of anything that might not fit in with conventional morality. To the contrary, purification consists of including and opening up in a fuller way the sexual currents and deep feminine heart of our beings (symbolized by the women being ready to serve Gawain) and seeing that this crucial part of ourselves is only problematical if denied.

Yet another peculiar castle is empty except for a set of chess pieces, which play against Perceval and checkmate him three times. Perceval loses his temper and threatens to throw the pieces into the castle moat, but a damsel rises out of the moat and warns him not to. The black and white of the chessboard and pieces represent the dualities of our own nature, which we must learn to play upon in order to navigate successfully through life. Later I will explore how the attaining of the Grail is itself a symbol of the uniting and resolving of duality: male/female, conscious/subconscious, secular/sacred, inner/outer, form and spirit, and so on. Perceval's defeat means he is not yet ready to unite these dualities in himself. He is still struggling with them and wants to submerge them, go "unconscious," which the maiden emerging out of the moat—his own subconscious—warns him against.

In a third castle the hero meets nobody but is served by invisible hands. These tell us that in many ways the forces of the unknown, toward which we strive, will look after us. They are a rather lovely symbol of the presence of God; how the presence of the divine works through the circumstances to help one achieve one's goal once one has committed oneself to it.

After overcoming the Red Knight, Perceval's next encounter is with a very different kind of knight called Gornemant of Gohort. Gornemant, realizing that Perceval lacks any kind of training as a knight, invites him to stay for a while and trains him in riding, jousting, and other knightly skills. He also advises Perceval to avoid overreadiness in speaking and asking questions. Gornemant's training of Perceval represents our conditioning: that imprinting of the patterns of the normal, socially acceptable world. And as I will show, these conditioned responses can get in the way of actually experiencing one's authentic self and fulfilling the Grail quest.

Soon after Perceval leaves Gornemant, he comes upon a castle and town under siege. He learns from the damsel of the castle, Blanchefleur, that they are being besieged by King Clamadeu. Perceval promises to help, and they pass the night together "side by side and mouth to mouth." In the morning, Perceval overcomes Clamadeu and sends him off to Arthur's court. This mirroring of male and female represents the mind and heart working together, with neither one overruling or controlling the other. This kind of self-mastery is important because it means that the conscious mind is able to hold steady and does not react when wild or ugly apparitions—feelings—emerge out of the heart realm. In this way the old emotional tapes can be erased: King Clamadeu is overcome. If, however, we react to the apparitions—in disgust or denial—the patterns become recharged with one's emotional energy and can sink back beyond conscious reach again, where they will continue to exert their illogical and often destructive influence on one's behavior.

At one point on the quest a devil appears and takes Perceval's horse. Then the devil turns into the form of another horse for Perceval to mount, only to disappear from under him when he makes the sign of a cross at a stream. This encounter enacts for us the problem of deceit, self-deceit for the most part, and the necessity of not being fooled by the appearance of things. The horse, that powerful animal whose energy we use to carry us, is yet another symbol of the power of the subconscious. That power can be subverted to evil ends, cleverly disguised to look the same as before. The figure of the devil is often associated with false appearance and has to do with the idea of substituting what is God-like for God. Hence this little piece of symbolism is also to do with the way we must struggle with our very ideals and *ideas* of God, because these things are not the reality but only images—graven images—of the reality. As such, they are potentially dangerous. We can get caught up in trying to be God-like—adhering to certain belief systems, obeying sets of rules and dogma—and be diverted from the true goal of the quest, which is not to become *like* God but to know God in ourselves. Perceval makes the sign of the cross at the stream. The cross is a much more ancient symbol than that associated with the crucifixion of Christ. It denotes the source of identity, the crossover point where the integration of the vertical and horizontal factors of identity—spirit and form—meet.

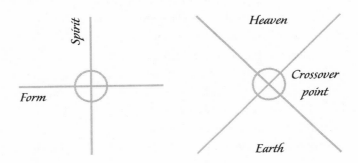

The cross does also of course evoke the presence of Christ, that is, a higher spiritual authority. The stream is a body of flowing water; thus truth is represented as a flowing energy: a presence, not a dogma. It is the presence of the living God that exposes the false appearance, the attempt to be God-like, and causes it to disappear from under us, setting us down with a bump.

In one version of the story, toward the end of his adventures Perceval comes upon a tree at a crossroads. In its branches are two naked seven-year-old children who guide him on his way to the Grail Castle. The children represent innocence: they are naked, and they are children. It is always the quality of innocence that brings us to the Grail Castle. The age of the children, seven, is also significant: the full spiritual stature of the human being is said to be of seven dimensions: three inner and three outer, with the seventh being the heart realm where inner and outer meet. This is the meaning of the seven golden candlesticks in the Book of Revelation whose shape echoes the tree in which the children sit. Experiencing the connection between inner and outer, spirit and form, is what is symbolized by the finding of the Grail. The position of the tree at the crossing of four ways tinges this tree with the

archetypal image of the World Tree that grows at
the center of the four quarters of the world, accessing the three planes of existence, or joining
the three levels of the human being: the inner,
outer, and heart realms.

Only one knight out of all those who begin
the quest is successful. This is usually Perceval but
in some versions is Gawain, and in one version
is Galahad. Many knights are unhorsed, endure
gruesome adventures, or are even killed. However, the low success rate of the knights does not
mean that very few people will ever be able to
succeed in the quest; it is simply yet another
metaphor for the process of clarification. Those
parts of ourselves that are unclear, or in "shadow,"
are going to have a hard time of it and may even
be vanquished in the process. Only the quality of
innocence, which the Perceval/Gawain/Galahad
figure represents, will allow us to find the Grail
Castle.

On first reading, the fantastic and multitu-
dinous encounters and tests of the quest appear
illogical and bewildering—which is rather like
many of the situations that arise in our lives. Yet a
closer look at the quest—and one's life—reveals
that all these incidents revolve around the twin
issues of fear and identity. Overcoming the fearsome knights and monsters, the emotional controls of one's subconscious, relates to handling
fear; exposing false conditioning, including a sense
of being "God-like," relates to clarifying identity.
In fact the quest is not so much a linear path from
one point to another as a spiraling around and
around slightly different rings of the same territory. On this rambling, inward curve, one encounters fear and identity "masks" in varying guises

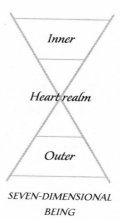

SEVEN-DIMENSIONAL
BEING

SEVEN GOLDEN
CANDLESTICKS

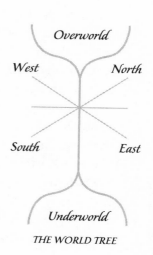

THE WORLD TREE

(and often one's experience seems to repeat, yet it is never an exact repetition, because it is a spiral and not a circle) until we arrive at the center, the hub of the spiral, and encounter the root fear and the central identity issue—and find that they are one and the same.

Not even the fear of death, faced at the Perilous Chapel, is as terrible as this first fear that lurks deep in the center of us. This is the fear that we might be nothing and that we might have no meaning. We cover this fear up with its opposite—the conviction that we are the center of the universe. This central fear, and its opposite pole of paranoia, is why we started to feel uncomfortable around King Arthur. His presence threatened us because it bruises our ego-self that has subconsciously confused itself with the center of the universe. His authority is a reminder that we might be wrong and therefore might after all be nothing. So this central misalignment gets nudged and pushed and prodded this way and that, until one day we meet the Wounded Fisher King and enter the Grail Castle and see it all there, laid out before us. For just as this central fear sits at the center of one's subconscious process, so the Wounded Fisher King and his home, the Grail Castle, sit at the center of Perceval's wanderings.

Perceval comes upon a river and sees upon it two men fishing from a boat. One of them directs Perceval to his castle, which is close at hand. Although Perceval does not realize it, the man who directs him is the Wounded Fisher King. At this point, Perceval does not see that this man is wounded. Nor at first can he see the castle, but then he suddenly comes upon it and finds that it is large and splendid. Inside he finds a man with graying temples lying on a couch in a large banqueting hall. It is the same man who was fishing from the boat. The man apologizes for not getting up but explains he is unable to and invites Perceval to sit beside him on the couch. A lad comes in from outside, bringing a sword that has been sent by the invalided man's niece. The lad gives the sword to the wounded king, who then immediately presents it to Perceval. A strange procession then takes place out of one inner room through the banqueting hall and into another inner room: "they passed by in front of the couch, going from one room into another." First comes a youth holding a white lance that drips blood, then two more (extremely handsome) youths carrying golden candelabras with ten candles burning in all, then a beautiful maiden carrying a grail or chalice of refined gold set with jewels, and finally another maiden with a silver carving dish.

One of many meanings laid out for us in this short but numinous sequence of events is the anatomy of our central fear: its nature, its cause, and its cure. The first stage of dealing with fear is the emotion itself. We feel fear—the wound, represented here by the Wounded Fisher King. Perceval first sees the wounded king fishing from a boat. The boat is on the river; the river (as water does so often throughout the myth) represents our own subconscious. The fear has surfaced—has emerged from the subconscious realm to the surface of consciousness—and we have become aware of it. The next thing that happens is that Perceval comes upon the Grail Castle and finds it to be large and splendid. Inside, he finds the king again, lying on a couch, and he realizes that the king is wounded. Up to this point, Perceval hasn't seen that the king is wounded—he has just seen the king. Likewise, at first we just perceive, feel, and "see" the fear; then we realize that the fear is caused by something. There is a wound somewhere; what is the nature of this wound? What is *causing* the fear? Well, suddenly all these people and objects start issuing out of one inner room and proceeding before us into another.

Although we don't know it yet, the Grail King, the heavenly energy that Arthur represented to us, already resides in one of those inner rooms. Does the castle belong to the Grail King or the Wounded Fisher King? The Grail Castle is large and splendid. It is the house of our being. Whenever we come upon the wound we are also in the vicinity of a healing power. They coexist in the same place. We don't believe yet that the presence of the Grail King is more powerful than the Wounded Fisher King—than the fear/wound. After all, we think the Grail Castle, our house of being, is the home of the Wounded Fisher King; it was he who invited us there, after all!

All the beautiful precious objects that proceed through the banqueting hall are different symbols of one's own being when illuminated by the connection to the Grail King. Supreme among them is the Grail chalice. There is already a lot of light in this banqueting hall. The fire is so large that four hundred people could be seated in front of it, and there are hundreds of candles. But when the maiden enters bearing the Grail, so great a radiance appears that the candles lose their brilliance, as the stars do at the rising of the sun. The squire and the three youths and two maidens all pass by between the couch, where lies the Wounded Fisher King, and the brightly blazing fire: "and [they] passed by between the fire and those seated on the couch." Here the fire is behind them, like the fire of love, not known directly but through the medium of our own beings when we are aligned with the heavenly king energy. So as Perceval watches, and the objects process by, here is symbolized the first stirring, the beginning connection to the light energy of the Grail King.

The wound, which is felt primarily as fear, is caused by the separation from the energy of the heavenly king; the wound is the closed door of that inner room where the Grail King lives. In some sense, without the open, experienced connection to the wellspring of ourselves, we *are* nothing. That is why we fear that we are nothing. Our identity is shaped around a mask, an outer sense of self only, one that is not sourced securely in a transcendent reality. So it feels fragile and builds defenses upon defenses around itself, like the ancient hill forts surrounded by circular ditches, earth walls, fences, and moats. These are the defenses that we have to slowly unwind, slowly spiral through on the journey of the quest. Instead of one's true self, one's inner king operating at the center of ourselves, it is the ego sitting there, an ego that thinks of itself as being God-like, instead of having a connection to God.

The wound is twofold. First, it is the fear that one is nothing; second, it is the attempt to cover up the fear of nothingness by constructing a falsely inflated human ego identity. The cause of this twofold wound is the separation from God, the sense of disconnection from the deeper spiritual dimension of being.

Perceval sees the Wounded Fisher King. He gets to see where and how the wound comes into focus. If we can see our fear, it means that it has begun to separate out from our consciousness; otherwise we would not be able to see it, we would simply continue to be controlled by it. The reason why we can see the fear is because we have stumbled into the Grail Castle and therefore into the presence of the Grail, the connection to the Grail King. So, paradoxically, when we draw close to the fear at the center of ourselves, it is not the fear we feel but the presence of love, the presence of the heavenly king. This is the Grail Castle epiphany.

I can remember lying in bed on the first night of my stay at the community in Caribou, knowing instinctively that I was in the presence of a force, a dynamic, that I knew would heal me. The experience would be challenging and would require everything of me, but I knew that here was a quality, a tingling something sensed in the very air, that could penetrate the fears and vulnerabilities that caged me. I could *feel* those fears and limitations, but I could also "see" them. They had separated out from me sufficiently for me to know that although they were in me they were not "of" me. They were not a part of who I really was. And it was during my visit there that my first visit to the Grail Castle took place. In that atmosphere, without fully realizing it, I began to open up and to shed some of my inhibitions and teenage sadnesses. And one evening, at yet another little social gathering in someone's small log cabin home, I was drinking tea, talking and laughing with everyone else, when something began to happen. I suddenly felt a power starting to build inside; a hugely powerful flow was welling up, rising up, like a great golden sun. Instantly I recognized that this energy is what is really meant by the word *love* and the word *truth*. This was it, and it was also me, it was who I really was, who everyone really was. It was the fire of core being: so strong and so radiant.

I started to wonder if anyone could see what was happening—if I was transfigured in some way. I said something about a power building up inside me and voiced concern about how I would handle this when I got home. A friend said something like "Don't worry, you'll know what to do." And I realized she did not understand what was happening. And then the power, the gold, subsided. It hadn't lasted very long, but I knew that it was what all the religions and mystery traditions were talking about. I knew beyond a doubt, from that time on, that the power of the heavenly king is real and is inside all of us. I knew it, but I did not understand it. Nor did I have any idea how to recreate that experience. Furthermore, even though I had the experience, it did not prevent me from subsequently stumbling back into the forest of emotional monsters.

Experiences of this kind, of greater or lesser intensity, are nowadays very often termed "altered states" or "peak experiences." No longer just the domain of the hermit of old or the visionary poet, they appear to be much more common than the prevailing cultural orthodoxy would have us believe, as is witnessed by the ever-increasing volume of literature on the subject. However, the Grail Castle experience may not be as dramatic as this: it can simply be a feeling of well-being, a lifting or clearing in consciousness, a sudden sense of the beauty of the world. Certainly my experience of transfiguration while at the community was a high point of that visit, and it was subsequently also a reference point of sure knowing while walking through many other landscapes of fear and doubt in my life. However, the whole five-week visit also became a touchstone in my life. Drying the white hot plates together at the back sink of the big communal kitchen, gathering wild camomile by the barn, joking with the "cowboys" who worked the ranch, the smell of the pines in the sun, the sweet beauty that I saw in the people, the depth of connection that I saw was possible between us, the way incredibly simple things, like having tea, could hold so much satisfaction when undertaken from a depth of presence—all of these aspects would remain like a window into true home in my memory and heart. This very unlikely Shangri-la, a somewhat ramshackle collection of huts and cabins nestled up in the Caribou plateau of British Columbia, was the place where I got a taste of what life could be if lived from a center of true being. It was where I connected with the true meaning of life, and ultimately with my life's purpose.

The hallmark of the Grail Castle experiences is that they emerge spontaneously and are not caused by something wonderful happening to us first. They are not feelings brought about because we have got something we always longed for or achieved something important to us or because we are in love. All these things will certainly make us happy in various ways, but they are not Grail Castle experiences.

I can remember another occasion at a youth hostel in Nice on the Côte d'Azur. A friend and I had hitchhiked across France, encountering many adventures. We had reached our destination; the showers were cold, our money was running very low, and there was the feeling that our adventures were far from over. It was our first night at the hostel, and I was staring out the window. A yellow moon was hanging in the sky. As I looked out at the moon, I felt a deep, strong upwelling of happiness flooding through me. The sense of assurance and unconditional joy was palpable and wonderful. In fact, the experience was so wonderful *because* there was no reason for it. It was not dependent on something pleasant happening. The implication, therefore, was that potentially this experience could always be available to me.

Perceval sits by the Wounded Fisher King and watches the procession, but, mindful of Gornemant's instructions, he does not say anything or ask any questions, thinking that it might seem rude to do so.

> The grail, which proceeded ahead, was of pure refined gold. And this grail was set with many kinds of precious stones, the richest and most costly in sea or earth: those stones in the grail certainly surpassed all others. Exactly as the lance had done, they passed by in front of the couch, going from one room into another. The young man saw them pass, but did not dare ask who was served from the grail, for he kept continually in his heart the words of that wise gentleman.

Instead, he decides he will ask in the morning. However, Perceval wakes at daybreak to an empty, silent castle in which the only door open to him is the main entranceway, where his horse awaits, saddled and ready. The drawbridge is already down, but as Perceval rides across, it starts to rise so that he and his horse have to jump to safety onto the opposite bank of the moat.

The Grail Castle, which appeared so suddenly and mysteriously and then drew up its drawbridge as suddenly again, symbolizes these moments of epiphany when the divine energy that lives at the core of us like a fire begins to be felt and known. Our own being starts to be illuminated by the connection to the Grail King, the door to the inner room opens, and the procession of beautiful objects moves through into it. But we don't yet know how to give ourselves into what is happening. During my epiphany experience of power rising up inside me, one part of my consciousness—the ordinary, everyday part—was *watching* what was happening. I can remember even feeling worried about how I would integrate this new power with my life back in England. So even though the power of the living God was pouring through my being, my conditioned consciousness was concerned with how it would fit "normality"! And as that worry surfaced in me, the golden power subsided. It is almost as if in these moments one gives greater credence to one's conditioning—to Gornemant's instructions—than to the experience itself. And so the light fades, leaving one knowing, but not understanding.

Gornemant represents the quality in people and traditions that has integrity and is honorable and well-meaning but is also ultimately obedient to the status quo. A Gornemant figure in one's life can nurture and assist us at many levels but is not equipped to help one find the Grail, because he or she does not recognize the validity of the spiritual context in anything but an institutionalized way. I remember one teacher in my high school who was kindly and encouraging toward me, where others thought me a bit of a pain. Her benign attitude meant a lot to me, but it became almost more difficult for my own inner questing than the somewhat cynical attitude of some other teachers, when I came to see that she didn't really give weight to the kind of crazy, visionary spark in me. In a paradoxical way, then, while on the one hand a Gornemant in our lives can give us some respite and help on our journey, on the other hand their very kindness and gravitas gives them more weight in our own eyes, so that their apparently wise and implicit assumption that our spiritual insights are nothing more than delusional shadows can be more undermining to our spiritual progress than a less benevolent figure.

Perceval follows tracks into the forest hoping to find some of the castle's occupants out hunting, but instead of meeting the fisher king or his retinue he meets a lamenting damsel with a beheaded knight on her lap. Immediately we know that something is amiss: her knight is dead; we are back in the wasteland. The Grail Castle experiences have a peculiar quality to them. When we are in the Grail Castle, in the presence of the Grail, there is no question that the experience is real, yet a few moments later, when the light fades, it is as if we were never there. The drawbridge snaps shut. Unlike memories of other pleasant times—a holiday, a reunion with old friends—one can start to doubt whether it ever happened, so different is the nature of the experience to what one is used to and so quickly and intensely do the conditions of the wasteland swarm in again to claim one's attention—and claim one's allegiance to their familiar, and apparently invincible, reality.

It is from this damsel that Perceval learns where he has been and who he has been with. The damsel identifies for him the fisher king and the Grail Castle and explains how the king was wounded: "he was wounded and indeed maimed in a battle, so that he has not been able to manage for himself since; for he was struck by a javelin right through both thighs." She then questions him about what happened to him in the castle. When she learns that he saw the lance, candelabra, Grail, and so on but did not ask about any of them, she reproaches him bitterly and tells him that if he had only asked questions he would have brought relief to the suffering of the king and his land. Up until this point, Perceval has "had the experience but missed the meaning." (T. S. Eliot, "The Dry Salvages," from *Four Quartets*). Perceval is innocent, but he is not yet wise. He is not yet conscious of what he is doing. He learns about everything after the event. Innocence—openness of heart, will get us into the Grail Castle, but wisdom is what we need to take us back there: "and approach to the meaning restores the experience / In a different form" (Eliot, "The Dry Salvages"). Wisdom consists of coming to understand the spiritual mechanics behind the Grail Castle experience and aligning with those mechanics in order to bring about the complete healing of the wound.

We have tasted what the Grail cup has to offer. We have drunk a little of the ambrosia of divinity, and now we know that there is an experience, a way to be that surpasses any ordinary joys that life has to offer. Moreover, we know that this experience of fulfillment is not dependent on outer circumstance and does not arise from an outer cause at all but from an inner source. This much we know. Now we must find out how to let the Grail Castle experience be a more ongoing reality, so that as we live from that place ourselves, we are in position to play the King Arthur mentor role for others and thus assist in their process of healing too. This means that we must consciously seek out—not just stumble upon—the Grail Castle and its wounded occupant again and ask the all-important Question that our conditioning and our fear prevented us from asking the first time.

When we come to the account in Chrétien de Troyes's poem of Perceval's first visit to the Grail Castle, we know that we have arrived at the core meaning of the story. All the rambling around has suddenly ended in a short passage into which is packed an astonishing concentration of symbol and meaning. We know we are at the threshold of understanding; and yet the understanding eludes us, just as it does Perceval—and before he and we know it, the interlude is over. In fact so charged and concentrated is the symbolism of this passage, that we cannot continue on with—nor fully understand—the rest of the story until we have explored further the meanings that are clustered together here. Five years of wandering will pass before Perceval gains sufficient understanding and clarity to find the Grail Castle again—but only three more chapters must pass before I will return there and elucidate fully the significance of the Question and many other matters.

3

THE FISH, THE CUP, AND THE ANATOMY OF THE WOUND

The conviction of the senses often shuts the door to the realities of being. —LLOYD MEEKER

What is the cup? It is your body, your form of being, which when it is filled with the water of truth can begin to quench the thirst in others. But until your cup does overflow you cannot give to others.
—LLOYD MEEKER

WHEN PERCEVAL stumbles upon the Wounded Fisher King and his home, the Grail Castle, he is coming, as I have described, to the center and peak of the spiral quest. He is uncovering the core fear that sits at the center of ourselves: the fear that we might be nothing and have no meaning. (This fear has a twin manifestation of its opposite, a sense of ourselves as the center of the universe, which is the attempt to cover up the fear.) This fear is symbolized by the presence of the Wounded Fisher King, or more specifically, by this king's wound. But at the Grail Castle Perceval is also close to discovering the means by which this wound can be healed, because the door to the inner room where the Grail King lives is open. The Grail King symbolizes the heavenly king energy, the presence of God or love that also lives within us and that floods us at moments of epiphany or "well"-being. Love, as it is said, casts out fear. This presence or power would, if accessed, heal the wound of fear.

Therefore we could say that the wound is the closed door of that inner room where the Grail King lives and is the sense of separation from the Grail King energy. But if the wound is caused by the closed door, the separation, why does the grieving maiden whom Perceval meets when he leaves the Grail Castle describe the fisher king's wound so graphically for us as caused by a javelin thrust through his thighs? "For he was struck by a javelin right through both thighs."

The wound in the thighs symbolizes impotency (this is why he is described by the maiden as "maimed"). This does not mean just sexual impotency but a loss of power, a loss of the life current, the feeling of powerlessness. And what does this lead to? Fear: fear of being defenseless; fear of being nothing.

The implication here is that the wound of fear that sits at the center of us (and consequently the attempt to cover it up) is a *secondary* wound, that there was a *prior wounding* that led to this secondary wound of fear. And this prior wounding is whatever caused that door to close, whatever caused the sense of separation from the Grail King energy. So how did this door get closed in the first place? What caused the separation?

Childhood, especially early childhood, is thought of as a time of wonder, and this is because, generally speaking, the sense of connection to the presence of love is dominant in the childish consciousness. The door has not yet been closed. But of course, as young children, we are vulnerable to the behavior of others, to the atmosphere of the larger world. Very early in my childhood, before I was old enough to be logical, I turned my heart away from my father. This was not something which, at the age of five, I decided to do, although I was aware that I had done it. I can still remember my mother, concerned about the change in my behavior, picking me up and taking me over to my father to be given a hug by him. She had to initiate deliberately this exchange because I had withdrawn so dramatically. I don't remember her trying again. Something sad and cold had settled over my heart, and it stayed there until my father's death. Why had I done this? It certainly wasn't because my father was abusive in any way. In fact he was an extremely kind and gentle man, and he loved me dearly. But he was also weak and unhappy, and at some point my childish mind and heart found this out, and my great love for him felt betrayed. This turning away was a deep wound to my psyche. It meant that the male animus had nothing to form around, and it tended to remain hesitant and doubtful, rather like my father himself was. At age eight a woman friend of mine had a terrible encounter with a would-be rapist. He was her neighbor and threatened her with death if she ever told about his attack. This ensured her silence, and the double fear of the attack and the threat caused the trauma to go underground. The memory did not surface until about 25 years later, and her life in between had been lived in a kind of disconnected ungrounded place—a situation she still has to grapple with. Many children suffer physical and sexual abuse from their own parents. My own wounding, though much less extreme, nevertheless inserted a sense that something was wrong. The world was not okay, not safe; I felt fearful.

In his book *Magical Child,* Joseph Chiltern Pearce argues that a young child's consciousness does not really differentiate between inner and outer:

> The brain as hologram is representative of the earth. So long as this is undifferentiated, the personality, or consciousness within that brain, receiving its perceptions from that brain, is literally an undifferentiated part of the hologram effect. It is part and parcel of the world system, which, because it radiates out from the child, places him/her at the center of thought, with the world a body extending from him/her.

No separation exists yet between the sense of self, which includes the numinous presence of love at the center of the self, and the outer world and the people in it. So when the parent/adult wounds this childish heart and consciousness, it is almost as if we have been wounded by God himself. The withdrawal of our sense of trust and openness from an outer source of love—the wounding parent or adult—correlates with a closing-over of connection to the inner presence. As a result, we do not go on to learn how to sustain our orientation to the core presence of ourselves, the door to the inner room from where the radiant energy of the Grail King emanates through us is closed.

Instead of growing naturally into our spiritual heritage, we inherit the conditioning of society, the conviction in those around us that fulfillment is to be found from an outer source of one kind or another, whether that be material possessions, intellectual achievement, career goals, relationships, even family and children. And deeper down, we are hoping that these outer forms and achievements will cover up our sense of nothingness and feed the spiritual hunger that the cutoff from inner source causes. Thus the wound of fear and its twin manifestation of ego-coverup of the fragile, separate sense of self is manifested and repeated generation after generation.

Perceval was brought up in an obscure part of the world, where he lived very simply and dressed in sackcloth. He represents a consciousness that is still open, that is not yet completely taken over by the addiction to, the lure of, the glittery world of form. This is the innocent quality of openness that can bring us into the presence of the Grail King. On the way, however, we have to meet the Wounded Fisher King, who represents not just our own wounded consciousness but the collective wound, and the ingrained, unquestioned belief of most of the world—our heritage—that consuming and acquiring these outer forms and facades is the way to happiness and meaning.

In two versions of the story, the fisher king is first encountered while fishing from a boat, and in Chrétien de Troyes's "Perceval" it is explained that ever since his wound in the thighs by a spear his only solace has been to fish. Just as we attempt to cover up our fear or feed our emptiness by consuming or accumulating more, so the Wounded Fisher King seeks to ease his wound by going fishing. This gives us a clue to the meaning of this mysterious fish symbol.

If we delve into Celtic myth, and ancient Mediterranean mystery religions, we find that the fish is a symbol with a long genealogy and many connotations. There are ancient Celtic sea deities who often fed on salmon, and there is a story in Irish mythology in which the hero Finn eats the "salmon of knowledge" and becomes a great poet. The fish is a symbol of immemorial antiquity associated with fertility and life, and the title "fisher" was often connected to deities who were themselves connected with the origin and preservation of life. The annual death and resurrection of such deities were thought to ensure the on-going fertility of the land by the cults who worshipped them. Sometimes ritualized maiming rites were connected with this worship. Fish, moreover, was the holy food of the ancient mystery religions, which existed in parallel with the fertility cults but whose concern was with spiritual regeneration. None of these connotations, however, explains either why the fish appears to be such a potent symbol or what its significance is in the Grail myths.

I believe the answer to both puzzles (as well as a clue to the genealogy of the meaning of the fish symbol) is to be found in yet another fish symbol, the *vesica piscis,* or Vessel of the Fish, which is the shape derived from two equal, overlapping circles, the circumference of one passing through the center of the other.

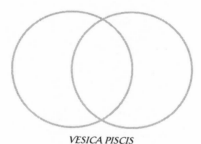

VESICA PISCIS

This ancient shape and symbol has been described by John Michell as "the matrix figure of sacred geometry." From it are derived the hexagon and sixfold geometry, including the pyramid. This symbol is also seen as depicting the vulva of the great Mother (matrix) Goddess, out of whom all life flows, just as all the primary shapes of sacred geometry come from the vesica. Using techniques developed by the renowned photographer Lennart Nilsson, film footage exists of the fertilized ovum as it begins the process of division that will ultimately build a human body. The nucleus of the cell divides into two nuclei, and the two emerging cells begin to move apart. As they do so, they form the two overlapping circles (only of course they are really spheres) of the vesica,

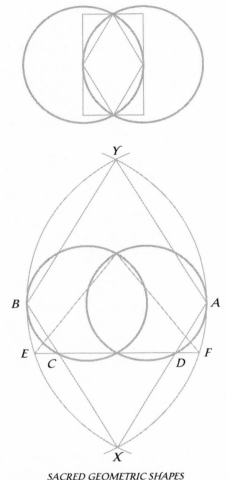

SACRED GEOMETRIC SHAPES
DERIVED FROM THE VESICA PISCIS

the circumference of one passing through the center of the other. Out of these two overlapping cells will come all the forms of life as they occur in the body.

In Tibetan Buddhism, as described by Lama Anagarika Govinda, the overlapping circles are called the solar and lunar circles. The solar circle is the inner world of mind, the universal or archetypal consciousness, and the lunar circle symbolizes the empirical, outer world. Where the circles overlap, the vesica, or vessel, is termed *manas*. In his

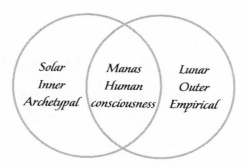

book *Time Stands Still,* Keith Critchlow notes that *manas* "has been etymologically linked via the archaic Indo-European language with the word *man*—the conscious animal." Here the vesica represents the consciousness of humankind that connects the realms of inner and outer. Thus the vesica symbolizes both the deep feminine, the source of creation, and the place of connection between spirit and form, heaven and earth.

What other symbol has such connotations? The Grail chalice itself: the feminine form and vessel of the chalice or cup, whose shape clearly echoes that of the womb and whose appearance in the Grail Castle signifies the beginning connection with the Grail King energy of the inner realms. In the British Museum there is a thirteenth-century Mycenean goblet that depicts the association between chalice and womb. It has two delicate oval handles, shaped like ovaries, while the triangular central part of the cup and its stem form the uterus and vagina. This shape is echoed by the stylized pattern on the cup of the tapering arms and long body of a cuttlefish. Here the fish connection reinforces the paralleling symbolism of Grail and vesica. The fish has also been associated with sexuality, which is explained by the vesica symbolizing the vulva of the Mother Goddess and the Grail chalice symbolizing the womb.

The Grail has essentially a twofold significance as a symbol: in its aspect of a container and in what it contains. Its lineage, like that of the Wounded Fisher King, appears to derive from both Celtic myth and ancient Mediterranean mystery cults. In Irish legend, one of the four treasures belonging to the godlike Tuatha De Danaan was Dagda's cauldron, which could feed an entire army without becoming empty. Welsh legend has several such magic containers: the slain could be

*THIRTEENTH-CENTURY
MYCENEAN GOBLET WITH
STYLIZED CUTTLEFISH DESIGN
(Credit: British Museum, London)*

brought back to life in Bran's cauldron; Caridwen's cauldron contained a drink that conferred wisdom and inspiration. When meat for a coward was put into the cauldron at Tyrnog it would not cook, while meat for a brave man was cooked at once. The basket of Gywddo Gahahir was one of the Thirteen Precious Things of the Island of Britain. If food for one man was placed in it, sustenance for one hundred was provided. Bran also had a horn of plenty—the cornucopia—and a similar symbol occurs in Irish myth as well.

The mystery cults had a tradition of a mystic meal served out of holy vessels. Eating the food out of this sacred vessel was part of a process of initiation into life. In its Christianized form, the vessel ultimately became the chalice of the Eucharist. According to the story in the "Grand Saint Graal," the Grail is the dish that Christ ate from during the last supper. Later Joseph collected the blood flowing from Jesus' wounds in the same dish, while helping to lay his body out in the tomb; Joseph eventually brought the dish to Britain.

The womb contains both menstrual blood or the newly forming baby. Both blood and baby are symbols of life. The magic cauldrons conferred life-giving properties. The cornucopia or horn of plenty holds all the abundance of creation: fruit, flowers, jewels, all the forms of life. The vessels of the mystery religions held food that initiated their tasters into life. The cup of the Eucharist holds wine, the symbol of Christ's blood and a symbol of life. So something is held in, or issues out of, the Grail that is life-giving. In one version of the stories, the

Grail mysteriously appears at Pentecost in the midst of a feast at Camelot. It passes around the room and serves each person food that is supremely satisfying to him or her.

Perhaps the most central meaning of both aspects of the Grail is given here in this beautiful and simple passage from the Psalm 23: "Thou preparest a table before me in the presence of mine enemies: thou anointest my head with oil; my cup runneth over." The cup runs over, the heart is full to overflowing with the presence of love, irrespective of outer circumstance—"in the presence of mine enemies." The heart that is open to the presence of the heavenly king energy, in other words the experience of union—connection—with the divine source: this is what finding the Grail symbolizes in the Grail quest. The container is the heart, and that which is contained within it, the life-giving substance, is the substance of love.

If the two circles of the vesica piscis symbol represent the inner and outer, the spiritual and material worlds, and the vesica shape is the place where the two connect, then finding the Grail also means to find the place of connection between these two worlds and to let them be joined instead of separated. This place of connection symbolizes the purified heart realm.

The esoteric name for Christ was Jesus the Fish. Early Christians, wishing to hide their true affiliation, used the initials of the words "Iesous Christos Theou Huios Soter" (Jesus Christ, Son of God, Savior) which together form ICHTHUS, the Greek word for *fish*. However, Jesus also spoke about his disciples who were fishermen being "fishers of men," and he performed the miracle of the loaves and the fishes. I believe that once again underlying all these fish connotations is the vesica symbol, which denotes the consciousness of union between God and human being, inner and outer, because this is the Christ consciousness: "I and my Father are one."

At the Chalice Well gardens in Glastonbury, England, the correspondence between the Grail and vesica symbols is graphically demonstrated. The symbol of the vesica piscis adorns the lid of the well that is said to be the place where the Grail chalice was hidden. Moreover, there are several other places in the gardens where the vesica is formed, including an ancient yew tree whose trunk divides into two and then

CHALICE WELL LID, CHALICE WELL GARDENS, GLASTONBURY, ENGLAND
(Credit: Bernard Chandler)

grows together again higher up, making the same shape as the central area of the vesica. This extraordinary feature of the yew has become known as the "vulva of the Goddess."

If the vesica piscis is a symbol of the Grail, the various fish found in the stories of the Grail quest must also be symbols of the Grail. In fact this parallel symbolism is enacted in Robert de Boron's poem, when Brons is instructed to place a fish that he has caught on the table opposite the Grail vessel. Those who sit at the table are then "filled with sweetness and the desire of their heart." Here the equivalence of fish and Grail is demonstrated in two ways: first by them being placed opposite one another, and second by the way they share the same mysterious ability to satisfy both physical and spiritual appetites.

And if the fish is the Grail, then when we come across the wounded king fishing from a boat, when he is given the epithet Fisher, and when

THE "VULVA OF THE MOTHER GODDESS," ANCIENT YEW TREE IN CHALICE WELL
GARDENS, GLASTONBURY, ENGLAND (Credit: Bernard Chandler)

we learn that his only relief from the suffering caused by his wound is to fish, a whole lot more meaning must be involved than merely an account of a king's angling hobby. In fact this insistent but unexplained fish symbolism is like one of those odd, illogical junctures in our dreams that don't quite add up until we "decode" them.

We remember that the Grail has a dual significance: first in its aspect of container and second, in what it contains. The chalice or cup will tend to denote the aspect of the Grail as container. The vesica piscis symbol, with its connotation of the vulva of the Mother Goddess through which all the forms of life emerge, tends to denote that which is contained in or pours forth from the Grail. So when the fish symbol shows up (i.e. the "vessel of the fish" shape) it is the precious substance contained in the Grail or that pours out of it that is being emphasized. Therefore, when the wounded king goes fishing, he is seeking to catch, and presumably consume, the substance contained in the Grail.

Through the vesica/Grail come all the forms of life—just as all the bounty and fruits of creation come tumbling out of the cornucopia or horn of plenty, which is a parallel symbol for the Grail. So the king is seeking to consume the fruits of creation (fish are themselves part of the bounty or fruits of life). What does this signify? The forms of life, the fruits and bounty that tumble out of the Grail/cornucopia are symbolizing here the visible, material realm of form. To wish to consume this fruit signifies an involvement therefore with the realm of form: polarization in the material realm and a consequent loss of connection to the spiritual realm.

Arthur demonstrated by his ability to draw the sword out of the stone that he was polarized in the spiritual realm. He represents the mentor figure who, because his connection to the heavenly king is open, can represent that energy for us and catalyze our process of inner clarification that is the quest, the aim of which is to become ourselves polarized in the inner, spiritual realm. The Wounded Fisher King is the opposite, shadow version of Arthur, because he is polarized in the material realm. He goes fishing whenever he can. And this of course is why he is wounded, because instead of being open to the Grail King energy he is closed off from it—"positive" to it, to use the electrical analogy—because of his involvement with form.

So the fisher king is wounded by turning his orientation away from the inner realms of the Grail King and becoming polarized in the outer realms of form. Once his consciousness has been separated from spiritual source, he feels fear, and to assuage his fear he consumes more: he goes fishing. In so doing the primary wound—loss of polarity in spirit—is entrenched, because his addiction to form deepens. This king is in fact, in a paradoxical way, wounded by the Grail—wounded by consuming/seeking the fish.

Why is he wounded when others are blessed? When the Grail passes through the banqueting hall at Camelot, the knights are all "filled with sweetness and the desire of their heart." All those paralleling symbols of the Grail, the magic cauldrons, the sacred vessels, the womb, the heart, and the life-giving qualities they serve us are supposed to nourish us and increase life, aren't they? Not wound us. And what about Finn, who eats the salmon of knowledge? He is not wounded but becomes a great poet.

When those who eat the fish/fruit are seeking fulfillment from it *because of the separation from the Grail King energy,* the fruit wounds instead of conferring blessing. This is the great paradox that is contained at the heart of the myth. The fisher king lives in the castle where the Grail is kept, and yet, although he is in the presence of the Grail, the dispenser of blessings and bounty, he cannot be healed by it. This paradox symbolizes for us the well-known but little-admitted fact that often no matter how much we have, we are never satisfied or content.

I remember once visiting a beautiful house on Long Island. It was large and gracefully laid out, with a big garden and a swimming pool. Its owners were both professionals in well-paid jobs, and they had two lovely children. Surely they had "everything." But the house, though beautiful, was in a mess, strewn with "stuff." In the little girl's room alone was a pile of over one hundred furry animals. Her mother was addicted to ordering things from catalogs: more and more toys, clothes, baby equipment, gadgets, ornaments, shoes—until there was simply no more room to put it all. The cupboards were full of unopened packages from catalog companies. This struck me as a poignant example of the Grail wound operating: no matter how much we can get our hands on, we find no sustenance from it.

Some religious or spiritual groupings have noticed this addiction to form and have decided that the way to deal with it is by complete denial. We'll be healed by living in a monastery and owning nothing, or we'll simplify our lives. But these approaches don't deal with the root cause of the wound, which is one's polarity. By arranging one's life so as to avoid being subject to outer things, one proves that one is still subject to them. The point is not that having things is bad and not having things is good; the point is to be free of the *need* for things. After all, these goals and possessions and relationships represent the blessings of the Grail. If we long for them, they probably belong to us, but we won't enjoy them for very long unless we have learned to be centered in the spiritual food from within first.

In a prologue called "Elucidations" that is sometimes attached to Chrétien de Troyes's poem "Perceval," the story is told of King Amangons, who "did wrong" to one of the maidens of the wells and springs and took away her golden cup. His men followed his example, and as a result all the maidens who had used to bring refreshment to travellers disappeared, the wells dried up, the grass withered, and the land lay waste. Somewhat confusingly, the story also tells us that the court of the Rich Fisher, which had filled the land with plenty and splendor, disappeared as well. Even though King Amangons and the Rich Fisher are not clearly associated, we are told that the latter knew much "black art," in other words was an evil king, so we can assume that they are two versions of the same character. The phrase "did wrong" and the taking of the golden cup have connotations of rape, of a violation of trust, and of taking something that did not belong to him. The maiden and the golden cup also symbolize the feminine Grail chalice. The wells dried up and the land withered as a consequence of a wrongdoing that involved the Grail. The king and his men took by force what formerly had been freely given.

Once the polarization in the inner realms has been lost, the door to the Grail King energy closed, then not only do we wish to consume more to fill our hunger but we come to believe that the bounties of creation—the Earth and her flora and fauna—exist merely to feed us. And to believe that we have a right to take whatever we like, consume as much as we wish, without regard to the consequences and with no sense of the sacredness of what has been freely offered to us through the magical kingdoms of Mother Earth.

The story of the wrongdoing of King Amangons, with its connotation of taking what did not belong to him, and the resulting wasteland contains echoes (along with other aspects of the myth we have been considering) of the even older layering of myths depicting what has been called the Fall. We are most familiar with the story of Adam and Eve, whose eating of the fruit of the Tree of the Knowledge of Good and Evil led to their expulsion from the Garden of Eden. But the story in Genesis is in fact just one version of a theme that is retold worldwide. In ancient Mesopotamia, Iran, Egypt, India, China, Australia, North and South America, and Africa, parallel stories can be found that all share the same two basic components: the existence of a paradisiacal state and its loss. The cause of the loss is usually the eating of a forbidden fruit or a spiritual amnesia (a forgetting or turning away).

Adam and Eve were told that they could eat of every tree in the Garden of Eden save the Tree of the Knowledge of Good and Evil: "for in the day that thou eatest thereof thou shalt surely die" (Genesis 2:17). Nevertheless, Eve, tempted by the serpent, goes ahead and eats the fruit, and Adam follows suit. In his book *Memories and Visions of Paradise* Richard Heinberg writes:

> In nearly all languages, the word *fruit* is used metaphorically to refer to the result of any creative process. Fruit is the ultimate product of the vegetative cycle of reproduction and growth. . . . Since all creative processes—from the growth of a tree or an embryo to the invention of a new technology—begin invisibly and end with a completed physical form, the image of fruit is metaphorically applicable to any finished product.
>
> To eat is to take something into oneself and allow it to become a part of one's body. But there are analogous emotional, mental and spiritual processes: we speak of devouring literature and of feasting on the sight of our beloved. Whatever fascinates us we incorporate mentally and emotionally into ourselves. The eating of the mythic fruit, then, was a fascination or union with the result, or end product, of creation, which is the manifest form of things.

Again, therefore, the eating of the fruit or fish depicts the reversal of polarity from orientation in the inner, positive source of life to an involvement with the outer realm of form. It is the process by which consciousness has become "positive" to the inner positive energy and therefore repelled—cut off—from that energy and instead "negative" to the outer realm.

When this reversal happens Adam and Eve experience a change of consciousness: "and the eyes of both of them were opened, and they knew that they were naked" (Genesis 3:7). The nakedness is the sense of separation from the source of being that has come about because of eating the fruit. Self-consciousness—"*they knew* that they were naked"— has taken the place of communion with God. As soon as this sense of separation is experienced two emotions are felt: fear and shame:

and they sewed fig leaves together, and made themselves aprons.

And they heard the voice of the Lord God walking in the garden in the cool of the day: and Adam and his wife hid themselves from the presence of the Lord God amongst the trees of the garden. (Genesis 3:7, 8)

They try to cover up their nakedness—shame—and now instead of knowing connection with the Creator, they feel fearful of him and hide.

So here is depicted the primary wound: the sense of separation from the higher king energy, the subsequent feeling of being nothing or naked, vulnerable, inadequate, and so on, the fear consequent upon this, and the attempt to cover it over with the fig leaves of ego identity. Layers of defense and pretense to both protect and hide the now fragile sense of self.

The fisher king, wounded in the thigh, feels powerless and fearful because of the loss of alignment with the Creator's power. The only solace for his suffering was to go fishing, in other words to eat some more, to consume more status, material goods, achievements, to cover up with more facades, to become even more deeply polarized in the realm of form and appearance.

In this way the original wound is reinforced—because the only time the wound is eased is when we do more of what it was that caused the wound in the first place. The only time an alcoholic feels good is when drinking. A vicious circle of addiction is initiated, consequent upon the primary condition of being "negative" to the outer, material realm of creation.

The complete anatomy of the wound can be laid out in four steps as shown in the illustration:

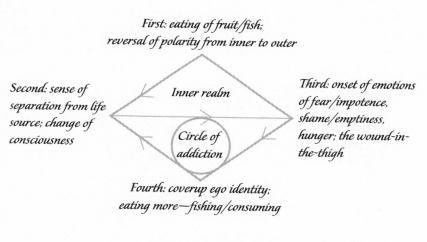

First: eating of fruit/fish;
reversal of polarity from inner to outer

Second: sense of
separation from life
source; change of
consciousness

Inner realm

Circle of
addiction

Third: onset of emotions
of fear/impotence,
shame/emptiness,
hunger; the wound-in-
the-thigh

Fourth: coverup ego identity;
eating more—fishing/consuming

ANATOMY OF THE WOUND

The eating of the fruit leads to the expulsion of Adam and Eve from the Garden of Eden, and the fishing/wounding causes the onset of the wasteland. The loss of paradise could be said to be the onset of the wasteland.

Strictly speaking though, according to the account in Genesis, paradise is not "lost" except in the experience of Adam and Eve. They are expelled from the Garden of Eden, but the Garden still exists somewhere: "so he drove out the man; and he placed at the east of the garden of Eden cherubims, and a flaming sword which turned every way, to keep the way of the tree of life" (Genesis 3:24). Both the Tree of Life and the Tree of the Knowledge of Good and Evil are described as being "in the midst of the garden." They are the same tree! But when we have "fallen" into the realm of form, of effects, and lost our sense of connection to the source of life, we have separated ourselves from the *experience* of being that Tree of Life, of participating in bringing forth the fruits of creation. Knowledge of good and evil implies judgment. When we judge what is good and what is bad, we tend to separate ourselves from the overview that sees how creation moves through cycles of completion and incompletion. We no longer understand how the dance of duality works, the natural dualities of male and female, light and dark, chaos and clarity. Our separated ego has usurped the position of the Creator, eaten fruit that was forbidden, taken what is not ours to take. And then we create another kind of evil: the evil of the fragmented human ego, which believes creation exists to serve itself and which imprints onto the world its fragmented viewpoint and consequently creates a wasteland. This is the consciousness that in its worst extremes creates a death camp, an atom bomb, and a devastated ecology. This is how we "surely die."

We could picture the vesica shape again; when the connecting place of the heart is open to the inner realms, we can become aware of the movement of the cycles of life that are the Tree of Life. When the heart is closed, the door is closed; we know only the outer realm, the visible effects of the invisible cycles: the Tree of the Knowledge of Good and Evil. We have lost the perspective of wholeness.

In the Irish myth, after Finn eats the salmon of knowledge he needs only to put his thumb into his mouth, and whatever he needs to know is revealed to him. This was a different kind of knowledge; what he needed to know was revealed to him as he needed to know it. This is the poetic knowing, the knowing that allows the inner realms to reveal their wisdom to one's outer mind. This is the fish of the vesica piscis, the means by which what is invisible, at the level of preform, becomes visible and becomes form. This is the way by which the invisible currents of life, moving and shaping the elements of seed, earth, water, and sun, turn into a tree and grow, and produce branches, leaves, blossoms, and eventually, fruit.

The Wounded Fisher King represents more than just one's own individual wound. He is a king: therefore, he has control over a kingdom. The wound is a controlling consciousness in the society. No matter what one's own experience of wounding has been, however extreme like my friend's or subtle like mine, it has arisen because of the presence of the fisher king wound in the larger world. We have been wounded by the wound in others. As is well known now from studies of sexually abused children and their parents, the evil deed is often done to the child because it was first done to the parent when he or she was a child; and abused children can have a propensity to go on and abuse their own children in their turn, and so on and so on.

So where did the wound start? Again, we can look back into history and prehistory and come up with all sorts of theories. Was it due to the sexual and emotional repression of the Victorian era? Did it arise with Descartes and the ascendancy of science over religion? Was it inflicted by the coming of Christianity and the burning of the witches? Did it originate with the violent invasions by barbaric tribes of peaceful and egalitarian Epipaleothic and Neolithic settlements, and the subsequent rise of a "dominator" mode that initiated the suppression of women and all things feminine, a pattern not seriously challenged until the end of the nineteenth century with the suffragette movement— and against which we are still struggling? But then, what caused the savagery of the marauding barbarians in the first place? Who inflicted the first wound, and why? To ask this question is like pulling on a thread that keeps unspooling without ever coming to its end. The theory of evolution does not help us to answer this question. According to this theory, humankind is the species that has survived the most efficiently on Planet Earth—as is witnessed by our near total destruction of the coexisting flora and fauna—thanks to our superior brain. If we have adapted so well, why are we so unhappy? Why do we abuse our children and wage wars if we are such a well-adapted species?

The strange fact is that despite all our modern sociological research, our technological innovations, our historical and archaeological data, the only source we have that gives us any real clue to the origin of the wound is in the ancient mythic records.

The Grail legend, while containing echoes of the much older layering of the loss of paradise myths, is not a retelling of the same theme but more a continuation of the original story. The Wounded Fisher King and his wasteland kingdom sit at the center of the story and of the quest, symbolizing the result, and ongoing presence, of the wounded state. When Perceval enters the Grail Castle and finds the Wounded Fisher King there, and when the Grail is carried in front of them into the inner room where the Grail King lives, we know we are not witnessing the *beginning* of this story but are present at its potential *ending*. That is what makes this myth so exciting.

4

THE FISHER KING AND THE DOUBLE WOUND

*He is the hoarder of the general benefit. He is the monster avid
for the greedy rights of "me and mine." The havoc wrought by
him is described in mythology and fairy tale as being universal
throughout his domain. This may be no more than his household,
his own tortured psyche, or the lives that he blights with the touch
of his friendship and assistance; or it may amount to the extent of
his civilization. The inflated ego of the tyrant is a curse to himself
and his world—no matter how his affairs seem to prosper. Self-
terrorized, far-haunted, alert at every hand to meet and battle
back the anticipated aggressions of his environment, which
are primarily the reflections of the uncontrollable impulses to
acquisition within himself, the giant of self-achieved independence
is the world's messenger of disaster, even though, in his mind, he
may entertain himself with humane intentions. Wherever he sets
his hand there is a cry (if not from the housetops, then—more
miserably—within every heart): a cry for the redeeming hero, the
carrier of the shining blade, whose blow, whose touch, whose
existence, will liberate the land.*

— JOSEPH CAMPBELL, *The Hero with a Thousand Faces*

SO FAR we have interpreted the symbol of the Wounded
Fisher King as relating primarily to an inner condition of
ourselves and of the larger society—that is, as representing a
central wound of fear and separation from spiritual source. King
Arthur, meanwhile, I have talked about in terms of an actual
flesh-and-blood leader or mentor figure. However, the Wounded
Fisher King can just as easily cross over into the "outer" world
and be understood and embodied as a very different kind of
leader, while the figure of King Arthur can be read as symboliz-

ing our own leadership potential and our own aligned, positive energy. In other words, both figures can be interpreted either as internal energies or as roles played by people in our lives. In this chapter, I want to talk about the impact and implications of the Wounded Fisher King when he shows up as a leader, both in our individual lives and in the larger sphere of society.

When we meet a King Arthur leader, we are empowered to set off on the quest, the aim of which is to heal our wound of fear and separation. But when one meets a Wounded Fisher King leader, something very different happens. If the fisher king wound, that is, the consciousness that has forgotten its connection to the higher king energy, has become dominant within an individual who plays a leadership role, there occurs a rather complex interaction between the leader's wound and one's own, the effect of which, far from healing either one's own wound or the leader's wound, makes both worse.

This interaction relates to the phenomenon of transference. Transference is the process, first identified by Freud in the early twentieth century, whereby a patient undergoing analysis develops strong positive and negative feelings toward the analyst. Through the means of this transference, the patient's symptoms acquire a new focus, the therapeutic relationship itself, which can then be worked on more directly in therapy. Freud observed that this phenomenon took place as part of a healing dynamic between patient and analyst. It was a process that could assist in the recovery of the patient. *No one tried to bring the transference about, it just showed up.* The crucial—and massively overlooked—fact, however, is that the phenomenon of transference *does not limit itself to the context of psychoanalysis.* The dynamics of the positive and negative transference constellate around any leader figure, whether it's the minister of the local church, a workshop leader, the organizer of a neighborhood association, or a president. Generally speaking, the more high-powered the role, the stronger the positive and negative currents that are directed toward him or her. Thus the leader of the neighborhood association may feel both appreciated and undermined, while a president may be first admired and later assassinated.

Most people have never been weaned from a childlike relationship with authority onto a more mature, peer relationship. Leaders are often related to with a toxic mixture of fear and longing, secret phantasies of ecstatic union and deep vengeful resistance. Underlying our sophisticated criticisms of leadership are infantile grievances of rejection. This is the syndrome of the unstable love–hate, worship-or-kill relationship with the spiritual leader. This is the phenomenon of the positive and negative transference. A pioneer in the practice of psychoanalysis, Jonathan Hanaghan (founder and first president of the Irish Psycho-analytical Association) asserted that the requirement for healing—for being made whole—is not restricted to a minority of dysfunctional patients but is needed by the majority of society. He saw clearly the need for leaders who were able to receive the currents of the transference:

> Now, although it seems to oppose all modern and rational expressions of society and of groups of society, until these movements of positive and negative transference occur towards leaders, it is impossible to heal society. Therefore the doctrine of the leader is the fundamental doctrine.

The aim of this relationship is the same as that of the spiritual quest, which is catalyzed by the presence of the King Arthur leader:

> I want to return you to your authority and I want to say to everybody—You have the divine authority of your real soul with God. You have a divine, authentic bond and contact with the Creator who speaks to you with the tongue in which he speaks with no one else. For you are unique, for He is your daddy, your Father. And when you lose this unique, intimate, personal, inward bond with God, your Father, you are lost.

The lost state is the condition out of which we all seek to emerge with the help of the spiritual mentor or leader. Indeed, it is vital that this occur, because until we are weaned from our dependence on the leader onto our own "authentic bond and contact with the Creator," the situation is unstable and fraught with dangers both for ourselves and for the leader.

If the leader is a King Arthur figure, one who consciously or unconsciously has a connection to the higher king energy, the energy of the transference will usually be handled safely because the currents of emotion directed at him will not be taken personally. Moreover, the dynamics of the transference can be allowed to work to bring healing to the individual who is orienting to the King Arthur leader, just as they can within a psychoanalytic context.

However, when the leader is a Fisher King, the currents of positive and negative emotion directed toward him will correlate with the dual aspects of his wound. The eating of the fish, which leads to the sense of being cut off from the life source, will correlate with the positive transference; and the stab wound in the thighs, which is the consequent sense of fear and impotency, will correlate with the negative transference.

In this way, his woundedness is reinforced, and at the same time one will find oneself oppressed and undermined by his presence, because instead of empowering us through his blessing and his challenge, the Wounded Fisher King leader will seek to take—to eat—one's power to feed himself. We have all met the Wounded Fisher King. He is the polar opposite of the King Arthur leader, and, sadly, we usually meet more examples of him than we do of King Arthur. He is the cold-hearted parent, the scornful teacher, the implacable and undermining boss, the tyrant leader.

According to Hanaghan, the first part of the transference is always the positive transference, and the eating of the fish is also the first part of the wounding. We remember that when the Grail appears as the fish (i.e. vesica) symbol, what is being emphasized is the precious substance that is contained in or pours out of the Grail. In the previous chapter I discussed this in terms of the bounties of Creation, and I mentioned that the fisher king's wound symbolized polarization in the material realm, caused and sustained by him going "fishing." But the Grail/vesica symbol also represents the heart realm, the opening through which the currents of love can pour into the world. These currents of love show up initially as the positive transference. We direct our love, our "adoration" in fact, toward the leader. This phenomenon of transference will start to work around any leader figure, whatever his or her potency, and whether that person be a King Arthur or a Wounded

Fisher King leader. But when the positive transference starts to be directed at the Wounded Fisher King, he eats it. He takes it to himself. And this wounds him again because it helps to magnify his ego and sustain his wound of separation from a higher source of energy. At the same time, it wounds us because we are not going to be able this way to be weaned from our transference. We will remain emotionally dependent on and, worse, probably also be emotionally further wounded by a fisher king leader. To quote Hanaghan again: "the positive transference is easy to receive and dangerous, flattering [the leader] and putting him into many difficult situations." In other words, positive feelings, attention, adulation are focused on the leader/mentor figure. If he is King Arthur, this positive response does not destabilize him because his connection with the Grail King is in place. He knows that the love and adulation coming to him are really directed at a higher source, whom he is temporarily representing. Therefore, psychically, he passes it on; he does not take it personally and does not allow his ego to be pumped up out of proportion by it. But the Wounded Fisher King is a different story. He is the leader who has no awareness or connection to any being or authority greater than himself. His own ego has covered over the opening to the presence of the Grail King. He is cut off from the presence and energy of that higher source, and therefore instead of psychically allowing this response to move on he takes the response to himself, takes it literally into himself—he eats it. He is tempted by the positive response to him. He is flattered; his ego grows and distorts. Whether in a subtle or gross way, he takes the response of the "kingdom" personally.

So the Wounded Fisher King's "transparency" to the upper sacred king has clouded over, and the life-giving flow of that higher king's presence is cut off. This is again how the fisher king is wounded by the Grail itself—the currents of the positive transference that come from people's hearts. In the process, corresponding distortions are produced in those around him. Those who flatter confirm his sense of self-importance; those who question are perceived as heretics and ultimately will be persecuted. People "adjust" themselves to fit the shape of the status quo determined by the king, which is one way the kingdom becomes a wasteland—a rigid, fear-ridden repetition of the Wounded

Fisher King's own obsessions. Far from a blessing, the Wounded Fisher King's presence is more like a curse. Individuals and nations who are subject to a Wounded Fisher King do not flourish; they are themselves wounded and suppressed. He rules over a wasteland.

I know of several hardworking, competent men whose working lives were made a misery by the cold, implacable emanations from their fisher king boss. I once worked for a woman who, while not directly malevolent, simply gave me no expression of friendship—or encouragement or even direction. Added to this was the presence of two senior colleagues who operated in somewhat the same way—not openly hostile but giving no help and functioning behind a wall of cold distance. The experience was a bit like being oxygen starved: I found myself unable to think clearly, and I kept making mistakes that should have been easily avoided. And of course the more I made mistakes, the more justification there was for the coldness, and eventually the coldness was able to show itself as outright hostility. The situation degenerated into a test of nerves: were they going to break me, or, worse, were they going to cause me to turn into one of them? For this is what will often happen under a fisher king. The subjects' need to be received and made whole is still driving them, but instead of being remade "in the image and likeness of God," that is, empowered and brought into their own unique awareness of God, they are turned into replicas of the fisher king and take on his wound. They become egotistical, ruthless, cold—whatever the particular flavor of the Wounded Fisher King is. This is what had happened of course to the two senior colleagues in my office. In this way the wound becomes multiplied and magnified by the "subjects" of the kingdom.

A fisher king leader may not necessarily be cold and unkind. He can just as easily be charming, outgoing, and charismatic, but ultimately those who serve him will come to realize that he is self-serving. His bottom line is self-interest, not the interests of his kingdom or his subjects. The former CEO of the bankrupted and corrupt Enron company, Ken Lay, is one example. In his book *Who Really Matters,* which examines the function of leadership groups in corporations, Art Kleiner likens Lay to Tim Matheson's role in *Animal House* "as the charmer who beguiled outsiders."

Again, many will mold themselves in this image. Much of the world operates this way; this is where the clichés of the "rule of the jungle," "survival of the fittest," and so on stem from, and they seem to be justified. More often than not it is corruption, not efficiency, that is the result of the fisher king's rule. If there is no integrity in the leader, there will generally be no integrity lower down in the ranks. Anyone who holds out for the truth and for fairness seems a fool, liable to miss out on easy benefit or to get his head chopped off—metaphorically, and sometimes literally, speaking.

Corruption nearly always leads directly to the expansion of the wasteland, again both figuratively and sadly also literally. One example comes from India, where a system exists to try to protect the Bengal tiger by awarding compensation to farmers whose property is damaged by the tigers, on condition that they do not shoot the animals. However, corrupt and incompetent government bureaucrats delay so long in awarding such compensation that the farmers go ahead and shoot the tigers, whose numbers, like so many other wild animals, are dwindling dangerously close to extinction.

Even within the context of the spiritual communities, the Wounded Fisher King might show up—inevitably, in a way, because until the work of the quest is finished in all of us, we all bear the mark of the wound. In my community experience, the syndrome was never manifested in extreme ways, but sometimes the openness of people around a leader was taken advantage of in subtle ways, used to build personal ego and miniempire; or the leader was unable to cope with the negative projections of those around him or her. For the most part, however, the people who took on leadership were exceptional and visionary individuals, and I have a profound respect for the way many undertook responsibility to provide spiritual mentoring so honestly and, for the most part, so honorably.

Be he or she charming or cruel, the energy that must naturally move toward the leader will be eaten up by that leader if he or she is a Wounded Fisher King. Just as we feel the current of blessing from a King Arthur leader, so anyone who has been in the presence of a Wounded Fisher King also feels it! His presence can be literally withering: we feel insecure and unsafe; we tense up. A very interesting exercise that I once participated in demonstrates how potent these "ener-gies" are. The exercise was part of an evening presentation, one of a regular series of meetings whose broad content was the art of spiritual living. The man who was presenting that night asked for a volunteer to step out of the room. Then he explained to those of us who remained what he wished us to do. When the person returned, the man asked her to hold out her arm. He would then try to push it down. The first time he tried, we were all to think positive, loving thoughts toward the vol-unteer. The second time he did it, we were to think negative thoughts— not seriously malevolent but tepidly negative thoughts, like "I don't like the way she's done her hair," and so on. The demonstration was dramatic. While we were all thinking kind, positive thoughts, the man could not push the volunteer's arm down. But as soon as we switched to negative thoughts, her arm went down with a whoosh, and she could not hold it up. The implications are astonishing, particularly be-cause none of us, including the man who presented the evening and did the arm pushing, had a strong connection with the woman volun-teer. We did not know her very well, and we held no strong views either positive or negative about her. Yet our superficial thought processes were able to affect her physiologically. Imagine how much more potent are the energies directed toward us by someone with whom we are in daily contact, in a working relationship, or in any situation where we are literally "in the power" of another.

This is how the situation can get very dangerous for the fisher king's subjects. The individual seeks healing; he or she is vulnerable to his or her own mainly unconscious need to be mentored, to be weaned onto his or her own authentic bond with God. Therefore such a one is vul-nerable to the fisher king's wound. He or she will hand over his or her power whether or not the leader is worthy of it; whether or not this temporal king can be trusted to pass that offering onto the Grail King, to God. And if the leader is not trustworthy, if he is a Wounded Fisher King, then that person is terribly wounded in turn. Instead of being blessed, empowered, freed up into one's own authenticity, one becomes bound and oppressed by the inflated ego of the wounded king. This is why the kingdom of the fisher king is a wasteland: because the door to blessing, that outflow of beneficence that naturally comes from the

King Arthur leader who is "transparent" to the "upper sacred king," and which is the first step in healing for the individual, has been closed by the king's wound. The Wounded Fisher King is taking all the energy, all the life flow, all the response to himself—he is feeding on it. He is not acting as a conduit for that energy to pass up to and down from the divine source: so the world stagnates, it turns into a wasteland.

Most of us have probably crossed paths at one time or another with a minor version of the Wounded Fisher King, but we have all also either witnessed or learned about some major Wounded Fisher Kings whose eras are dramatic demonstrations of the destructive impact of the wound that are writ large and indelible in the historical record.

In the spring of 1990 I had the opportunity to witness something of the legacy of one such figure when I visited Romania as part of a team making a film for British television's Channel 4 that documented the first elections to be held there since the 1940s. We gained a sobering overview of the "reign" of that country's recently executed leader, Nicolae Ceausescu, who had been in power for over 20 years: demoralized people, a decimated middle class, entrenched resistance to work, corruption, fear, chaos, dire industrial pollution. But it wasn't until I walked around the massive Casa Republicii, or House of the Republic, built entirely at Ceausescu's whim, that the full extent of his power and his vanity impacted me. Raised up on three enormous grassed terraces, the monstrous edifice—a cross between an oversize Italian palazzo and a prison—dwarfed the square and avenue that led to it. Pedestrians walking on the street and cars passing looked out of scale, Lilliputian. Despite a profusion of arched windows, Corinthian columns, and meter on meter of architrave and corniche, the sheer size of this flat-roofed, concrete block facade, stenciled over with hundreds of windows, betrayed its origins as the malformed brainchild of a totalitarian regime. The building dwarfed anything I had seen in western Europe, including Versailles, the court of the Sun King himself. (Apparently it is the world's second largest building after the Pentagon.) It housed a thousand rooms, hung with hundreds of crystal chandeliers. One room was so large it looked as if Grand Central Station could fit inside. Many of the chandeliers were covered in huge plastic bags to protect them from gathering dust, as the interior was only half finished. You passed from one room with hand-carved wooden paneling, white marble, and plush curtains into a corridor with a rough concrete floor. A whole neighborhood of old Bucharest had been bulldozed to make way for this gigantic folly and the long avenue in front of it, lined with brand new civic buildings, libraries, and museums. Many of the people whose homes were destroyed to make way for the new development were given only hours' notice to leave and no recompense. A bitter irony for those evicted from their homes was the book awaiting visitors at the end of their tour asking for suggestions as to what to do with the building now!

Ceausescu, like many another good communist leader, was in fact pure dictator. Over the 23 years of his rule he maneuvered constantly to concentrate power in his own hands: purging rivals, conferring positions of power on his wife, his six brothers, and on collaborators deeply indebted to him and using the usual fear tactics of secret police, informers, and forced labor sentences to keep the population subdued. He amassed an array of offices and functions that was unmatched by any other communist leader, even Stalin: he was head of the Communist Party as its secretary-general, president of the State Council, supreme commander of the Armed Forces, president of the National Defense Council, and president of the Socio-Economic Development Supreme Council and of scores of lesser institutions, including the Communist Academy, which he created. He also awarded himself the title of president of the Socialist Republic of Romania—an empty gesture, since he already had supreme power, but one that satisfied his overweening vanity.

However, Ceausescu was not only vain but also acted in ways that defied all rationality. Enormous civil engineering projects were pursued seemingly for their own sake rather than any practical need. Despite petrol rationing, tunnels and viaducts for new highways were built. The Danube–Black Sea canal (grave of at least one hundred thousand, some say two hundred thousand, forced laborers), finished under Ceausescu, ran at only 10 percent of its capacity, yet plans were made to link Bucharest to the Danube with another canal. In 1967 the Romanian fleet was scrapped; but three years later Ceausescu decided to build up

CEAUSESCU'S "PALACE OF THE REPUBLIC," OR CASA REPUBLICII, BUCHAREST, ROMANIA (Credit: AP/Wide World Photos)

a maritime industry with powerful warships—though the only likely opponent, the Soviet navy, could have disposed of the fleet virtually overnight and despite the fact that the vessels, based on outdated Soviet and Chinese models, would be impossible to sell; the whole exercise thus added up to a monumental waste of money.

Exports of foodstuffs to help fund these projects led to food shortages, as did the general neglect of agriculture, with peasants encouraged or forced to become urban industrial workers and an incompetent system of food collection, storage, and distribution. Then there was Ceausescu's obsession with the "homogenization" of the population, which meant his desire to "radically wipe out the major differences between towns and villages." Translated into policy, this meant the demolition of eight thousand ancient villages and the relocation of five to eight million people into uniform modern blocks of flats. Of course in practice, these were poorly built, often without running water, and demolition proceeded ahead of reconstruction, so that in many cases up to six families would be sharing one kitchen and bathroom. The difficulty of finding enough to eat was also exacerbated by the fact that under these conditions it became impossible to keep pigs and goats or grow vegetables.

Despite the fear tactics of the secret police, the presence of informers, and the threat and reality of forced labor, and despite food rationing, severe shortages of gas and electricity, denial of the more costly healthcare procedures to those over sixty, and a virtual outlawing of contraception and abortion, Ceausescu insisted that Romania was blessed by "the most just social system mankind has ever seen" and could not understand why so many Romanians were desperate to leave their country.

This blinkered and out-of-touch view of the populace, the syndrome whereby the people go hungry and their health deteriorates while the leader builds useless monuments to his own ego, unrestrained by anyone or any institution, is reminiscent of the "Let them eat cake" attitude, when a monarch had absolute power over his country and people and became completely cut off from a sense of reality and proportion, as happened under Louis XIV in eighteenth-century France.

When a Wounded Fisher King finds himself in a position of power, the situation is aggravated by his ability, as leader, to more easily eradicate people and elements that might challenge his ego coverup conviction that he is the center of the universe. Here instead of the "political king" having a open connection to the "higher king," *he has identified himself with that higher king.* Moreover, all the energy coming to him from the kingdom is being poured into the limited container of his ego; madness and loss of perspective are the result.

Ceausescu ruled like a king with absolute power over a suffering kingdom. The kingdom of Romania lay in waste because of its king's own dysfunctionality. Both king and kingdom were wounded by an egotism swollen out of all proportion, all meaningful relationship. This was plainly there to see in the Casa Republicii. Everything was wrong about it: wrong scale, style, proportion. Everything too big, too much, unrelated to its context. Moreover, it was not just aesthetically wrong, it was morally wrong—built on the bulldozed lives of helpless people; and it was also "wrong" at a practical level, because no use could be found for it. I was walking around a physical symbol of Ceausescu's ego.

Under communism, power was supposed to be taken away from its former traditional repositories such as church, monarchy, and the aristocratic or intellectual elite and to reside in "the people." However, all that happened was that once those old institutions were eradicated or weakened, power accumulated in tenfold concentrations in the leadership. Once Ceausescu came to power, it was therefore quite easy for him, in this fragile and newly evolving structure, to maneuver himself into a position in which no one and no institution could challenge his unbounded egotism or set limits on his sense of limitlessness.

The late Professor David Bohm once defined egotism as the attributing of "the significance of the unlimited to the limited. . . . We generally behave as if the ego regarded itself as the universal 'I am' beyond all limits of time, space and conditions." This is a very good description of Ceausescu.

Cruel and wasteful as Ceausescu's "reign" was in Romania, it pales in comparison with the rules of other Wounded Fisher Kings. In fact, Ceausescu remains a relatively obscure Wounded Fisher King in a century that has abounded with far more terrible figures. As appalling as the fate of the one or two hundred thousand who died in forced labor was, and the suffering of millions more, under the harsh conditions imposed by Ceausescu, these numbers and this suffering appear almost negligible when compared with the 60 million who lost their lives in the vast network of prisons and labor camps set up by Stalin. And horrifying beyond words though Stalin's reign of terror was, nothing is quite as awful as the coldblooded system of mass murder practiced at the death camps of Treblinka, Chelmno, Sobibor, Belzec, Majdanek, and Auschwitz-Birkenau under the auspices of the fisher king Hitler (whose actions ultimately led to the deaths of around 50 million in all, taking into account those killed in World War II, which Hitler initiated, as well as those who died as slave labor or were executed in the death camps). Under a Wounded Fisher King the land always lies waste.

The demonic cloning effect of the Wounded Fisher King showed itself under Hitler as the SS (Schutzstaffel, the Blackshirts) and the Gestapo; and under Stalin as the NKVD (People's Commissariat of Internal Affairs, Soviet secret police, 1934–1943) and the KGB (State Security Committee, Soviet secret police, after 1953).

These two regimes are especially interesting because both Nazism and communism were strictly materialistic. That is to say, *they recognized no higher authority than the temporal leader, namely Hitler and Stalin.* Western democracies have on the whole succeeded in preventing such tyrants from taking over, but the democratic system deals with the symptoms of the problem, not the cause. It prevents power gathering in one person for too long. But it cannot guard against Wounded Fisher Kings being in power, and it cannot guarantee the presence of King Arthur leaders. This is why Churchill was right when he said: "no one pretends that democracy is perfect or all-wise. Indeed it has been said that democracy is the worst form of Government except for all those other forms that have been tried from time to time." However, it is worth noting that in the two longest established and most successful democracies, Britain and the United States, a higher focus of power than the merely temporal has always been acknowledged, even if for the most part it may have been only a superficial recognition. America has always been referred to as "one nation under God," while in Britain church and state are still intertwined, and the continuing presence of the monarchy, though having now no temporal power, has been a useful representation of a higher authority.

It may be that the acknowledgment of a higher focus is a helpful brake on the harmful accumulation of power in a prime minister or president, as well as, of course, the constitutional checks and balances that make up a democratic system. Certainly the forms of a democracy correlate with the spiritual principles that are patterned in King Arthur's court. Democracy holds as primary the rights of the individual as long as they do not threaten the integrity of the state—that is, the collective formed by all the individuals. A democracy also seeks the participation in government by individuals through the voting system, referenda, local government, a free press, public demonstrations, and so on. In King Arthur's court, the establishment of the Round Table symbolizes Arthur's desire for the participation in government of all his knights. Arthur, being the leader whose connection to God is open and in place, knows that Godhead, that is to say *authority,* does not reside in just the leader but in all people. Therefore, all people must have the opportunity to participate in the government. Otherwise the expression of God—which is the sacred kingdom—would be incomplete.

Under both Nazism and communism the individual was completely subsumed by the state: everyone's power was taken and eaten up by the fisher king leader. No individual rights or free thinking of any kind were allowed to threaten the supercharged egos of either Hitler or Stalin. There is a telling excerpt from Aleksandr Solzhenitsyn's great work *The Gulag Archipelago* that demonstrates graphically how independent-minded individuals were ruthlessly hunted out and eliminated during the poisonous reign of the fisher king Stalin. It is quite a long passage but worth quoting in full:

A district Party conference was under way in Moscow Province. It was presided over by a new secretary of the District Party Committee, replacing one recently *arrested*. . . . At the conclusion of the conference, a tribute to Comrade Stalin was called for. Of course, everyone stood up (just as everyone had leaped to his feet during the conference at every mention of his name). The small hall echoed with "stormy applause, rising to an ovation." For three minutes, four minutes, five minutes, the "stormy applause, rising to an ovation," continued, but palms were getting sore and raised arms were already aching. And the older people were panting from exhaustion. It was becoming insufferably silly even to those who really adored Stalin. However, who would dare be the *first* to stop? The secretary of the District Party Committee could have done it. He was standing on the platform, and it was he who had just called for the ovation. But he was a newcomer. He had taken the place of a man who'd been arrested. He was afraid! After all, NKVD men were standing in the hall applauding and watching to see *who* quit first! And in that obscure, small hall, unknown to the Leader, the applause went on—six, seven, eight minutes! They were done for! Their goose was cooked! They couldn't stop now till they collapsed with heart attacks! At the rear of the hall, which was crowded, they could of course cheat a bit, clap less frequently, less vigorously, not so eagerly—but up there with the presidium where everyone could see them? The director of the local paper factory, an independent and strong-minded man, stood with the presidium. Aware of all the falsity and all the impossibility of the situation, he still kept on applauding! Nine minutes! Ten! In anguish he watched the secretary of the District Party Committee, but the latter dared not stop. Insanity! To the last man! With make-believe enthusiasm on their faces, looking at each other with faint hope, the district leaders were just going to go on and on applauding till they fell where they stood, till they were carried out of the hall on stretchers! And even then those who were left would not falter. . . . Then, after eleven minutes, the director of the paper factory assumed a businesslike expression and sat down in his seat. And, oh, a miracle took place! Where had the universal, uninhibited, indescribable enthusiasm gone? To a man, everyone else stopped dead and sat down. They had been saved! . . . That, however, was how they discovered who the independent people were. And that was how they went about eliminating them. That same night the factory director was arrested.

In this incident the three symptoms of the Wounded Fisher King's rule are at play: the demonic cloning of the fisher king himself in the form of the NKVD, the unquestioned support of the status quo as represented by the fisher king and his clones by all the people in the hall too frightened to stop applauding Stalin's name, and finally the persecution of those individuals who might question or be independent in any way, in this case the capable factory director who was arrested (and given 10 years' hard labor) for the terrible offense of being the first to stop applauding. This passage reads like a fictional scene from a nightmarish fantasy: a place where the king has gone mad and the kingdom is suffering under his delusions. It reads in fact, like a myth—the strange case of the fisher king's wound! Everyone knows that it is sheer madness in a leader to punish initiative, to get rid of your most capable men and women, to execute all your best generals at the outset of war. But all these things, and worse, Stalin did.

What constitutes madness? Paranoia—delusions of grandeur—is a recognized form of psychosis. A psychological dis-ease or imbalance.

Here is another way of describing the wound: as madness. The fisher king has lost his connection to the Grail King. As a result, all the energy from the kingdom is coming to him and accumulating in his ego instead of being "handed on" to the higher king. This overaccumulation of energy causes a malfunction—like an overloaded circuit.

When we consider the excesses of Ceausescu's regime, the irrationality and terror of Stalin, and the horrors of Nazism, not to mention the insane policies of Chairman Mao's so-called cultural revolution, it is as if we are not reviewing events of recent modern-day history but some phantasmagoric mythical story of mad tyrants and impossible scenarios that are too overblown to be real. The world of myth and the so-called modern-day world prove to be not that far apart. The myth tells us that we are subject to forces and responsible for choices that decide in the end whether our lives have meaning and whether our potential is fulfilled.

Somewhere deep in all our hearts we long for the king. We are hardwired to respond to him, to obey the positive and negative law and to be healed of our wound. And while this compulsion remains unfulfilled and unresolved it can lead to an abdication of responsibility. We need to become more fully aware of how this longing plays itself out in our lives, both individually and collectively, because its dynamics underlie some of the worse excesses of the 20th century. No one doubts the potency of leadership. Indeed, sometimes history has been interpreted purely as the effects of certain dominant figures for good or for ill. However, what we may not have understood so well is *why* these people are so influential. It is not possible for leaders to accrue such power as Stalin, or Hitler, or Ceausescu without there being something in the hearts of people that allows them to have that power. No matter what the political realities of history were, this longing has been the underlying dynamic that has allowed such an accumulation to happen. Nor have we understood very clearly how great the difference is, nor fully articulated *what* the difference is, between a King Arthur and a Wounded Fisher King leader. A King Arthur figure can cause those around him to undertake the quest for spiritual fulfillment and thus "grows" leadership in others. But a Wounded Fisher King leeches away moral authority and encourages ambition without responsibility. Under his rule there will be individuals who prosper and gain power, but it will always be at the expense of their souls.

The renowned journalist Gitta Sereny, in her book *Into That Darkness,* examines the mind and motivations of Franz Stangl, who, as commandant of Treblinka, the largest Nazi death camp, oversaw one of the most awful aspects of Hitler's wasteland kingdom, namely the efficient slaughter of approximately one million men, women, children, and babies. Beloved by his daughters and wife, Stangl emerges not as a moral monster but as a classic example of a man who made a Faustian pact with the devil and sold his soul for the sake of his ambition. He wanted to do well, he wanted promotion, and he got it: from a post in one of the main centers of the euthanasia program, to running the Sobibor camp, to commandant of Treblinka. Stangl claimed that if he had turned down the positions offered him, he ran the risk of execution himself. But this seems unlikely, particularly in the early stages of his career; and many documented instances exist of officers on the Eastern Front who went unpenalized for refusing to carry out Hitler's orders to murder civilians. Stangl therefore accepted no responsibility for what he was doing (and dealt with the horror by finding ways to avoid thinking about it), maintaining that he was merely a pawn in the hands of a system beyond his ability to change.

Stangl was never mentored by honorable leadership, and he never set off on the quest for his true strength and authority. He remained subject to his fears and desires, seeking outer roles to give him importance (which is how ambition is so often translated) and thus he perpetuated the wasteland kingdom of the Wounded Fisher King Hitler. In another place, at another time, Stangl would probably not have developed into a mass murderer. He might have been a somewhat ruthless but extremely effective head of department in a big corporation or a senior police officer.

Gitta Sereny also interviewed and studied in depth another former Nazi, Albert Speer, one of Hitler's closest aides, first as his chief architect and then as his armaments minister. Although a highly intelligent and gifted man, Speer was nevertheless in such thrall to the fisher king Hitler that he was blinded to, or avoided seeing, the essential evil of Hitler's regime. It was only at the very end of the war, when Hitler ordered a scorched-earth policy for his own country, that Speer allowed himself to recognize that Hitler was mad; and even to the very end of his days, Speer could not bring himself to admit that he had known what was happening to the Jews. He could not bear to accept the awful fact that by his involvement in leadership and his self-deceit, he too was responsible for those terrible crimes. These two men's stories are lessons in the destructive potency of a fisher king's rule.

Our compelling need to respond to the king is also what lay behind the Jonestown and Waco disasters and the suicide pact of the Heaven's Gate group. The would-be messianic leaders of all these cults were able to tap into their followers' longing for the king. Their adherents responded by literally handing over their lives and dying as part of a final glorification of their leader's swollen egos, rather like the doomed retinues of the entombed pharaohs of old.

The positive transference precedes the second wounding, the negative transference. This is the kill-the-king instinct. When instead of the wonderful feelings of empowerment and love while in the presence of my spiritual mentor I began to feel resentful and insignificant and found him daunting and uncomfortable to be around, this was the beginning of the negative transference following on from the positive. This is how Hanaghan describes the negative transference:

> the negative transference is another thing, and my judgment is: woe betide the man who does not ease off . . . the real fundamental leaders of mankind must ease off onto their Creator, for there is no man capable of receiving the negative transference of humanity unaided. There is no man born of woman who has the capacity to engage all the hate, the bitterness, the suspicion, the illusions, the delusions, the cruelties of the heart by which the man who receives them is wounded again and again.

Here, using slightly different terminology, is yet another recognition of the crucial relationship between what Bly calls the "middle political" leader or spiritual mentor and the "upper sacred king," or the Grail King. The temporal leader or spiritual mentor must be open to the presence of the higher king, or of God, in order to bear the transference from his followers and therefore bring healing to them by allowing them to be weaned onto their own direct contact with the higher king energy.

It is important for the leader's own safety to have this connection, because he or she cannot bear the transference in his or her own strength: he or she will be wounded, perhaps mortally wounded, by the transference. Until the individual is thus weaned, he or she has a love-hate relationship with the temporal king: on the one hand worshipping the king and on the other wanting to destroy him.

Many people who find themselves in positions of leadership, not ever having been weaned themselves on to a relationship with the Grail King, simply do not know how to cope with either the positive or negative transference that automatically surrounds them. Hanaghan talks about the reluctance of even the qualified leader to take on the transference: "they want to go right away from it. They do not want it. They don't willingly accept it."

The unqualified leader, that is, someone who has never himself or herself been weaned on to his or her own authority, usually learns to deal with the resistance he or she meets through the use of fear. He or she takes on the crueler aspects of the Wounded Fisher King as a means of survival. He or she knows that both false flattery and outright hostility mean the same thing: the "subject" wants to kill the king and rule in his place.

An ailing king can also mean a weak king. Not strong enough to assert his will directly, he uses indirect means and stratagems to get his way. He may appeal for, or seem to offer, sympathy and help, but underneath this apparently friendly veneer he is treacherous. If his subjects are strong, they threaten him, and he will give them no support; if they are weak, he will manipulate and take advantage of them.

Another way of dealing with the problem of the transference, particularly the negative transference, is to adopt an attitude of cool distance. Unable to deal with the currents of either adoration or hatred that are coming his or her way—unable to transform them by passing them on and in the process allowing the "subject" to come into his or her own birthright of power—the leader keeps everyone at a distance, thereby neither allowing transformation nor invoking total destruction.

This was the leadership style of the British civil service in India during the empire—those few thousand men who ruled many millions. The cliché of the "stiff upper lip" symbolized their stance of cold aloofness, as this passage from James Morris's marvelous trilogy about the empire aptly puts it:

> The British kept their distance . . . paternal nearly always, fraternal very seldom, sisterly almost never. Cruelty was rare, and almost never official. . . . Physical violence was seldom to their taste, paternalism was their forte and anyway to be distant was enough. Their most vicious weapon had always been contempt.

Although it was mainly benign and outwardly was sensationally effective, British rule in India, and elsewhere for that matter, was never really going to foster maturity and growth and prepare the indigenous populations to govern themselves. This is why Ghandi said "Give us chaos." He knew that when the British went, order would go with them, but he also realized that chaos was the price of freedom to develop.

The instinct to kill the king has very deep roots. It is worth examining these roots to understand some of the layering of unconscious belief and custom that even today drive our attitudes to the leader figure. As I have shown, there are elements within the Grail myth, specifically related to the Grail/fish and the wounded king figure, that may echo ancient fertility rites and the worship of vegetation gods. In the ancient cultures of the eastern Mediterranean, Adonis, Attis, and Osiris were worshipped as the divine yet mortal lovers of the Mother Goddess, lovers whose union with the Goddess ensured the fertility of the land. Winter represented the sexual maiming and death of the god. It is these deities, whose maiming correlates with the barrenness of the earth, that appear to be echoed in the figure of the Wounded Fisher King and his wasteland kingdom.

The various practices that emerged from these cults seem to have been based on the belief that by simulating the death and resurrection of the male god, the people could ensure the return of the Goddess and of life to the land. In rites associated with Attis, a pine tree dummy dressed like a corpse with an effigy of Attis attached to it was tied to a tree, while the priests worked themselves up to a frenzy cutting themselves and splattering the dummy with blood. In earlier times the dummy was most probably the high priest himself. Human sacrifice was often an aspect of these kinds of rituals. There is an interesting parallel in Norse mythology: human victims dedicated to the god Odin were hanged or stabbed and then tied to a tree and ritually wounded with a spear. The youthful Adonis was said to have been gored in the thigh by a boar's tusk. These woundings prefigure the wound in the thigh or genitals that caused the fisher king's impotence. Osiris was a vegetation god, a kind of Egyptian John Barleycorn. Images of him were buried during seed time to rise with the corn. In an interesting leap, seed-covered models of his mummified form were also buried in human tombs as a pledge of resurrection.

Similar beliefs and customs also accrued around the king himself. It was believed that the king was wedded to the land, to the kingdom itself, and was therefore one-with—joined with—the kingdom. In many cultures this union of king and land was symbolized by the monarch sitting or standing on a sacred stone, which symbolized the land or kingdom, during his crowning ceremony. The British monarch is crowned on a medieval wooden chair that holds a sacred stone in a compartment under the seat. There were two parallel implications to this belief. The king—like the vegetation god—was the husband/lover of the Earth Goddess, and somehow his life force was what impregnated her so that she brought forth all the forms of life: crops, animals, babies, and so on. If the king was impotent, ill, or aging, he would not be able to ensure the continuing fertility of the kingdom. Similarly, because he was joined with, one-with, the kingdom, whatever happened to him would be reflected in that kingdom. In *The Golden Bough* James Frazer writes of ancient cultures: "the king's life or spirit . . . (was) sympathetically bound up with the prosperity of the country." So again, if he was ill, aging, or impotent, or if he had sinned, committed a wrong, this would mean that the kingdom would turn into a wasteland as a reflection of his own literal or moral wounding. On both counts, the king would need to be killed—sacrificed—in order to ensure the ongoing fertility of the land, and replaced with a more satisfactory king.

King-killing persists today in the form of the assassination of leaders who displease or threaten in some way either special interest groups or the status quo. Remember the killings of the Kennedys and Martin Luther King (and how interesting that his name was King). Malcolm X can also be added to this list. Sadly, too, elements within the extreme right wing in Israel reverted to the practice of king-killing with the assassination of Prime Minister Rabin. We blame the leader for all our problems; we project onto him our own ills.

So the king-killing instinct stems in part from an abdication of responsibility, but there is a deeper and stronger layer of motivation here, and that is fear. It was the fear that the earth would lie barren if the king's life-force ebbed that caused the ancients to kill him. This fear was ultimately the fear of death, because if Mother Earth did not reproduce her crops and offspring, humankind would die.

This linking of the fear of death with the regicide instinct is shown to us in the myth when Mordred mortally wounds King Arthur in the battle that closes his reign. Mordred is a very interesting name. If we break it down we have "Mor"—La Mor, death, and "Dred," dread, fear. Fear of death kills the king. This symbolism unfolds further when we realize that Mordred was the offspring of an incestuous union between Arthur and his half-sister Morgana. Not recognizing who she is but enthralled by her beauty and sexuality, Arthur slept with Morgana and she conceived Mordred. Incest indicates wrong-relationship-with, or reversed polarity. Mordred, himself the product of incest, goes on to attempt an incestuous act himself when he tries to marry Guinevere. Even though this would not technically have been incest, as she was not his mother, nevertheless she is his father's wife. There is an intriguing parallel here with the myth of Oedipus, who killed his father and married his mother. These stories symbolize the polarity in the material creation, in "the mother," the vesica/Grail, instead of in "the father" or the divine energy, the Grail King.

We remember that the result of the wound of separation from the life source is fear, and its close corollary, coverup. The fear that we are nothing surfaces again when we meet the spiritual mentor, because his or her presence and authority show up the false coverings and "push the button" of the core wound. So we want to get rid of the mentor; the fear that we are nothing causes us to want to kill the king.

This is precisely why Jesus was crucified. There was in fact no logical reason for Jesus' death. The Romans weren't out to get him. It was simply that the presence of his spiritual authority threatened that of the scribes and Pharisees and other Jewish sects of the time and brought into play within them deep and lethal instincts. Those instincts surround any leader. By crucifying him, we get rid of the threat to our ego, the threat to our place at the center of the world. Once he is dead, the way is clear for us to worship him, without having to change ourselves or take any personal responsibility. After all, he did it for us already by dying! The sacrificial mindset will always ignore the intent of the true leader. That intention is essentially quite simple, and always the same: it offers loving encouragement to mature spiritually and to take responsibility for contributing our unique aspect of divinity into the world.

So it is the King Arthur leader, the spiritual mentor, who is most vulnerable to this second wounding, the king-killing instinct. Christ was crucified, King Arthur was mortally wounded, modern-day visionary leaders are assassinated. The Wounded Fisher King leader usually manages to strike first. He will often kill his followers—either literally, like Saddam Hussein, or metaphorically, like a ruthless boss—before anyone gets a chance to kill him.

5

THE WASTELAND

What are the roots that clutch, what branches grow
Out of this stony rubbish? Son of man,
You cannot say, or guess, for you know only
A heap of broken images, where the sun beats,
And the dead tree gives no shelter, the cricket no relief,
And the dry stone no sound of water. Only
There is shadow under this red rock,
(Come in under the shadow of this red rock),
And I will show you something different from either
Your shadow at morning striding behind you
Or your shadow at evening rising to meet you;
I will show you fear in a handful of dust.
— T. S. ELIOT, "THE WASTELAND"

WHERE THERE IS A WOUND, there is always a wasteland. In the previous chapter, I traced some of the ways our individual wound interacts with leadership to create a wasteland. When our individual wound of incompleteness causes us to hand our power over to a Wounded Fisher King leader, his grip tightens over his wasteland kingdom, whether that be an office with an icy and inhibiting atmosphere, or a gulag, or a death camp. And equally, when our fear of nothingness causes us to kill the King Arthur leader, a wasteland ensues because of the loss of his benign influence. After King Arthur was mortally wounded by Mor-dred (even though it is not certain whether he actually died or not) Camelot and the reign of peace and plenty gave way to battle and chaos. After President Kennedy was shot, the Vietnam war was stepped up; following Prime Minister Rabin's assassination, the Middle East peace talks foundered.

The consequences of Christ's crucifixion are probably too momentous to be summed up in a few sentences. First there was the persecution of Christians, and then, as the church became established and powerful, there was the persecution of just about everyone else by Christians—the burning of witches and heretics, the Crusades—and the ushering in of what have been called for good reason the Dark Ages.

But even without the exacerbating interrelationship of our wound with leadership, the wasteland still shows up, because the wasteland begins as a state of consciousness. To the extent that we experience a sense of emptiness, futility and inertia, we are living in a wasteland right inside our heads.

This is the condition that T. S. Eliot was writing about in his famous poem "The Wasteland," in which he drew on Jesse Weston's then new ideas about the derivation of the Grail myth from ancient fertility rites and mystery religions. Embedded in the lines from the second stanza of this poem, quoted in the epigraph, are two echoes from passages in the Bible. The first echo is the phrase "Son of man," which is used throughout the book of Ezekiel. The other echo is from the well-known passage in Eccelesiastes that begins: "Remember now thy Creator in the days of thy youth." The two passages to which these two quotations refer represent the two states possible to human consciousness: the first is the experience of connection to spiritual source, of correct polarity; the second is the wounded state, the sense of separation, or reversed polarity. The prominent placement of these two quotations—the first of many such echoes—very close to the opening of the poem helps to underline the poem's central theme, which is that the wasteland is essentially a spiritual condition, one emanating from the ancient wound of separation from the divine life source.

The opening two chapters of the Book of Ezekiel are a description of Ezekiel's amazing vision of the Lord, and "Son of man" is how the Lord addresses Ezekiel in his vision, an appellation that is repeated throughout the rest of the book:

And above the firmament that was over their heads was the likeness of a throne, as the appearance of a sapphire stone: and upon the likeness of the throne was the likeness as the appearance of a man above it.

And I saw as the color of amber, as the appearance of fire round about within it, from the appearance of his loins even upward, and from the appearance of his loins even downward, I saw as it were the appearance of fire and it had brightness round about.

As the appearance of the bow that is in the cloud in the day of rain, so was the appearance of the brightness round about. This was the appearance of the likeness of the glory of the Lord. And when I saw it, I fell upon my face, and I heard a voice of one that spake. (Ezekiel 1:26–28)

And he said unto me, Son of man, stand upon thy feet, and I will speak unto thee.

And the spirit entered into me when he spake unto me, and set me upon my feet, that I heard him that spake unto me. And he said unto me, Son of man, I send thee to the children of Israel, to a rebellious nation that hath rebelled against me. (Ezekiel 2:2–3)

Ezekiel falls upon his face before the Lord, and is told "stand upon thy feet." As the voice spoke, "the spirit entered into me . . . and set me upon my feet," in other words, here is a description of someone coming into an experience of oneness with God and therefore with his own inner power or divinity. (There is a strong parallel here with the passage from Revelation when the angel says to John "See thou do it not" when John wants to fall down and worship the angel.) The whole book of Ezekiel is concerned with the union between the human being and God (as is, it could be argued, the whole Bible), and Ezekiel's vision describes his experience of union.

The passage in Eccelesiastes is describing the opposite condition, the state of man when separated from God, from his divine source:

Remember now thy Creator in the days of thy youth, while the evil days come not, nor the years draw nigh, when thou shalt say, I have no pleasure in them;

While the sun, or the light, or the moon, or the stars, be not darkened, nor the clouds return after the rain:

In the day when the keepers of the house shall tremble, and the strong men shall bow themselves, and the grinders cease because they are few, and those that look out of the windows be darkened. And the doors shall be shut in the streets, when the sound of the grinding is low, and he shall rise up at the voice of the bird, and all the daughters of musick shall be brought low;

Also when they shall be afraid of that which is high, and fears shall be in the way, and the almond tree shall flourish, and the grasshopper shall be a burden, and desire shall fail: because man goeth to his long home, and the mourners go about the streets: Or ever the silver cord be loosed, or the golden bowl be broken, or the pitcher broken at the cistern.

Then shall the dust return to the earth as it was: and the spirit shall return to God who gave it. (Ecclesiastes 12:1–7)

Here the prophet or preacher is exhorting us to connect with the divine source, the Creator, before we grow old and it is too late. However, the symptoms of old age, when everything seems a big deal, when "fears shall be in the way" are also the symptoms of the separated state of human consciousness, of the internal wasteland that can set in at any time if one has lost touch with one's vital core. People grow old before their time; they are alive but not fully alive, like the ailing fisher king who can neither live fully nor die, in those "evil days . . . when thou shalt say, I have no pleasure in them." This is the separation from the life source and the spiritual and social wasteland such separation engenders that Eliot is addressing in his poem, just as the preacher Ecclesiastes was doing in his verses. The dust is not just the dust of parched land—"nor the clouds return after the rain"—but the dust of our very bodies without the quickening element of the spirit: "Then shall the dust return to the earth as it was and the spirit shall return to God who gave it." The last line of the epigraph from Eliot describes the condition that occurs when separation—the source of all our fear—is complete, namely, death: "I will show you fear in a handful of dust."

The passage from Ecclesiastes also contains some beautiful metaphors for the human body and for the moment of separation that is death: "or ever the silver cord be loosed, or the golden bowl broken, or the pitcher broken at the cistern." The cistern and the golden bowl remind us of the Grail chalice, wrought of refined gold; and the sparkling water, that never dries up or stagnates, of the life-giving substance that is contained within it.

Eliot's whole poem evokes a state of stale, weary inertia, the condition that ensues when "desire shall fail." It is not merely sexual desire that fails, key though this is, but vitality, desire for life itself. Despite its constant literary and therefore historical excursions, the poem is set more or less in the London of the 1920s, and one of the ways Eliot achieves the atmosphere of the contemporary wasteland is by brilliantly evoking a city exhausted by the weight of its own history, trundling along on tradition, but no longer inspiration:

> Unreal City,
> Under the brown fog of a winter dawn,
> A crowd flowed over London Bridge, so many,
> I had not thought death had undone so many.

The city is tired and worn, and so are the people eking out their shabby lives within its nooks and crannies.

In this poem, London was the capital not just of Britain but of an empire, and in conjuring the spirit of this place Eliot evokes not only a city but a civilization weary from empire, tattered, dusty, and, although no one knew it at the time, tottering on the brink of its final dissolution in the flames of World War II:

> What is that city over the mountains
> Cracks and reforms and bursts in the violet air

Why is it all so tired, so etiolated? What is the reason for the vapid atmosphere of this wasteland? It is the wound of the fisher king, the wound of forgetting. The preacher's words, "Remember now thy creator," have gone unheeded. The fruit or fish or dust has been eaten, has been chosen, leaving the wellspring of the spirit to dry up.

As is well known, Eliot used the device of literary echoes extensively throughout his poem, so that there is barely a line that does not contain a reference to some other text, whether it be the Bible, Dante's *Inferno* or *Purgatorio,* Saint Augustine's *Confessions,* the Buddha's Fire Sermon, Herman Hesse, Webster's "The White Devil," Ovid, *Tristan und Isolde,* and so on. This literary referencing has the effect of mimicking culture itself. We think we are reading a line of Eliot but in fact we are stumbling upon something else: older ground, a line from Spencer or from Baudelaire. We may think we are dealing with a "modern" malaise, but in fact we are exploring an ancient and perennial condition, the wasteland of a myth with its roots in the mists of time. There is nothing new about the wasteland; nothing new about the wound of separation.

The promise inherent in the Grail myths is that finding the Grail chalice will heal this wound of separation. When I experienced the transfigurative energy of the Grail King on my first visit to the community, the words *love* and *truth* were what came into my mind, as the experience happened, to describe the power that filled me and the nature of my own being, even though they were by no means included in my everyday vocabulary. It was as if some part of me was saying: "Oh, *this* is what those words mean." And these words, in their primary sense, do denote something that is beyond the grasp of intellectual understanding alone. Several years later, I was to explore the meaning of these words again when I returned to the community to attend a spiritual education class. During this time I was introduced to the thinking of a man named Lloyd Meeker, a visionary leader whose spiritual insights had led to the founding of that community, along with several others in different parts of the world. One diagram based on Meeker's work is particularly pertinent to the Grail symbolism (see the illustration).

This diagram depicts the seven-dimensional nature of humankind, as symbolized by the seven-year-old children in the tree who guide Perceval to the Grail. There are three inner and three outer planes, and the fourth plane is the realm of the heart which either connects or separates the two aspects. *Love, truth,* and *life* are simply words that denote frequencies of our being, which are rarely experienced directly by us. We are most familiar with the physical and mental planes of ourselves,

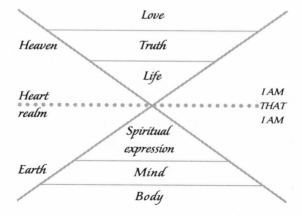

and may have a sketchy understanding of what Meeker termed the *spiritual expression* aspect of being. Meeker had an extraordinary insight into what could be termed the mechanics of consciousness and sought to dispel what he called the "sense of personal disassociation with the divine." Essentially, according to him, at these higher frequencies of being we are already in contact with, or part of, the divine, and what needs to be changed or rather dissolved are the subconscious blocks and habits that keep us from responding to this inner source. This is yet another formulation of the theme of correct polarity. To be "negative" to heaven means to be open and receptive to heaven and therefore "positive" to and in a position to bless earth. Meeker likened the subconscious mind to a cistern that, if purified and kept fresh by openness to God—to the "waters above"—becomes a source of never-ending inspiration. This was, he suggested, the meaning of genius: a person who by some fluke managed to keep this channel to inspiration open and the subconscious full of newness. But genius is really the birthright of all people:

> But whosoever drinketh of the water that
> I shall give him shall never thirst;
> but the water that I shall give him
> shall be in him a well of water
> springing up into everlasting life. (John 4:14)

This is how life is meant to be lived—not as a jaded, encrusted round of habit, which is what life can become when the cistern itself becomes stagnant and polluted. At the time Jesus spoke these words, he was playing the role of the spiritual mentor or leader who had a connection to God; therefore, he gave this water because response to him would lead to a connection with God for oneself and ultimately one's own divine source. In its meaning as a vessel that is ceaselessly replenished, the Grail could also be said to represent this purified subconscious, or "cistern."

The shape of the diagram shown here has always reminded me of the traditional Grail chalice whose base is as wide as the rim of its cup (see the illustration).

The meaning of both the quotation from the Psalm 23, "my cup runneth over," and the famous beatitude "Blessed are the pure in heart, for they shall see God," is further clarified by this diagram. If the heart is "pure," has been purified by going on the quest, and if polarity has been returned to the inner realm, then the inner dimensions of love, truth, and life, which are the characteristics of the Holy Trinity, of God male and female, can spill or "run" over into experience in the other levels. Equally, one begins to "see" God, to perceive and experience the nature of the divine, which is one's own nature: "made in the image and likeness of God." When the heart realm is clouded over with

NINTH-CENTURY DERRYNAFLAN CHALICE (Credit: National Museum of Ireland)

fear it forms a veil between the worlds. Perceval's name could be broken down to mean to "pierce the veil": to clear the connection between God and man, heaven and earth.

So we begin to see that finding the Grail, opening up the portal of
the heart to the higher frequencies of being, heals the wound of
incompleteness—heals that fractured, fragile sense of self that has been
so carefully constructed over the fear of nothingness. Finding the Grail
therefore means making whole what was formerly a partial identity.
Another way of saying this is that the finding of the Grail, the clearing
of the heart realm, is the healing of duality. The vesica piscis shape,
formed by the overlapping of two circles, symbolizes the place of
union between all the polarities: God and man, heaven and earth, male
and female and—most important—the inner and outer dimensions of
our own being.

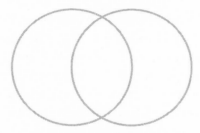

VESICA PISCIS

Thus the "vesica," or Grail, represents the balancing place in consciousness that as the Tibetan Buddhist Lama Anagarika says "either
binds us to the world of the senses or which liberates us from it." If we
have ourselves "pierced the veil" of separation, then we have achieved
the consciousness that is freed up from the—apparent—limitations of
the outer world: "And ye shall know the truth, and the truth shall set
you free."

This is supremely important, because if we do not master duality, it
will master us and often in its most debased form. The world is full of
the conflict arising from dualities: white versus black, Protestant and
Catholic, Tutsi and Hutu, Serb and Croat, and so on. This conflict and
hatred is another manifestation of the wasteland consequent upon the
wound.

If we operate in life from only one of the circles of consciousness, oriented in the material realm and without the connection to the larger spiritual source, we have a partial identity, one that relies heavily on outer form such as cultural tradition and roles for a sense of validity. Anything that threatens those outer cultural norms therefore appears to threaten us. Back in 1954, nine black students attempting to enter a "white" school apparently threatened the identity of practically the whole town of Little Rock, Arkansas, particularly that of a large mob who stood outside the school and yelled and screamed abuse at the sober and terrified teenagers. So much so that federal troops had to be sent to safeguard the nine, the state troops having been stationed to turn them away!

This fractured identity operates in someone who has not undertaken the quest—to find the connection through to the unifying place of the Grail. The work of subconscious clarification has never been done, and the transferences are flying about and exploding all over the place. What is like us is good, what is different is bad, hateful. We project onto people who are different all our own unresolved neuroses. We load them up like a scapegoat with all our ills and try to turn them out into the desert to perish. Every now and then, the irrationality and injustice of such processes get pointed out. Only a few voices are raised at first, but gradually these will swell into a huge chorus, such as the suffragette movement at the close of the nineteenth and the opening of the twentieth centuries, or the civil rights movement in the 1950s and 1960s in the United States. Such movements mark civilizing evolutions in the collective functioning of society and are of course crucial to that process. They help loosen the cultural embedding of duality conflicts and prepare healthier ground in which to raise following generations. However, as everyone knows, these changes do not cure the root of the problem. The civil rights movement did not eradicate prejudice against African Americans. It removed the machinery of discrimination but not its cause. Prejudice itself, whether against African Americans or against Jews or anyone else, subsides more gradually, sometimes over generations, as people die and their encrusted structures of consciousness dissipate with them. Flare-ups of such attitudes can still ignite, especially if economic or other pressures create unease in the status quo of the majority, or the habit of prejudice can just find a new focus—Muslims, for instance.

Many of those who hate each other are very similar. Protestants and Catholics in Northern Ireland, for instance, are both white and worship the same God. Superficially at least, there seem to be more similarities than differences between Arab and Jew, Turk and Greek, Armenian and Azerbajani, Iranian and Iraqi, African National Congress supporters and Zulu or Inkatha members, Albanian Kosovars and Serbian Kosovars. The film *The Life of Brian* made this point brilliantly when in an early scene it depicted the "Jewish National Liberation Front" as hating the Romans only a fraction more than it hated the "National Jewish Liberation Front," and vice versa.

The conflict between those who are similar, however, has its roots in the same process as that between groups who may be said to have genuine differences, such as color of skin. Often when someone is similar to oneself, he or she can "press buttons" in us that someone who is quite different does not. One's own inadequacies are mirrored back more obviously, and this is objected to and projected back again, and conflict ensues.

When a conflict has gone on for a long time, it gets hardened over by blood feuds, revenge, and simple economic and material self-interest. Indeed, the conflict can become a way of life. This happened after World War II when the so-called Cold War began to set in. Gradually this standoff between primarily the United States and the Soviet Union solidified into a status quo in which virtually the whole of the rest of the world then became invested. And when the Iron Curtain fell, the Western military industrial complex was probably as dismayed as the former communist generals.

Many duality conflicts tend to splinter into subdivisions of dualities. In a mixed-race dialogue group I once organized, I remember never being able to find the nub of black–white conflict. Instead, the conflicts that people in the group had experienced seemed to keep changing shape, turning into male–female conflict, or class, or African–British or rich–poor issues. We often forget that it was black Africans who sold their own people into slavery; and that the Arabs were buyers long before the white traders came, and long after the British government declared slavery illegal (which was also several decades before the American Civil War).

Simply put, conflict is the state that exists between people who have a partial or fragmented identity, because there is literally no common ground to join them. That common ground lies in the deeper, spiritual realm of consciousness, where it is found that in fact we are all aspects of the same life energy:

> Out beyond ideas
> of wrong doing
> and right doing
> there is a field.
> I'll meet you there.
> —JALALUDDIN RUMI

I would suggest that while a person's consciousness remains unhealed, that is, unweaned, not "whole," that person cannot be trusted. Indeed, such a person cannot be *known,* because he or she does not yet know his or her self, does not act or think yet from his or her deeper roots. Moreover, a partial person is someone without morality. Even if, as a child, some form of morality has been inculcated and laid out, unless the parents have been true "God-parents" and allowed the child to develop his or her spiritual dimension of identity, that morality will often break down in later life if enough pressure or influence is extended.

For instance, I am certain that many of the ordinary German people who participated in the hounding and later the genocide of the Jews were decent, law-abiding citizens, with a basic set of exterior morals in place. Despite this outer morality, they had no *inner* morality, because they participated, before and after the rise of Hitler, in a virulent program of mistreatment of Jews, culminating of course in the mass executions and gassings of the Holocaust. According to Daniel Jonah Goldhagen,

> the program's first parts, namely the systematic exclusion of Jews
> from German economic and social life, were carried out in the
> open, under approving eyes, and with the complicity of virtually

all sectors of German society, from the legal, medical, and teaching professions, to the churches, both Catholic and Protestant, to
the gamut of economic, social, and cultural groups and associations.
Hundreds of thousands of Germans contributed to the genocide
and the still larger system of subjugation that was the vast concentration camp system.

How can people do such wrong and call it right? The abuse leading to
mass murder of Jews in Germany is probably the most blatant example
of our ability to rationalize unspeakably inhuman actions. However,
many other examples abound in what is termed history or even current
affairs, and probably most people have experience of lesser acts of inhumanity, injustice or betrayal, not so extreme of course but still potent
because closer to home.

My husband is a filmmaker, and as a result I have had a fair amount
of exposure to people who work, or aspire to work, in the television
and film business. For the most part it is not a pretty picture. Indeed, the
world of film and television seems to be one of the more arid parts of
the wasteland of human consciousness. In this world a few genuine
thinkers and artists have to contend with an abundance of paranoia,
overinflated egos, and underskilled wannabes. I can count six "friendships" in as many years that have foundered in the process of making
films or attempting to get projects off the ground. In at least two cases,
the people in question had been "friends" for many years, but this did
not stop them from reneging on agreements and slandering our name,
behind our backs, to a major cable company and potential employer. In
another instance, a "friend" and partner repeatedly professed his loyalty
and support before also going behind our backs in an attempt to take
over a project, aided and abetted by another "friend," who was looking
out for his own interests, before he told us what was going on. This
kind of dealing between people produces a state of unreality—another
aspect of the wasteland: "Unreal city . . ." In particular, the language
we use starts to lack meaning, because the fine words we employ are
not anchored to honorable motive or action. A condition of mistrust
prevails, especially between men, who find themselves cut off and
alone, without any deep friendships and dependent on wife and family

for all emotional nourishment. It is a desperately sad state and one in sharp contrast to the high-intensity comradeship and honor represented by the knights of the Round Table. It is a wasteland much favored by the fisher king, who knows all about "divide and conquer" and encourages mindless competitiveness at the earliest stages possible.

As long as we live from a partial consciousness, we are all capable of committing acts of minor or major atrocity, as well as liable to experience them from others. Solzhenitsyn meditates on this grim truth in *The Gulag Archipelago* after describing his own willingness to act in exactly the same way as the investigators and executioners of the secret police:

> I credited myself with unselfish dedication. But meanwhile I had been thoroughly prepared to be an executioner. And if I had gotten into an NKVD [secret police] school under Yezhov [head of secret police], maybe I would have matured in time for Beria [Yezhov's even more brutal successor]. . . .
>
> So let the reader who expects this book to be a political exposé slam its covers shut right now.
>
> If only it were all so simple! If only there were evil people somewhere insidiously committing evil deeds, and it were necessary only to separate them from the rest of us and destroy them. But the line dividing good and evil cuts through the heart of every human being.

It's no use trying to be "good"—trying to obey a list of rules. That's how we still tend to think about morality, as a list of do's and don'ts:

> Thou shalt not kill.
> Thou shalt not commit adultery.
> Thou shalt not steal. . . .

Any such laws are only valid in the longer term as a first step in an outer morality, from which we must foster an inner morality. We have to understand ourselves at the deepest levels: both the pollution and the clear waters of origin. We have to undertake the quest of clarification of our hearts or subconscious minds and find the Grail, the state of union between heaven and earth, God and human being. We have to know in our own deepest heart the connection between ourselves and God, and therefore our own individual aspect of God; and know that the rest of us makes sense only as it is illuminated by this connection, as stained glass is made beautiful when sunlight shines through it.

> Thou shalt have no other gods before me.
> Thou shalt not make unto thee any graven image,
>> or any likeness of anything that is in heaven above, or that is in
>> the earth beneath, or that is in the water under the earth:
> Thou shalt not bow down thyself to them, nor serve them.
> (Exodus 20:3–5)

What is being said here? That we obey the positive and negative laws, that we discipline ourselves to stay centered in the spirit, that we cease to eat the fish or the apple or the dust of the ground. We cease to worship "graven images": that is, the *form* of things, as opposed to the spirit.

The extreme atrocities committed in Nazi Germany were the result of a lethal failure, both collective and individual, to realize this deeper, spiritual dimension of identity. Over the course of the nineteenth century the German people had been seeking to consolidate their sense of collective and individual identity, to consolidate a series of shifting princedoms into a nation. This process was badly undermined, and thus given more urgency, after the humiliation of defeat in World War I, with the subsequent abdication of the monarchy and national bankruptcy. As in all instances where identity is partial, the Germans sought to define themselves through the "form" of things, that is, through factors of nationality, religion, and race. Throughout Christian Europe in the Middle Ages, the Jews were universally shunned because they had supposedly rejected and the Messiah and turned him over to the Romans to be crucified. This religious prejudice gradually receded as the church's power waned with the coming of the Enlightenment, Darwinism, and the rise of the liberal middle classes. However, in Germany (as well as parts of central and eastern Europe, notably Poland and Lithuania) this prejudice lingered on longer, possibly in part because the heritage of Martin Luther, who was violently anti-Semitic, was so strong.

During the nineteenth century, with the upsurge of ideas about eugenics and evolution, this religion-based prejudice was gradually replaced with racially based prejudice. The Jews, it was somehow concluded, were a race, distinct from and inferior to the Aryan race, which was the true German stock. As such, the Jews were held to be irredeemable, even by conversion to Christianity. Here was a clear example of the worship of graven images. Form was imbued with authority and meaning: race, bloodlines, genetic inheritance. These were more important than quality of character. The Germans identified themselves by what they were *not* as much as by what they *were*. And what they were not were the Jews. Thus the presence of the Jews in Germany was seen as a threat to the newly formed (and therefore fragile) sense of identity, which gave rise to the most deadly duality conflict the world has ever seen—again always a symptom of partial identity. The Germans projected all their negativity onto the Jews. Everything that was wrong with their nation, from losing the war to economic collapse, was laid at the feet of the Jews. So the Germans loaded up their scapegoat and, under the auspices of the fisher king Hitler, who both had a personal fixation about the Jews and used the anti-Semitism inherent in the nation to gain power (a fisher king always appeals to the basest instincts of his subjects and will exploit their subconscious projections to gain more power; a King Arthur leader on the other hand will encourage the best in people and not tolerate bigotry and deceit), they proceeded not only to send their collective scapegoat into exile but to kill it off as well.

We start to see that the wasteland created by the wound of partial identity has many different aspects to it. The wasteland that starts inside our heads—the inner wasteland consciousness of fear and inertia, evoked by Eliot's poem—turns into a wasteland "out there": the wasteland of conflict and atrocity, the perennial, doleful tale of man's inhumanity to man (and women and children); and, increasingly difficult to avoid these days, the ecological wasteland condition of our planet and, closely associated with that, our treatment of animals, both wild and domesticated. There can be little doubt that today we are fast creating a global wasteland. The litany of statistics has become frighteningly familiar: a species made extinct every 25 minutes; an area of rainforest the size of a football field burnt and cleared per second—that's 86,000 acres destroyed every day. According to the United Nations Global Environmental Outlook 2000 statement (see Appendix III), tropical forest destruction has gone too far to prevent irreversible damage. It would take many generations to replace the lost forests, and the cultures that have been lost with them can never be replaced. It is too late to preserve all the biodiversity our planet once had. It is probably too late to prevent global warming as a result of increased greenhouse gas emissions. In addition, the world water cycle seems unlikely to be able to cope with the demands that will be made of it in the coming decades; and more than half of the world's coral reefs are threatened by human activities. While some may yet be saved, it is too late for many others.

How does the wound create this physical, literal wasteland? A good part of the reason is that the partial state of identity brought about by the separation from the higher frequencies of being cannot see wholeness. A fragmented consciousness can only see the world in a fragmented way. The material, rational consciousness assumes that matter is matter—that trees are trees, not nature spirits; that animals are products for consumption, or simply inconveniences; that the planet is a complex and evolved but chance clustering of molecules, not a living entity. Of course, to an extent, the advent of quantum physics threw a spanner in these works, as matter seemed to disappear altogether at the quantum level and become energy, vibration—dare one say spirit? But the implications of these discoveries are still kept severely in check by the scientific community. Certainly they do not yet impact the assumption that the Earth, its minerals, and its flora and fauna are commodities to be bought and sold for our profit. Thus we cut down forests because we want to make money from chewing up their wood into pulp and selling toilet paper, kitchen towels, and tissues.

This was the attitude that so stunned the North American Indians when the white man talked about buying and owning the land on which they lived. This was a concept that made the Indian people extremely uneasy: How can you own the land? How could you buy and sell the sacred, living home of earth? *Sacred*—this was how the Indians viewed the land. What does *sacred* mean? Holy, whole, a way of seeing that does not fragment, that sees the holiness, the wholeness, of creation; that sees the two worlds as one. The buffalo, of course, is the other well-known symbol of the differing worldviews of white man and Indian. The buffalo too was sacred, just like everything else. This attitude did not preclude the Indians from hunting the buffalo, but it had everything to do with how they hunted. Out of the vast hordes that used to roam the prairies, the Indians would kill only a few—whatever was needed for their own survival. Moreover, every single part of the buffalo was used: flesh, skin, bone, innards. And prayers of thankfulness were offered to the spirit of the buffalo that had given itself so generously so that the tribe might live. The white man, on the other hand, hunted the buffalo in the hundreds of thousands, for sport—an easy sport, given their guns and the huge size of the herds—and left the carcasses to rot on the plains.

The materialistic attitude found its apogee under the communist regime of the former Soviet Union. I have already discussed the human cost of the communist system, particularly as it existed under the tyrant rule of the fisher king Stalin. But there was also an enormous ecological cost. It is not a coincidence that a regime with no recognition of the spiritual realm at all resulted in the land becoming the most polluted area in the world. The disaster at Chernobyl, with the subsequent loss of thousands of miles of rich farming land, not to mention the terrible human cost in lives, health, and livelihood, was headline news when it happened. Perhaps not so well known was a catastrophic explosion in 1957 at the Mayak nuclear weapons plant in the closed city of Chelyabinsk-65, which contaminated 9,200 square miles and prompted authorities to evacuate 10,000 residents from neighboring regions. The Chelyabinsk region has been called the most radioactive place on the planet because of accidents and Soviet-era nuclear waste dumping into lakes and rivers. Artificial lakes containing more than 14 billion cubic feet of waste from the Mayak nuclear processing plant are filled to capacity and within a few years may leak into the region's rivers. A British documentary made not long after the fall of the Soviet system featured one lake that was so heavily contaminated with radiation that anyone who sat on its shores for an hour or more would die from radiation sickness. Over three quarters of Russian lakes and rivers are so contaminated by nuclear pollution they cannot be used as drinking water. And this is just the pollution from the nuclear industry, never mind that from the oil and chemical industries.

However, though slightly less extreme, the former communism of the East was and is well matched in its profligacy by the consumerism of the West. North America has its own extreme examples of the polluted wasteland: Love Canal in Niagara, where an entire community was allowed to be built up on top of a toxic waste dump; Port Hope in Ontario, whose location next to the site of a former nuclear reprocessing plant resulted in the town being so polluted that all the sidewalks and roadways had to be dug up and the topsoil replaced—to this day if you dig in your garden there you have to get permission from the Atomic Energy department; the ecosystem of the Great Lakes, in which seven hundred to eight hundred chemical pollutants still persist; the dioxin pollution at Times Beach, Missouri.

Of course, for many of us the wasteland may not seem to impinge very much, if at all. Our lives are comfortable. We live perhaps in leafy suburbs, a buzzing city center, or a rural setting. We may have gardens or balconies full of flowers, and access to supermarkets and farmers' markets brimming over with fruit and vegetables and produce of all kinds. Things seem pretty good, particularly if we don't delve too closely into any of the more serious newspapers and magazines. And for the most part, in the United States at any rate, we can usually rely on the television to avoid anything too distressing—except the weather of course. But now the physical aspect of the wasteland is ending up inside our very bodies. Every human being harbors in his or her body about five hundred synthetic chemicals that were nonexistent before 1920. The effects of these chemicals both individually and mixed together is largely unknown, but there is growing evidence that at least two effects are cancers and reduced fertility in both men and women.

And what do you say when your child wakes up crying about the "aminals being extimpt," as my young daughter did? It made me remember how as a child I cried in bed at night thinking about elephants being killed in Africa because they strayed into rubber plantations. We take for granted the intense love all children have for animals, but doesn't it point to something fundamental to our nature—that inherently we know there is a different way to function? Doesn't it stir a memory that once, long, long ago, the animals did speak to us, there was a design of stewardship between us and all living systems on the planet, the violation of which is so ancient and so painful we have blocked it out almost completely?

The love that children have for animals is certainly a far cry from the attitude toward the animals we raise for food in a process that is no longer farming but "agribusiness." In his bestseller *Diet for a New America* John Robbins exposed to a wide audience the concentration camp–like conditions of millions of cows, calves, pigs, and chickens. Chickens are raised to be either broilers (for eating) or layers (for eggs). All are cooped up, five to a cage that averages about 16 by 18 inches in size, indoors, in an artificially controlled environment. They have to have their beaks cut off, which is very painful to them, lest in the collective madness induced by their unnatural environment they peck one another to death. The broilers have been bred to grow so fast that their bones and joints cannot keep pace. Most can barely stand under their own weight, skeletal disorders are common, and they must crouch or hobble about in pain on flawed feet and legs. Chickens have been found that have literally grown into the cages: their toes get caught in the wire mesh and in time the flesh of their feet grow around it. Their diet is designed not for health but solely to promote either rapid growth or high egg production. It is laced with antibiotics, sulfa drugs, hormones, nitrofurcans, and arsenic compounds. Without the supply of drugs, none of the chickens would live long enough to return enough profit to the business. They are riddled with disease: over 90 percent of them have cancer. Robbins quotes Fred C. Haley, the president of a 225,000-hen Georgia poultry firm: "The object of producing eggs is to make money. When we forget this objective, we have forgotten what it is all about." Another illuminating passage in Robbins's book comes from a "Farmer and Stockbreeder" magazine: "The modern layer is, after all, only a very efficient converting machine, changing the raw material—feedstuffs—into the finished product—the egg—less, of course, maintenance requirements." These two passages illustrate in blood-chilling clarity the inhumane extremes that result from the pursuit of material happiness by people who know only a material, two-dimensional sense of identity in themselves and therefore in everything around them, specifically, in this case, the thousands of unfortunate chickens in their "care." The same deadly consciousness is responsible for the torture of the other familiar "farm" animals. Pigs are also kept all their lives inside a windowless factory building, confined in small cages, often in several layers, so that the droppings of the pigs above fall down through the slats of the cages onto the pigs underneath. Robbins writes:

> It is difficult for us to fathom the suffering of today's pigs. They are crammed for a lifetime into cages in which they can hardly move, and forced against their natures to stand in their own waste. Their sensitive noses are continuously assaulted by the stench from the excrement of thousands of other pigs. Their skeletons are deformed and their legs buckle under the unnatural weight for which they have been bred. Their feet are full of painful lesions from the concrete and slatted metal floors on which they must stand.

Because the pigs, like the chickens, go mad under these conditions, they can start to cannibalize one another, biting tails off. To try to overcome this problem, they are sometimes kept in complete darkness, or their tails are cut off. Their diets are also laced with antibiotics and sulfa drugs and routinely include recycled waste, which consistently contains drug residues and high levels of toxic, heavy metals such as arsenic, lead, and copper. Often they are simply given raw poultry or pig manure to eat. Not surprisingly this does not make for very healthy animals. According to Robbins, over 80 percent of pigs have pneumonia at the time of slaughter. Other diseases that are rampant include dysentery, cholera, trichinosis, pseudorabies and African swine fever.

Cows fare no better. The majority of beef herds have long since disappeared from open pasture land and also lead their lives confined indoors in feedlots:

> Some of the larger feedlots have as many as 100,000 "units." Here the animals are fed a diet designed for one purpose only—to fatten them up as cheaply as possible. This may include such delicacies as

sawdust laced with ammonia and feathers, shredded newspaper (complete with all the colors of toxic ink from the Sunday comics and advertising circulars), "plastic hay," processed sewage, inedible tallow and grease, poultry litter, cement dust, and cardboard scraps, not to mention the insecticides, antibiotics and hormones. Artificial flavors and aromas are added to trick the poor animals into eating the stuff.

Then there is the fate of the dairy cow:

The industry points today with considerable pride to the fact that the average commercial cow now gives three or more times as much milk in a year as her bucolic ancestors. They don't mention that her udder is so large that her calves would have a hard time suckling from it, and might easily damage it if they were allowed to try. Nor do they mention that under natural conditions Old Bessie would live 20 to 25 years. In the unbelievably stressful world of today's dairy factories, however, she is so severely exploited that she will be lucky if she sees her fourth birthday. Old Bessie may spend her whole life in a concrete stall, or, worse yet for her legs and feet, on a slatted metal floor. She is pregnant all the time, and her nervous system has been made so ragged by breeding practices devoted exclusively to milk production and a lifestyle that affords her no exercise, that this most mellow and patient of animals has become something else. She is today so tense, nervous and hyperactive that she often has to be given tranquilizers.

The worst tortures of all are reserved for the cow's poor male calves in the interest of producing lower cost gourmet veal, meat that is tender and whitish. Normally this is achieved by slaughtering the calf shortly after birth, before it has started to eat anything but mother's milk or started to exercise and develop muscles. However, a company called Provimi Inc. dreamt up a system of prolonging the life of the calf while still achieving the white tenderness of its meat. The calf is confined, from birth, in a tiny stall, too small to let it move around in. It cannot even lie down. All its instincts to suckle and romp around are denied. It is fed an iron-deficient diet, designed to keep its meat white, and denied water so as to force it to consume the government-surplus skim milk and fat mixture it is fed to fatten it up. The calves are also kept in darkness except for the two daily feeds, with the result that many go blind. Many die, soon after going blind, and all require a massive and constant supply of antibiotics and other drugs such as nitrofurazone (a carcinogen) and chloramphenicol (which even in infinitesimal concentrations causes a fatal blood disorder in a significant percentage of humans) to stave off pneumonia and enteric diseases, to which they have become severely susceptible.

In Britain the scientist who cloned a sheep is now looking to clone a human being. In the United States, the scientist who cloned two cows now talks about herds of identical cows who will have medications that we need genetically engineered into their milk. How will we treat these cloned animals of the future, given the way we treat the ones now whom we have merely genetically or hormonally altered?

The Monsanto Corporation of America has genetically engineered soya bean seed that is resistant to Monsanto's own brand of herbicide, Round-Up. The company is selling its seeds to farmers, who are then not allowed to plant seeds from the subsequent crop but have to buy the seed again the following year from Monsanto. The beans will of course be heavily sprayed, because they will not be affected, and the killing of weeds makes growing and harvesting easier for the farmer. Monsanto's profits will increase because more of their herbicide will be used, on more of their beans.

Thousands of tons of herbicides, pesticides, and chemical fertilizers are poured onto crops and soil every year all over the world, with the result of course that the earth of the Earth grows steadily more poisoned and depleted. Microscopic trace minerals and vitamins essential to plant and human health are increasingly missing. Chemical substitutes do more harm than good, although no one admits it; and we wonder why there is such a hemorrhage of bad health, especially in the "developed" nations.

More recently there is the attempt by the Mexican billionaire Alfonso Romo and a handful of giant agrochemical conglomerates to seek to own (and alter) the genes of all the seeds that produce our food and fiber. Their means to full control includes phasing out traditional seed production in favor of genetically modified, or transgenic, seeds, which are patentable. Every major seed and agrochemical enterprise is developing a version of the Terminator—genetic technology that renders seeds sterile. The latest is so-called Traitor technology, which produces sterile seeds whose desired genetic traits, such as drought resistance, can only be activated by the company's patented agrochemicals.

Recently on a PBS *Scientific American Frontiers* program I heard a geneticist, in all seriousness, describe humanity as a "random event." The implications of such a viewpoint are astonishing. If humankind and the flora and fauna of the planet and the planet itself are nothing but a series of random events, chance outworkings of DNA and amino acid combinations, then it really doesn't matter what we do to nature or to one another. The dinosaurs were wiped out by such a random event, so why not the Siberian tiger, and the panda, and the one hundred or so other species that disappear daily, wiped out by another random event— us? If the Monsanto corporation is successfully surviving by genetically altering the basic stuff of life and then drenching it with poison and selling it to us as wholesome food, why not? It's only a random event after all. What's more, it really doesn't matter what happens in your life, what you do, what you strive for, how you bring your children up, because it's all random and meaningless.

What kind of mentorship is this? What is a young person to think? To look forward to? In the face of such reductionist, materialist orthodoxies, we urgently need to embark on the quest and return with the Grail, or we have no moral ammunition to challenge such madness and greed.

6

THE QUESTION AND THE UNTRIED SWORD

"SEEKERS"

Oh seekers, when you leave off seeking
You will realize there was never anything to seek for

You were only seeking to lose something,
not to find something,
when you went forth so vigorously in search.

—D. H. LAWRENCE

WHEN, three chapters ago, I broke off from Perceval's story, he had just left the deserted Grail Castle, where he had stayed the night, and was being scolded by a maiden whom he found grieving over her dead knight in the forest, where he had ridden to look for the Wounded Fisher King and his retinue. The maiden was telling Perceval off because he had asked no questions about the Grail or other objects that had proceeded before him while at dinner with the wounded king in the castle banqueting hall. During a three-chapter detour I examined the anatomy of the fisher king wound—how it is caused and how it operates—and also traced the way the wound gives rise to the wasteland; whether an inner, metaphysical wasteland; the wasteland of social abuse, war, and atrocity; or the physical, ecological deterioration of our planet and the extinction of its species. As we start to comprehend the impact of this wound, we realize that whatever it takes to bring healing must be of supreme importance. Therefore, even though we don't yet understand why asking a question about the Grail will heal the fisher king, we nevertheless begin to understand the force and bitterness with which the maiden upbraids Perceval for his silence when in the presence of the Grail. Because if asking a question about the Grail will heal the fisher king and restore the wasteland, then this must be the most vital thing that Perceval, or anyone, can do.

However, even though we may be starting to understand that asking the question is extremely important, Perceval, at this point in the story, does *not* seem to understand this. In fact all the information the maiden gives him concerning the fisher king and the Grail does not appear to register with Perceval much at all. This may be because the maiden tells him so many things, most of them either strange or shocking, including the fact that his mother has died of grief on his account. Not surprisingly, this sad news does get through to Perceval and, more than anything else the maiden has told him, causes him to think anew about where he is going: "why should I go seeking any further? Because I was going that way for no other reason than that I wanted to see her. I must take another road." As far as Perceval is concerned, he isn't aware of being on a quest at all. He was searching for his mother. He is still not particularly conscious of what is going on.

Along the way, Perceval has done a number of worthy deeds, and he continues to do so after his visit to the Grail Castle. For the most part these deeds take the form of overcoming various wayward knights and sending them packing to Arthur's court with their promises to place themselves at the king's command. As these powerful but now vanquished knights show up at Camelot or Caerleon, and as the rumors of Perceval's deeds circulate, Arthur vows that he must be found and fêted. Accordingly, king and retinue pack up and set out to track him down. Perceval is duly found and brought back to the court, where celebrations are held in his honor. On the second day of festivities, while everyone present is bent on celebrating him, a terrible hag appears, riding on a yellow donkey, and reproaches Perceval for failing to ask about the dripping lance and the Grail when he had the opportunity. Because of this failure, she goes on, the king has not been healed of his wound, and therefore his kingdom will continue to suffer:

It is unfortunate for you that you remained silent; for had you asked, the rich king, now in distress, would at once have had his wound quite healed and would peacefully rule his land, of which he will now never hold any part. And do you know the fate of the king who will hold no land or be healed of his wounds? Through him ladies will lose their husbands, lands will be laid waste, maidens left orphaned and helpless, and many knights will perish: all these evils will be of your doing.

Again, like an echo of the grieving maiden, the hag shows no compunction in laying this enormous responsibility fully and squarely on the bewildered Perceval's shoulders. And this time Perceval hears the message and realizes, perhaps for the first time, that he is on a quest. He sets out with renewed purpose, vowing to spend no more than one night in any place until he finds the Grail Castle again.

However, despite this vow, five years of wandering will elapse before Perceval comes to the place in himself that would make return to the Grail Castle possible. During this time, Perceval again appears to forget the hag's instructions, because although he pursues many deeds of chivalry he forgets to turn his mind to God. At the end of five years, he meets ten ladies who are traveling on foot as a penance for their sins since it is Good Friday. They are escorted by three knights. This company is surprised to see Perceval fully armed and oblivious to the holy occasion. Perceval learns that they have come from confessing their sins to a holy man who lives nearby. Having been brought to his senses by their rebuke, Perceval seeks out the hermit himself and confesses to having forgotten about God and to having failed to ask about the Grail.

The question is key to the success of Perceval's mission. It is not enough to find the Grail Castle and come into the presence of the Grail; he must ask this question if the king is to be healed and the land restored.

Chrétien de Troyes's version of the story is unfinished, and so Perceval never gets to visit the Grail Castle a second time and ask about what he saw there earlier. However, in various continuations of the work and in other versions, a question is asked, or questions are asked, about the meaning of the Grail, the lance, and the other wondrous and precious objects that proceed out of the inner room and through the castle hall. The wording is different in the many versions, but the questioning is common to all. According to Chrétien de Troyes, Perceval during his first visit to the Grail Castle: "did not dare ask who was served from the Grail." This is repeated shortly afterward: "and the young man did not ask who was served from that grail," and again, "he does not know who is served from it." The implication here is that there is both a general requirement to inquire about what Perceval has seen, but also a very specific question to be asked concerning whom the Grail serves.

The word *question* grows out of the word *quest,* which can be both noun and verb. And as well as being a process of purification, the quest is the formulation of a question—a very important question. The formulation of this question is not a simple, clear-cut affair. It may take place over many years and involve the whole of one's life and understanding. To ask this question one must be able to survey one's worlds, one's resources, the whole gamut of human activity, history, culture, and creation, and ask: Why?

What is the meaning and purpose of all the abundance of forms that pour forth from the cornucopia Grail? It's the What's-it-all-about, who-are-we, why-are-we here, meaning-of-life question. To ask these questions in more than a fleeting, half-glance way means to pause and to step back. It means we don't just stretch out our arms and grab and pillage as much as we can, without waiting and without thinking. To ask may mean letting go of ordinary goals and markers and launching oneself into a kind of free fall, like Alice falling down the rabbit hole. Yet it isn't necessarily something one can consciously choose to do. During the wilderness years of my twenties, nothing much seemed to have been achieved. Looking back now, however, I have come to realize that what appeared to be lost years were actually spent in formulating the question. Without choosing or at some level wishing to, I was learning to let go and trust to the deeper purposes of life and to a coherence that was not discernible from the surface level of events. Just like Perceval, I did not realize that I was on a quest until I came to understand that there was something very important to understand: the answer to life's fundamental question.

When I eventually moved to the community, it was by no means the end of my quest. In fact, if anything, living there came to represent a more intense and deeper phase of the journey through the forests of my heart. The community in England was one of a network of 12 communities in all worldwide, all of which acted as hubs for a wider circle of people. A wide array of classes, events, and meetings were held, and as much as possible a healing atmosphere was strived for. Central to all of the activity was a coherent system of leadership. There was usually one person or a couple who held the spiritual leadership for each community, and those who lived there were encouraged to develop a deep, loving, and open connection with the leadership. The leader in turn had another person of authority or leadership with whom he or she developed a deep connection, and very often this was the overall leader of the network, the man who most closely of all played the King Arthur role for all of us. This network of spiritual leadership was accessible by anyone anywhere, and so what developed in part was a tremendously complex and vibrant system of heartfelt connections. If some individuals did not get along very well with their "local" point of spiritual mentorship, they could always connect at some other point on the grid, as it were. The reason that this patterning and process of leadership was so emphasized was because it was clearly recognized that such openhearted connection to a trustworthy mentor figure was key to the process of spiritual emergence.

Obviously deep connection between people is not something that can be mandated; it has to arise organically and voluntarily. However, just as it would be extremely uncomfortable to work in a company where one continually avoided any meaningful connection to one's boss, so it did not in the end work very well if a person tried to live in such a community without at the very least an openness to the person playing the role of spiritual leadership. The depth of connection was entirely up to the individual to choose, and in this sense each person got to choose also the nature of his or her quest through his or her own heart. For this was and is the terrain of the quest. The invitation to live in openness and a certain vulnerability of heart with others can be— certainly in the opening stages of the process, anyway—a formidable challenge. The forces released within one's own subconscious when in the presence of an authentic spiritual "God-parent" are not to be underestimated. Primary among them is fear, particularly fear of rejection and rewounding, and shame—feelings of inadequacy and self-loathing. Mixed in with this potent emotional mix are equally strong feelings of longing to be close. In essence, some of the stronger emotional patterns from childhood get replayed; only now that one is an adult the process is even more intense, because it feels like there is more to lose. I first started thinking about the stories of the quest while living in this context. In particular I remember noticing how the more one could access innocence in oneself, the easier the process became; and the more convoluted or guarded one's mind and heart became, the more difficult it was. This was similar, I realized, to the adventures the different knights have on the quest. Some have gruesome adventures: they are hung from a tree, are marooned in the Perilous Chapel, fight with monsters. Others find themselves transported to the Grail Castle.

I can well remember my own feelings as a young woman—shame, fear, and terrible vulnerability—on going to speak about my sexual anxieties with a woman who at one stage played the role of spiritual mentor or "God-parent" to me. Making the appointment to see her, going into the room where she was, and sitting down beside her took all my strength. At every step of the way I had to walk through tremendously strong "walls" of emotion. And at the same time there was another pressure: the requirement, within that still, clear atmosphere, to speak accurately and innocently. Not to withhold, not to embroider, and not to diverge to any degree from what was true. The pressure of speaking absolutely truthfully and through strong emotional blocks in the presence of a nonjudging, loving, but uninvested witness was an amazing growth experience. Not only did this interchange help me— in the space of a few minutes—cut through issues and emotional fog that had dogged me for years (and some months later it bore fruit in the shape of a sexual relationship that was fuller than I had experienced before) but also it gave me a taste of, and an experience of, being entrained into the razor's edge of my own spiritual presence. Because that was where I had to speak from. Not just from my mind or from my emotions but from the fine-tuned point of being. This was potent magic!

The hermit whom Perceval meets after his five years of wandering explains to him that it is the older man in the inner room who is served by the Grail: "that king who has himself served from the Grail . . . [is] he, whose life is so spiritual that all it needs is the host that comes in the grail."

So it turns out that the Grail serves not the Wounded Fisher King but the Grail King, an elderly man with pure white hair who lives in an inner room of the Grail Castle. As I have mentioned, this figure is a symbol of God, or of a higher or whole order of energy. In other words, it is the purposes of God that are to be served by the Grail, *not the purposes of a human ego that has become divorced from an awareness of that greater whole* and has substituted its own image in the place of God's (has tried to be God-like instead of knowing a relationship with the reality of God). If an individual tries to have the Grail serve his or her own limited purposes, separate from the larger whole, the Grail does not bring blessing but only a curse, a wound—that Grail wound whereby we pursue happiness and consume more and more but never feel fulfilled or content.

The question and answer are in fact another formulation of the theme of polarity. They tell us that if we seek fulfillment from the material world alone, we will fail. We must turn the face of our response around, away from the forms of the outer world and back to whence they arise in the spiritual realm. We must reverse polarity from the outer to the inner. The question is seeking to correct the attitude of the fisher king, who thinks that the Grail serves him. That's why he eats the fish, which is a symbol of the Grail, and of course, this is what has wounded him. King Arthur, on the other hand, has already asked the question and knows the answer. He knows that the kingdom serves a presence and a purpose greater than himself alone. That is why he could pull the sword from the stone and that is why the kingdom came to him; the Grail served him because he served God. The sword here parallels the Grail symbol in its representation of the kingdom.

However, it is not the transcendent presence of the Grail King alone that is served by the Grail. The Grail also serves the differentiated presence of Godhead within each person who has learned to ask the question. This is symbolized in the "Queste del Saint Graal" when the companions of the Round Table are present at Camelot for a grand banquet and the Holy Grail mysteriously enters the hall and moves along the tables. As it passes, each person is provided with whatever food he or she most desires. As we serve the purposes of the Grail King and cease from the attempt to wrench fulfillment from the Grail, so we are served by the Grail with whatever it is we most desire. This is akin to Jesus' words: "Seek ye first the kingdom of heaven, and his righteousness, and all these things shall be added unto you." That is, turn your response around to the spiritual source within you, learn to act from that place (righteousness—right-useness) and all those things that you long for, both tangible and intangible, all the forms that flow out of the horn of plenty, will come to you in season just as inevitably as the sword came to Arthur. The sword belonged to Arthur because he was king; therefore, it came to him. What we long for usually—not always—but usually is what belongs to us; that's why we long for it, after all.

When something comes to us in this way, our enjoyment of it is not tainted by any hint of either guilt that we don't deserve it or fear that we may lose it. True enjoyment involves innocence: the stance that delights in and savors but does not crave the fruits of the Grail cornucopia.

In the story the quest is undertaken in order to heal both the fisher king's wound and his wasteland kingdom. The condition of an emotional or spiritual wasteland leads to a search for meaning: an attempt to find healing, to fill the emptiness. In other words, a quest for the Grail. Thus the quest begins by looking for something outside of ourselves to bring fulfillment. This attitude parallels the fisher king's wound because it means that we are oriented in the outer world, in the kingdom, and not yet in the inner world of the Grail King. The quest can only end when this attitude reverses: when meaning is no longer sought externally but accessed internally. This is what finding the Grail symbolizes. Joseph Campbell elucidates these themes in *The Hero with a Thousand Faces*:

> Professor Toynbee uses the terms "detachment" and "transfiguration" to describe the crisis by which the higher spiritual dimension is attained that makes possible the resumption of the work of creation. The first step, detachment or withdrawal, consists in a radical transfer of emphasis from the external onto the internal world,

macro- to microcosm, a retreat from the desperations of the waste land to the peace of the everlasting realm that is within.

To complete the quest, therefore, as I have already described, we must undergo a process of deep healing and change, which will involve looking into the "jadestone" of our own shadow energies:

> the first work of the hero is to retreat from the world scene of secondary effects to those causal zones of the psyche where the difficulties really reside, and there to clarify the difficulties, eradicate them in his own case.

So the quest begins as an attempt to find something—fulfillment, the Grail, the meaning of life; and ends, *if* it ends, in the act of letting go, of losing our old lives, and releasing past conditioning. When Perceval arrived at the Grail Castle the first time and failed to ask the question it was because he was inhibited by the instructions of the father figure Gornemant not to ask questions. In other words, here was some conditioning that stood in the way of achieving the quest. Perhaps it means that we have to give up our loyalty to the "grown-up" or so-called real world, and think and act in ways that might sabotage sensibleness and social taboo. We have to dare to be who we really are—a truly terrifying thought!

Instead of congratulating Perceval on all his feats of conquest and rescue, the hag accuses him of dire failure. He did many worthy deeds but not the one crucial thing. The hag is someone we need to hear even though we often resist what she has to say. She is the voice that deflates the false positivity in us. When our ego is celebrating its conquests and achievements, she reminds us of their hollowness if the essential question has not been asked. She shows up the attempt to substitute what is God-like for our own unique expression of God. The hag could also represent wasted Mother Earth: she is not going to be restored by "good works": exposing evil, paying our subscriptions to Greenpeace, feeding the poor. We have got to do something much more personal and fundamental. We have got to reverse our polarity, complete the quest by asking the question, if we are going to restore the wasteland. However unwelcome the hag is to us, we must learn to listen to what she has to say if we want to succeed on the quest.

If the quest does not end, paradoxically it can lead to making the wasteland worse, and too often the quest never ends because the attitude never reverses. The quest becomes translated in material terms, whether that means literally money and material possessions or more intangible goods: status, intellectual weight, expertise, relationships, and so on. All of these things may belong in our lives—they are the bounty of the Grail, after all. The problem arises when we are oriented in, or "negative" to, the material world and do not have the connection to the inner source of divinity in place. Then we start to believe these things will fill us, will satisfy *in themselves,* and we remain dependent on them for our sense of well-being, fulfillment, and identity. In this way, we act out the fisher king's wound, taking the bounty of the Grail to ourselves and wanting more and more of it. And here is the other way that the ecological, physical wasteland results from the wound, because we try to assuage our spiritual hunger with material goods. We consume more and more goods, utilities, trees, and land and in turn cause ever-increasing pollution and ever-decreasing habitat for wildlife. The recent surge in popularity of the four-wheel drive sport-utility vehicles is a good example of the questing/consuming mentality. These cars consume an enormous amount of energy, not only in gas (some monsters only do 8 miles to the gallon) but also in their manufacture. Despite everything we now know about global warming from carbon emissions, air pollution, toxic waste created by car manufacture (and demolition), these expensive cars are selling like hotcakes. The materially translated quest mentality is deeply embedded in our society. It is even written into the Declaration of Independence as the "pursuit of happiness"—the *pursuit* of, not necessarily the finding of. The United States is the greatest consumer of the world's goods and the most reluctant to cut its carbon emissions: a graphic example of how the material quest mentality extends the wasteland. The pollution caused by all countries is at least in part related to the belief that their gross national product must increase. This conviction is repeated in the unquestioned tenet of faith of most corporations: that they must grow in order to be profitable and provide a return to their shareholders. As I have already noted, there can be little doubt today that we are creating a global wasteland. And still the supermarkets stock half an aisle with over 15 different kinds of kitchen towel, only one of which is manufactured from recycled paper. And still vested interests lobby to drill for oil in the last unspoiled coastal wilderness of Alaska, oil that is not needed and that, according to the geological surveys, does not exist in the kind of quantities that would make economic, let alone ecological, sense.

The hermit gives Perceval absolution and furthermore explains to him that it is the Grail King who is served by the Grail. It is significant that Perceval learns (from the hermit) the answer to the question about the Grail before he returns to ask it. To ask the question is to understand its answer.

When Perceval asks for a penance that he can do to atone for failing to ask the question and forgetting about God, the hermit says, among other things, "Love God, believe in God, worship God." This is another formulation of the requirement to change polarity. To ask whom the Grail serves is to understand the requirement to be polarized in the heavenly king energy. To be oriented this way, so that we become the vessel of this experience, is what *worship* actually means. The word *worship* is derived from the Old English words *worth* and *ship,* and its original meaning had to do with deserving to be held in esteem or high repute, that is, to be recognized as a container—a ship—of worthiness, like the Grail itself.

To ask the question and understand its answer also carries the connotation of graduating. One is no longer dependent on the mentor figure for orientation in the radiance of spirit but has graduated into one's own direct connection to spiritual source. We have been weaned from that volatile state onto our own relationship with God. Now, instead of subjects or disciples, we are peers. There is a wonderful description of this process toward the end of the Book of Revelation when the angel who has been "talking" with John gives him a similar admonishment to worship God as opposed to himself, the angel:

> And when I had heard and seen, I fell down to worship before the feet of the angel which shewed me these things.

> Then saith he unto me, See thou do it not: for I am thy fellow
> servant, and of thy brethren the prophets, and of them which keep
> the sayings of this book: worship God. (Revelation 22:9)

These two brief verses form an astonishingly concise statement of fundamental issues: "See thou do it not": that is, don't bow down and worship me even though you have received this revelation of the divine from me; "for I am thy fellow servant": having received the revelation, you are now ready to stand with me and to see that I am now your peer. "Worship God": now, instead of worshipping me (the spiritual mentor) you must worship God, that is to say, sustain your own relationship with the divine, not a vicarious one through me or "your brethren the prophets"—or any other leader. The requirement is simple and clear: you are now expected to graduate into your personal connection with the Grail King. This is the whole meaning and purpose of the revelation.

When that angel says to us "See thou do it not"—however that realization comes to us—it is the pivotal point of our spiritual evolution, and a moment of liberation. "Worship God." Everything is condensed down to those two words. "Worhip God": meaning, for one thing, don't worship anyone else, that is, your spiritual mentor. Don't take a vicarious route; go direct, go to the source, and become aligned with that source so that you are a "ship," a container, of worthiness, of the presence of God yourself. Be true to the true nature of yourself. Be your own man or woman. Be free: "And ye shall know the truth, and the truth shall set you free."

Do we from this point on find that we have suddenly cast off all our subconscious conditioning of limitation and fear? No, we don't. But the difference is that now we take over responsibility for the ongoing healing of our minds and hearts and bodies. We do it *consciously*, knowing that while much of the "clothing," both physical and emotional, through which we express ourselves needs further healing, the spirit that we are, the core identity, does not; and we work gradually to align the instrument of our incarnation with the incarnate spirit that we are. When the monsters rise up, we have to vanquish them. When fear fills us, we must overcome it. The way is still both path and epiphany, effortful and effortless, a process to endure and an instantaneous arrival. But now instead of journeying toward the center, we journey outward from it.

This conscious carrying on of what was unconsciously begun relates to the symbolism of the sword, which I will now examine more closely.

When Perceval makes his first visit to the Grail Castle and is seated talking with his host, the Wounded Fisher King, before anything else happens, a lad comes in at the house door carrying a sword. The lad gives the sword to the wounded king, who immediately presents it to Perceval. The sword is obviously the partnering symbol to the chalice, the masculine to the Grail's feminine. I have said that the Grail, among many other things, represents the heart realm, and more specifically, the purified heart realm. So the symbol of the sword represents the partnering, masculine element of the conscious mind, and more specifically, the conscious mind that is in alignment with what I have called the wisdom of Merlin, the deep purposes of life. We remember that Merlin needed ordinary mortals to achieve his purposes. The subconscious wisdom requires the alignment of the conscious mind. This conscious alignment is represented by the sword given to Perceval.

This sword has never been used. When the fisher king hands the sword to Perceval "[h]e thanks him for it and girds it on, but not too tightly, then draws it naked from the scabbard. Then, having looked at it for a while, he returned it to the scabbard." Perceval, on arriving at the castle and seeing the wounded king, has had his first insight into the true nature of his consciousness. He has separated out enough from his own wound of fear to be able to see it, and even though he does not know it yet, he is in the vicinity of the healing presence of the Grail King and, seated in the banqueting hall, is beginning to take ownership of his own house of being. However, this realization, this sword, is new—untried and incomplete. He puts on the sword but doesn't fasten it too tightly—he doesn't completely own it yet. He takes it out and looks at it and then puts it back. He turns the discovery over in his mind but does not yet realize its full implications. "And you may be sure that it fitted splendidly at his side and even better in his hand; and it really seemed that in time of need he ought to put it to valiant use." This realization cannot remain just a wonderful insight; it will need to be acted on. We are told that this sword can never be broken except in one particular perilous circumstance. The next morning after Perceval has left the Grail Castle and been rebuked by the grieving maiden, she asks him where this sword came from and warns him: "I know well where it was made and also who forged it. Take care never to rely on it, for it will certainly betray you when you get into a great fight, since it will fly into pieces." The realization will need to be acted on, yet it will also prove to be untrustworthy. The sword will break and have to be re-forged. To begin with, our newly received sword—our newly grasped understanding of the mechanics of consciousness—exists predominantly as a concept, a mental construct, somewhat brittle and untried. This mental construct—like all concepts about spiritual matters—will break apart when applied to the rigors of harsh reality. The sword will fly into pieces. We will be left defenseless and with the sense that we know nothing of spiritual reality. This is a necessary part of the process, because if we know something with our minds only, we don't really know anything. It is not until we know with our hearts that we truly know.

In many of the tellings of the Grail quest story, this is symbolized for us when the broken sword cannot be mended until the knight in question—usually Perceval, Gawain, or Galahad—has proven his worthiness by finding, and asking about, the Grail, or the heart. In the "Grand Saint Graal" the broken sword will only be mended when the Grail quest succeeds. In the Gerbert continuation of Chrétien De Troyes's "Perceval" the hero is unable to mend the sword because of his having indirectly caused the death of his mother, and he must set out again in search of the Grail to amend this act. When he reaches the fisher king's court, he asks for the Grail, which appears followed by lance and sword. Perceval pieces together the sword, and the king embraces him. In the Gautier continuation, it is Gawain who is at first unable to mend a broken sword and is told that his inability proves he is not yet worthy of his quest.

However, there is a paradox here. The sword, or the mind's knowing, will not become strong and reforged, turned into assured experience, without finding the Grail, without the heart's knowing also. But equally, the Grail cannot be found, the heart cannot be healed, without the sword, without the understanding of the mind. The sword is as potent a symbol as the Grail. In Manessier's continuation, for instance, the sword breaks when it is used to kill the fisher king's brother, Goon Desert. When the fisher king picked up the broken pieces, they wounded him. Goon Desert's daughter foretells a knight who will mend the sword, avenge the death of her father, and thereby heal the fisher king. Here, therefore, the mending of the sword parallels the finding of the Grail as a healing, restorative act.

So the mind needs the heart, and the heart needs the mind. The interdependent symbolism of the broken sword and the Grail quest is speaking of a process of coemergence of clarified consciousness, both mental and emotional. Both mind and heart have to be healed. The mind's healing relates primarily to alignment with the purposes of Merlin and the Grail King; the heart's healing relates to purification. Our minds have a part to play in breaking the habit of addiction, deliberately turning attention away from involvement in the outer realm, and reorienting in spiritual source, thus giving space for the heart realm to yield up and cleanse its patterns—primarily of fear and shame. As I pointed out in chapter 2, the patterns of fear and shame that constitute the wound exist in those levels of the subconscious that lie just beneath consciousness. They do not really penetrate down to the deeper levels of magical presence where Merlin "resides," where the astonishing automatic pilot of the subconscious mind keeps so many marvelous systems of our physical bodies functioning.

This whole process is one of trial and error though; it's a bit like taking one step forward and two steps back, because even after we have been given the sword and have grasped some understanding about our real identity, when the emotional controls of fear leap out at us again, our sword will probably break. Our wonderful spiritual concepts will be thrown to the winds as we find ourselves enmeshed again in the strong currents of feeling that have always got the better of us before. Nevertheless, if we stay with the process, if we keep being reminded by the various grieving maidens and terrible hags that we meet on the way, our sword can be reforged in the fires of experience, will slowly strengthen and be tempered, and will become much more useful in the process of freeing up the heart realm from its shadow patterns.

Important though the work of reforging the sword is, it is not why we went on the quest. *We did not go on the quest for the sword—we didn't need to. It is given to us!* Some years after my first visit to the community in British Columbia, I returned to attend a class there. The class essentially laid out the larger spiritual context of the quest for me: that is, it laid out in very clear terms what the true nature of identity was and showed and offered the means to become "weaned" onto this deeper source of myself, as well pointing out why realization of the deeper spiritual source of identity—the "Grail King"—is the most important contribution anyone can make to a troubled world. In other words, I was handed the sword of conscious understanding—freely, abundantly, and with almost no effort on my part.

Perceval is given the sword in the Grail Castle, and he too doesn't really have to do anything to earn it. However, he still does not fully realize the implications of the sword and his experience in the castle. The grieving maiden tells him the significance of where he has been and what he has seen, but he still doesn't really hear her. It is not until the terrible hag reprimands him that he finally "gets" that he is on a quest, and even then he forgets after a while and rambles around rather futilely for five more years.

In my own experience, too, even though I was given the sword, even though the theory and design of the ultimately divine design of my own consciousness and being were laid out for and in my conscious understanding, and even though I was told I was on a quest and the bigger context had been spelled out for me, the real implications of both did not really begin to kick in until I started to prove out these things in my heart realm. Returning to the swarming flux of ordinary life in the overwhelmingly concrete and worldly—almost world-weary—context of London, it was always easy to forget that I was on a quest. Or the possibility of being on one could seem like a feeble delusion when weighed against the massive bulwarks of professional sensibleness and the granite realities of having to pay my way in one of the most expensive cities in the world. And it was all very well to tell myself—when the first relationship I had had for many years broke up (living within the confines of those drawn to the spiritual network meant that available and suitable men were in short supply) or when a job (that I really loved) as an upcoming (and promising) journalist at a small medical newspaper disappeared when it was taken over by a larger company or when I simply had no money or opportunity to explore the teeming possibilities of life in my twenties (which other "ordinary" people seemed to have available to them)—that being in touch with the deeper level of myself was enough and would bring the experience of knowing that "the kingdom of heaven is at hand." If I wasn't actually having the experience of this in my heart, which for a good amount of the time I wasn't, then the sword—the conscious understanding that this was possible—was not much comfort.

We do not go on a quest for the sword, we go on a quest for the Grail, for the heart. It's time for another look at that diagram of the seven levels of our being in which the three inner and three outer planes are either connected or separated by the fourth plane, which is the heart realm (see the illustration).

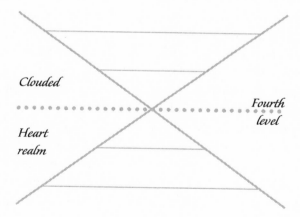

If this realm is clouded over—is wounded—it forms a veil between the worlds. Perceval's name, meaning literally to "pierce the veil," to clear the connection between God and human being, heaven and earth, indicates that this veil is cleared by the work of the quest, the work of purification of the heart realm. Hence the beatitude "Blessed are the pure in heart, for they shall see God." The quest, in order to succeed, must be a process whereby this realm is clarified and one's connection to the "upper" or Grail King, is restored. The ability to ask the question and understand its answer signifies the conscious understanding of this process—the mended and aligned sword. Finally, Perceval has become wise. He is not just stumbling upon the Grail Castle epiphany through his innocence, he understands who the Wounded Fisher King is, he understands the purpose and meaning of the Grail, and he understands that he is on a quest.

As I have said, the sword is naturally the masculine symbol: phallus, scepter, wand. All relate to the masculine domain of potency, government, purpose, power. I remember when my two-year-old son picked up the detachable wooden handle of a bath brush—two-thirds his height—and instinctively thrust it high above his head and commanded his eight-year-old sister to get out of the bath. As a mother I have a sense of ambivalence at the idea of my son playing with toy swords and guns—an ambivalence that I probably share with many other mothers. Don't they just foster aggression? Shouldn't he be denied them? But watching him, I realized that this symbol is the natural and innate property of the masculine. He was not being aggressive—he was sparkling and giggly and delighting in his own fierceness. To refuse him that, I realized, would be to suppress and inhibit an inherent essence through which he will need to express himself. The myths tell us in fact that this masculine power is only misused when it is not in partnership with the feminine of the Grail and is wielded by a consciousness that has not learned to stay polarized in the spiritual realm. The pommel of the sword given to Perceval was of gold—the symbol of love. So we could say that the true sword is always held in love. The broken sword can also in fact symbolize the misuse of power. In Manessier's continuation the sword broke when it was used to kill the fisher king's brother, Goon Desert, and it will only be mended when the deed is avenged and the fisher king is healed by finding the Grail.

If we think of the sword as representing purpose, while the Grail represents identity, we can see that the myth is confirming an additional meaning: namely that without the healing of identity it is impossible, or at best very difficult, to have one's purpose line up coherently in one's life. In Gautier's continuation, Perceval pieces together yet another broken sword at the Grail Castle, but a little crack remains. Even if everything seems almost perfect—in one's career, relationships, family—a tiny crack remains. A doubt, a flaw, an element of discontent. Something we don't want to think about too much, something that causes us to avoid intensity because we know instinctively that any pressure will cause that crack to break. Very often what one thought was one's purpose, one's goal, even one's closest relationships may break up en route to the Grail Castle as motivation and identity shift. The false purpose must break up and be reforged into a true blade, a true form for one's expression.

The most famous sword of all, of course, is the one that is pulled from the stone by Arthur at the commencement of his reign. Here the sword clearly represents our individual power, and to draw the sword from the stone is to take back power that we have invested outside of ourselves. As we have already outlined, this power is often given away primarily to a leadership figure, whether to a Wounded Fisher King, who doesn't want to give it back, or to a King Arthur figure, who insists we take it back. But there are secondary depositories of our power: our institutions, our corporations, our possessions, and our healthcare insurance plans, medical doctors, and experts of various persuasions. We invest power in our institutions and corporations because they are so large or long established that we assume they are wiser than us; we invest power in our possessions because we believe they give us meaning and status; in healthcare plans because we think they will look after us; in doctors and experts because we think they know better than we do how to look after our health, our children, our money, and so on. Obviously there is a place for all these institutions and professionals in our lives: but it is a balanced interaction, in which we are respectful, but not unquestioning, participants—in which we weigh advice against our intuition and other sources of information. And very often we project authority onto a Wizard of Oz, some person or entity that appears on the surface to be very impressive and powerful but is found in the end to be only a bald-headed little man hiding behind a shiny screen while working machinery to create magical effects. We think a government agency of some sort will be able to sort something out for us and find that it turns out that they are just as inept, if not more inept, than we are ourselves.

Very often these corporate or institutional structures are found to be running according to a preprogrammed patterning. They have become crystallized, like quartz stone, and no longer flexible or relevant to the purposes of life. One good example is the area of orthodox, allopathic medicine. The "software" that runs this "hardware" is the idea that our bodies are primarily material, machinelike objects that can be fixed up and reoiled like a car engine, when often there are much subtler levels of "malfunction" that need to be taken into account. This crystallized patterning of thought that then runs the larger structures of society is symbolized by the fate of Merlin, who is eventually trapped in a crystal cave. Merlin is the wisdom of the subconscious, we remember—the wisdom that is always released when the sword is taken out of the stone. When we access our own intuition and power and no longer look to find it in others.

Drawing the sword from the stone is an act of power. We find that power is not to do with the domination of others through force or manipulation but with a reversal of attention, a change of polarity so that we trust ourselves and our own power and no longer rely so much on outer forms.

The climactic scene in the film *Star Wars* is a great metaphor for this process, dramatically depicting Luke's change of polarity as he flies his fightercraft through the central channel on the surface of the Death Star. All the other rebel planes have been routed, and R2D2 has been rendered inactive. Darth Vader is close on his tail, and everything now depends on Luke getting close enough and firing a shot accurate enough to enter the one vulnerable spot on the Death Star. As Luke pulls down the visor to activate the computer-aided missile launch, he hears Obi-Wan Kenobi's voice speaking to him from the inner realms: "Use the force, Luke." "Let go, Luke." "Luke, trust me." The tension-fraught circumstances would all conspire to draw Luke's attention away from his inner intuition, but he hesitates one split second longer and then turns off the computer. Darth Vader, in hot pursuit, says: "The force is strong in this one." Luke uses his own sensing as to when to launch the missile, and his shot goes home. Darth Vader's craft is attacked by Han Solo on a surprise return and change of heart seconds before he can fire on Luke; the Death Star blows up split seconds before it was about to fire on the rebel base. As Luke pulls away safe, he hears Obi's voice once more: "Remember Luke, the force will be with you—always."

This action-packed sequence is a marvelous depiction of a spiritual truth. The universe is saved from the forces of destruction—the Death Star, or the wound—by the hero's deliberate change of polarity. Instead of giving his attention to and vesting his power in the material realm and its technology, he lets go to the "Force" within, the radiant power of the heavenly king, and as a result his shot goes home: he wields his power accurately. While the quest for the Grail, and achieving inner union and fulfillment, is essentially an inner act of being, drawing the sword from the stone is external, of the world, and has to do with action: the walking of our talk. It is the outer corollary to the inner experience of union. Alignment with the heavenly king energy assures that the power so wielded will not be misused.

7

BLESSINGS OF THE GRAIL

*There was a time when a traveler, if he had the will and knew
only a few of the secrets, could send his barge out into the Summer
Sea and arrive not at Glastonbury of the monks, but at the Holy
Isle of Avalon; for at that time the gates between the worlds
drifted within the mists, and were open, one to another, as the
traveler thought and willed. For this is the great secret, which was
known to all educated men in our day: that by what men think,
we create the world around us, daily anew.*

— MARION ZIMMER BRADLEY, *The Mists of Avalon*

*The "Wall of Paradise," which conceals God from human sight, is
described by Nicholas of Cusa as constituted of the "coincidence of
opposites," its gate being guarded by "the highest spirit of reason,
who bars the way until he has been overcome."*

— JOSEPH CAMPBELL, CITING ANANDA K. COOMARASWAMY'S
REFERENCE TO NICHOLAS OF CUSA'S "DE VISIONE DEI," IN
The Hero with a Thousand Faces

S O THE SYMBOLS of the sword and the further wanderings
of Perceval are telling us that if on our first visit to the Grail
Castle we, like Perceval, have the experience but "miss the
meaning," the internal work of the quest and of reforging the
sword of conscious awareness will eventually bring us back there
for a second visit and allow us to both experience the epiphany of
union once more and also to understand its meaning:

And approach to the meaning restores the experience
In a different form.

— T. S. ELIOT, "THE DRY SALVAGES," IN *Four Quartets*

It is a different form because now we have some perspective on what is happening; it is more familiar; and we know it belongs to us. This time we will be able to ask the question "Whom does the grail serve?"—we will be able to consciously align with the Grail King's energy.

The Grail Castle epiphany and the finding of the Grail symbolizes the condition of union between one's heart realm and the heavenly king's energy. I have described this energy as love. The heart knows love. That is what hearts are supposed to be about, aren't they? The heart knows love and is filled with love instead of fear, doubt, and hesitancy. Whom does the Grail serve—whom does the heart serve? It serves God; it serves the Grail King, who eats "a single consecrated wafer" from the Grail: something very refined. The Grail chalice was described by Chrétien de Troyes as made of "refined gold." Gold is the symbol of love. Our hearts serve God, literally serve the refined fire of the current of our love to the inner source of being. And as soon as we give, we receive: we receive the returning current of love and therefore are able to "serve God," or serve love, to others—to serve the current of blessing to others. To paraphrase Yeats's poem, we are blessed and can bless.

And suddenly the Grail serves us—we eat food from it that satisfies everything in us. The sacred food and wine are found to be simply what the world already offers—only lit up, transparent to the holiness that is the source of everything. Everything is sacred when bathed in this light: our sexuality, our history, our contribution of insight and essence, our ambitions and hearts' desires. What seemed to be wrong or shameful is found to have been merely incomplete. Now filled out in the light of the spiritual dimension of identity, it is found to be perfect, if not yet perfectly expressed. The Grail blesses all; the Grail is all blessings.

This was something of my experience on what could be called my second visit to the Grail Castle, which took the form of an extended stay on the community I had visited for a shorter time at the age of 18. It was during this longer stay, several years after my first visit, that I attended an intensive two-month-long class and stayed on for a further month or more living and working communally.

On the surface, there was really nothing very remarkable about what we did. The routines were quiet and steady: breakfast together, then gathering in the meeting room, which was one of the original log cabins, for a morning of classes. These would take the form of papers or audiotapes (later some videotapes too) of addresses given by the two founders of the network, Lloyd Meeker and Martin Exeter. These would be mixed with classes on the "Story of Man," using predominantly a symbolic interpretation of the Bible, anatomy, nutrition, and a nontouch healing practice called attunement. We would also do some presentations ourselves, particularly practicing the art of public speaking. We had a midmorning break and lunch, and in the afternoon would split up into smaller groups for what was called the "work pattern." This meant whatever was needed on the community: cleaning, cooking, heavier work on the ranch, maintenance, and so on. The idea was to put into immediate practice the spiritual principles that we may have begun to absorb in the morning. There were usually evening sessions as well, and a fairly early bedtime.

The atmosphere sustained in both the class sessions and the community itself was so rich and serene, so imbued with magic, that the presence of spiritual identity was magnified beyond what is normally discernible in the busy, everyday world. In this sacred space my own internal atmosphere was stilled and the background noise in consciousness turned down to the point where I was able to perceive and experience more consciously a deeper dimension of my own presence.

While in this atmosphere of spiritual presence—both my own and that of others—everything fell effortlessly into place. The shadowy dualism of the world lined up and clicked into oneness. The Grail experience of union was mine. I knew deeply, beyond intellectual "knowing about" or emotional "feeling for," and with a great sense of relief and joy, that everything was bathed in the outpouring blessing of the Grail. The world was made young again, sweet and tender. All its delights, desires, and intensities were meant to be; no taint of wrongdoing remained. My deepest longings were allowed to align fully within me, no longer shadowing me in self-doubt and hesitation.

An analogy used by Lloyd Meeker to illustrate how the higher levels of identity become discernible when our internal atmosphere is still and full is of a mountain by a lake. When the surface waters of the lake are still and calm, the reflection of the mountain is perfect (see the illustration).

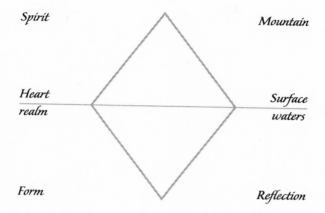

Spirit

Mountain

Heart realm

Surface waters

Form

Reflection

If the heart realm is clear and still, the reflection of spirit is perfect. Again we see the meaning of Jesus' saying "Blessed are the pure in heart for they shall see God." When he admonished "Let not your heart be troubled," it wasn't just a comforting idea but an absolute necessity if spiritual identity was to be known. The mysterious sea of glass mentioned in the Book of Revelation is also a reference to this same clarified state of consciousness:

> And I saw as it were a sea of glass mingled with fire: and them that had gotten the victory over the beast, and over his image, and over his mark, and over the number of his name, stand on the sea of glass, having the harps of God. (Revelation 15:2)

The beast refers to the emotional controls that bind us; the harps of God are our own forms, all seven dimensions of them, now expressing our larger identity because the heart realm has become the "sea of glass"—see-through, transparent—and "mingled with fire"—woven with the power of love.

When the waters are ruffled by emotional storms, the image breaks up or disappears completely (see the illustration).

The mountain is still there: it didn't go anywhere, but it is no longer known or experienced by us.

We can also talk about the mechanics of spiritual consciousness in terms of sound. If a bell is tolling in a vacuum, we cannot hear it. Air

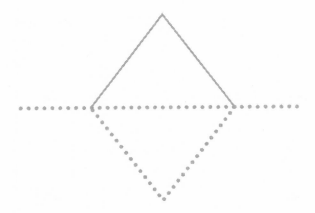

is needed to form the vibrations that carry the sound to our ears. Similarly, if there is no inner atmosphere in ourselves, we cannot hear the voice of spirit. However, if we come into a place where this atmosphere is available through others, or even into the presence of one individual who carries this atmosphere, we can become entrained into the hearing of the tone of spiritual presence. Perhaps at first we perceive it in others, but following on from that we begin to experience the reality of this golden presence living in us as well.

Whatever the nature of our Grail experience—a heightened state of awareness, a sense of being blessed, of being filled to overflowing with love, of transfiguration—there comes always the requirement to return, whether literally a return to our homes and everyday responsibilities or simply a return to a more "ordinary" level of consciousness. In my case there was a physical return involved as well as a return in consciousness. After my extended stay on the community, set in "New World," open ranching country, the time came when I could no longer avoid going back home to the musty confines of the Old World, literally the old world of England and the crowded, dusty streets of London, laden down with tradition and worldly cynicism. This correlation of spiritual and physical return was both helpful and confusing. It was useful to have a place "set apart" from my normal world, a place dedicated to allowing the Grail union to be grounded in experience because it made it easier to change habits of consciousness, to open up and allow in fresh insight. However, the association of the spiritual with rural and communal North America and of the physical with the busy streets of London made for such a dramatic contrast that ironically it was tempting to associate the spiritual with the material and believe that it was impossible to live from that new spiritual place in the old physical setting. There appeared to be an almost unbridgeable gap between the two worlds.

In his account of the hero's quest, Joseph Campbell described the great dilemma that faces anyone who has completed the Grail quest: how to return? Or even, why return at all? "The first problem of the returning hero is to accept as real, after an experience of the soul-satisfying vision of fulfillment, the passing joys and sorrows, banalities and noisy obscenities of life. Why re-enter such a world?" Return is fraught with danger. The first danger is memory. After the revelation has receded in the cycles of tension and release, we must let it go: otherwise the memory of purity will freeze us. Nothing else will ever match up; we will cling to the precious memory and hold the world at bay lest it seep in and rob us of those glittering fragments. Instead of blessing, we hold ourselves apart and exclude the world. Instead of the flow of water that would restore the land, the purity turns to ice: sharp-edged, brittle, cold, exclusive, fanatical; and we watch, helpless, as the green tender world grows rigid and white around us.

The second danger is a more frightening prospect than the first— amnesia. We can foresee the possibility that the pain of living in the low-flying, suburban gray, while the fire that consumes us within finds no answering flame without, will be too great, and we will therefore opt instead for oblivion. We fear that in fact we will come to hunger for normality in order to quench the knowledge that gnaws at us; that we will come even to loathe the drumming of intensities that seem to bar us from ordinary pleasure, and that we will long to be easily contented, happy to accumulate what is left to us of the good life and to start worrying about career, children's schools, and pensions.

Campbell wrote that in order for the hero's journey to come full circle, there was the need for him not only to return to the world but to bring with him the boon he had won—be it the Golden Fleece or runes of wisdom or the Grail consciousness of union—so that it might benefit humanity as a whole. Campbell wrote:

he has yet to re-enter with his boon the long-forgotten atmosphere where men who are fractions imagine themselves to be complete. He has yet to confront society with his ego-shattering, life-redeeming elixir, and take the return blow of reasonable queries, hard resentment, and good people at a loss to comprehend.

At this stage, there can occur, as documented in many myths, what Campbell termed the "refusal of the return." The prospect of returning to the realm of the normal and attempting to integrate his or her vision there is more daunting to the adventurer than was the original quest! "Even the Buddha, after his triumph, doubted whether the message of realization could be communicated."

My assumption that the new spiritual place could not exist in the old physical setting made it easier to avoid the responsibility that is inherent upon our return of integrating the one with the other. Instead of returning to Arthur's court bearing the Grail—instead of weaving back together heaven and earth—I started to become an accomplice in the conspiracy to keep them apart.

Obviously the two worlds of spiritual community in North America and a small house in London were very different, as different as Harry Potter's two worlds of Hogwarts and Number 4 Privet Drive, but the key reason for their difference was the absence of magic, the absence of the atmosphere that can reveal the shimmering of spiritual presence. My own process of spiritual growth had been helped by living in the relative abundance of the communal atmosphere of spiritual presence, and I was extremely reluctant to leave. When I did return to London, I felt starved of that atmosphere; it was like gasping for oxygen. But what I was coming up against, at least in part, was the fact that I had as yet a lot of "work" to do in generating my own atmosphere rather than relying on that provided by other people. Return involves, in short, yet another duality to be mastered—perhaps the most important of all. So that we neither reject on the one hand the mundane world or on the other the kingdom of heaven but come to learn how to knit them back together. We must handle anticlimax—we must accommodate the step-down in power—without losing access to its higher intensities. We must find practical solutions to the problems of joining back the worlds.

We return to a world that is much the same as when we left it, but *we* are not the same, and our task now is to find a way to integrate our new understanding with the world the way it is, to leaven the lump, as it were. Our return is also our reply. We have learned to ask the question and understand its answer: now the rest of our life will be about bringing that reply to the world.

Does the work of the quest, of asking the question, and of return last ten years or ten months? Both and neither of these, for the way is at once path and epiphany, a process of growth that takes place in and out of dimensional time, so it is difficult to measure. I believe there is some fundamental work constituted by the quest, the question and the finding of the Grail that, once completed in oneself, does not need to be repeated. I know in myself, for instance, something changed to do with fear. I don't know the exact day, but I know that one morning on waking I realized the familiar tingle of fear that had for years accompanied my return to consciousness, like the chimes a computer sounds when switched on, had gone, and it never returned. No more cold little curl of half-admitted fear—at what the day might bring, at what the future would bring.

However, the need to stay centered in one's inner presence remains a lifelong discipline of daily, momentary living. The extent to which I do this is up to me. To a very high degree, I both choose and control the nature of my life's experience—choose to remember that there is a little circle at the center of things, a circle that is still like a well, safe and calm; choose to remember that it is me, this core strong place, and it never goes away but is always there, in the middle of the rush of life, of the feelings of exhaustion, dejection, or elation and whatever current conflicts and problems surround me.

On the other hand, the instantaneous aspect of coming into the Grail Castle gives the lie to the idea that spiritual enlightenment takes years and years and is extremely difficult to attain. I do not think this is a concept that serves us well. The condition of alignment with one's spiritual core is something really quite natural to us and not so far removed from what we term "ordinary" human experience, with its full complement of emotions and perceptions. Enlightenment may not necessarily mean some exalted and superhuman state. As with most conditions, there are degrees of enlightenment: all the way from the full trance of the shaman to a quiet sense of the translucency of things, an awareness of depths within, fluid and sourced beyond mood and biography.

We could say that after the work of quest, question, and return comes the work of mastery. Mastery involves coming to the point in ourselves where the experience of union is ongoing. Where there is, in a sense, no more return, because we know that "the kingdom of heaven is at hand." The two worlds have become one in our experience. We have closed the gap, passed through the mists, and can see that Avalon exists in the same place as "Glastonbury of the monks."

This is the key to joining the worlds together: the realization that they were never separate to begin with, except in human consciousness. Campbell again: "the two worlds are actually one. The realm of the gods is a forgotten dimension of the world we know." This innocent yet wise attitude also signals the overcoming of "adult" reason; the intellectual, rational approach to the world, which mutters "nonsense, nonsense" at the illogical truths of the heart and does not see the "unremembered gate" that myths and children's fairy stories open up for us and that is also the gate in the "Wall of Paradise" that, as Nicholas of Cusa tells us, is guarded by the spirit of reason. The gate can only be open when this spirit has been overcome.

The overcoming of reason is also an overcoming of time. The Grail experience of union, as I noted earlier, happens instantaneously, out of time: "here, now, always." Of course we only ever live in the present moment, but rarely does our consciousness become focused exactly within it. Yet it is only then that the intersection of the two worlds is really known, and at the same time this sharp focus in the present moment creates a further trilogy of consciousness and understanding: throwing new light on the past and anticipating the shape of the future. Just as one listens to music, there is only one note playing at a time, one patterning of sound that is heard, but as we listen we have a memory or impression of the music that went before and a sensing of what is to develop out of it. Time is like music: we only really experience it in the present, but we sustain an awareness of both what is past and what is to come.

When the kingdoms are woven together again, there is nowhere that the fire of being is not. This was the illumination that Moses had when he saw the "burning bush." The bush and everything else had always been burning—the sacred fire continually consumes and renews ourselves and all creation; he just hadn't noticed it before.

But how? How can the fire, the spiritual kingdom, be present in a polluted earth, a benighted human being? Two personal experiences of mine go some way to answering this. One concerns a beach that is my favorite place in the world; the other the death of my father. The beach is on the north coast of Cornwall, the southwest peninsula of Britain and, thanks to the National Trust, is unspoiled by development. It has golden sand, massive cliffs, and above all the most beautiful green glassy waves that rise and fall in ferocious surf and crash into white lace. I have visited it since early childhood, and I always experience a deep sense of cleansing and renewal there. The four elements of water, air, earth, and fire combine there quite naturally; my body feels liberated in the bracing water, the breeze, the hard sand under my feet and the sun on my back. On one occasion I remember sitting on some rocks gazing at the waves advancing, rising, and curling over as the tide came in. I was quite close to the water's edge, and the waves rose up in front of me like green transparent walls. I noticed that suspended within their crystalline sheen were thousands of small black specks. I looked down at the rocks and saw the familiar black smudges—oil. Somewhere a tanker had spilled its cargo, and now some of it, rather a lot of it, was washing into this bay, polluting these beloved waves of mine. I waited for the sickening thump of horror in my stomach, but it didn't come. Instead I found that I was watching the waves from a deeper place. Yes, the pollution was there, unmistakably. The oil was suspended in the green water, yet it was *not* the water. It could not blend with the water, become inextricably joined with it. It would do damage, yes, but ultimately, it would separate out again, and those green waves would no longer be spotted with black. This became an analogy for me not only about the physical pollution of the earth but the emotional pollution in human beings. That the fire and the rose are one, that the pure state exists despite what might have got temporarily mixed up in it.

My father was dying of cancer. During the last few weeks of his life, I spent quite a lot of time with him, in a way that I had not since early childhood. These weeks were extremely painful, not simply because I was confronting death for the first time, and the death of a parent, but because I was also brought up against all the unfinished, desperately unhappy feelings I had toward my father. My father was a kind but, to my mind, unutterably sad man. I pictured him as sort of small and squashed by life. Nothing had ever seemed to enliven him, to make him merry or robust. My withdrawal from him at a very young age, while it had been a source of pain for him (half admitted because so bitter, as he had loved me very much) had also of course been a source of great pain for me. All these things and more were surfacing in me during those weeks. Three days after he died, I came back to the house after having been away. My mother was out, so the house was empty. My father's body of course had been removed, and was lying in the funeral home, which happened to be across the road. I can't remember now why, but I went up to the small, spare bedroom in which he had been and where he had died. I pushed the door open, and I stood just inside, but didn't want to go in any farther. There was something happening in the room. The best way I can describe it now is as a kind of fountain; but rather than falling, this was gushing up; there was an almost tangible vortex of energy upwelling in the room, tremendously powerful, and then also a great feeling of joy, of something unspeakably vast and dynamic released from a state of unbearable limitation. I called to my boyfriend, who had come in with me but was downstairs. He too could sense something: it wasn't just me, or imagined. After that, I had to leave the room, and I did not really want to go back in. The energy gradually faded away. I was left with a feeling of soul-wrenching thankfulness and relief. I knew that vast being full of joy whom I had sensed was the spirit who had been incarnated in the form of my father. I felt an exchange with this spirit that was full of understanding, of love—something I had never been able to share with him when in the form of my father. I knew that there really was no death—just the separation of the dust from the spirit, as described in Ecclesiastes. And I felt the whole sad, limited saga of my father's life evaporate, burned from the records. No doubt he had fulfilled something while on earth, but he was now released back into reality once more. Here again, the pollution was suspended within the spirit, but it was not that spirit, and when the time came, it separated out and was no more.

"Thin places" is the phrase used by the Celts to describe locations in the landscape where the two worlds merged, or where at least it was easier than elsewhere to "cross over" into Avalon, or fairy land, or the other world. Many of the megalithic sites seemed to have been built in a manner and from materials to create similar conditions of "thinness." However, it is no use trudging around dolmen and stone circles if nothing is going on inside us. We cannot beat on the wall of Paradise and hope to be let in. Similarly, if something is going on inside us, anywhere can become a "thin place" because we ourselves have thinned the pollution in the heart that prevents the connection from being known.

8

THE UNFINISHED THEME

The riddles of our individual lives
are found woven into huge coherence.
  —DIANA DURHAM, "DANCING"

EVEN THOUGH there is enough of an ending to the Grail story for us to be able to unravel the implications of the broken sword, the second visit to the Grail Castle and the asking of the question, there is a sense in which when we come to the end of this story we find that in fact there is no ending. There is no ending partly because, as I showed in the previous chapter, the work of healing the wounded patterns of our minds and hearts and of centering in the inner dimensions of our being, which these events and symbols relate to, constitutes an ongoing process in our lives, something that itself does not have an obvious and final ending. However, and more significant, there is also no ending in that the most central theme of the myth still hangs unfinished. If we recall, the promise and purpose of undertaking the Grail quest was to heal the Wounded Fisher King and restore the wasteland. Yet this is not exactly what happens—either in our experience or in the stories.

Our own inner wasteland experience may have been restored,

but we still find ourselves living in a world that is a wasteland, both in respect to the fragility of relationships between people and nations, and in an ecological sense. And in the stories, this central theme is not resolved either.

Only two of the tales, "Parzival" and the "Didot Perceval," go some way toward expounding coherently the central theme of healing and restoration. In the former, Parzival asks a question about the Grail that frees King Amfortas and his land; in the latter, when Perceval comes at last to the Grail Castle for the second time, he asks to what use the Grail is put, and at once the king is cured. However, there is no mention of the wasteland being restored; instead it is the enchantments of Britain and of the whole world that are ended. And even in these two versions, there is something perfunctory about the way the crucial issues are reported, almost as if they were minor details and not the urgent central concern around which the whole story turns. Meanwhile, Chrétien de Troyes's "Perceval," which seems to demonstrate the clearest grasp of the theme and meaning, is literally unfinished, so that we hear nothing more of Perceval after he has received absolution and understood the answer to the question. There is something so tantalizing about this— there he is, poised and ready to complete the quest and bring resolution, but the poet never finished his tale! In all the other stories, the themes of the question and the restoration of both king and land are scattered arbitrarily around, with some of the pieces included but not all. In the Gautier continuation, for instance, while Perceval does ask questions about the meaning of the Grail and other talismans that accompany it, there is no mention of the fisher king being healed or the land restored. In the "Diu Crone," Gawain asks about the Grail and releases an old king from a living death, but there is no restoration; instead the whole court, including the Grail, disappear and are to be seen no more.

What is the meaning of this unfinished theme and partial restoration? In part what is being addressed here is the problem of the impact—or not—of the individual revelation on the collective experience. Without doubt, we as individuals are impacted by the work of finding the Grail. We have been entrained into a greater experience and understanding of our own inner core of divine power, or into the presence of the Grail King. Our own wound, our own version of the Wounded Fisher King consciousness, has begun to be healed, and as a result our own consciousness is no longer a wasteland of separation and alienation. Here then the blessings of the Grail and the resulting restoration are felt primarily at the individual level. However, as we all know, especially since the advent of quantum mechanics, we are not separate from the wider world, the wider consciousness. And what happens to us as individuals will affect that wider field. As our consciousness changes, the world we live in also changes. It is no longer seen as such a barren place but full of fertile possibility. Moreover, as our own wound is healed, we are automatically weaned from our dependence on leadership. Therefore, whoever has played the role of Wounded Fisher King in our lives is released from our transference. He has lost his potency in our lives and therefore is free—at least within our sphere—to once again achieve his own correct relationship with the Grail King and therefore also be healed.

So to some degree we can measure the extent of our individual impact on the larger world. Yet there is more to it than this. I have said that the Grail quest story delineates primarily the individual path toward wholeness, while the stories of Arthur pertain more to the collective story of humanity. But the presence of the Wounded Fisher King in the Grail Castle connects this myth—*and our process*—to that larger world. Why is this? Well, the Wounded Fisher King is a *king*. He rules over a wasteland *kingdom*. He represents the *controlling consciousness in society.* His is the fundamental assumption of most of the world that consuming the fruits of the Grail—pursuing happiness—is the way to fulfillment. He is the material, sophisticated, technologically astute, intellectual, cynical, even nowadays enlightened man (and woman) who does not value the voice of the heart, the voice of spirit, but on the contrary mocks the wisdom and intuitions of the heart, does not challenge the guardian of reason at the gate of Paradise (yet underneath his rationalist philosophy he is fearful, primitive, aggressive) and therefore remains in and sustains the wasteland, in grand denial of his wound. And he is also, I might add, the well-meaning liberal or Christian who believes that we will save the world by social programs and other "good works," as well as the radical socialist who believes that political works will do it. All of this is a form of arrogance—an arrogance that springs from the separation from God and the consequent attempt to be as God and that therefore *gives no weight to what would heal the wound, gives no weight to the solution.* He gives no weight to what would heal the wound because he doesn't even admit he is wounded. It is this consciousness itself, the controlling consciousness of the wounded king, that needs to be addressed.

The exciting news that this myth is telling us is that we have the ability to do just this. The presence of the Wounded Fisher King in the myth means that when we come to the core fear that sits at the center of our spiraling quest, we touch not only our own personal version of the wound, but the wound of the fisher king. It is not just our wound but "the" wound—the consciousness that, in its worst extremes, creates a death camp, an atom bomb, a polluted planet: a wasteland. If we complete the process of alignment with the Grail King energy that begins when the door opens and the Grail appears—in other words, if we complete the inner work of the quest signified by asking the question— we are in position not only to heal our own consciousness but also to loosen the grip of that fisher king consciousness, to begin to address the fundamental cause of suffering and desolation in the world. Right there in our consciousness, we hold the key to restoration. That's why the grieving maiden and the dreadful hag were so hard on Perceval when he failed to ask the question! If we ever feel that our lives have no significance, or that we lack the ability to do anything to help the world's ills, we might ponder that reproachful maiden and the accusing hag. The fact is that we hold within our own consciousness the key to healing the wound. It could be said that nothing else we can do will be as important, as potent as asking this question; that all other achievements and worthy deeds pale into insignificance beside this.

Nevertheless, when we face up to the misery, degradation, and poverty of millions of peoples' lives, and when we recognize that the ecological damage we are inflicting on the planet seems to gather pace with each day that passes, it would amount to either spiritual crassness or self-delusion to believe that the process of restoration is over. Obviously, the larger world is far from being healed. So what does this mean? In part it relates to the saying "While some are bound, none are free." What this saying means of course is that we are all connected, we are all one. Consequently, while some are still suffering, others are not free, but equally if some have experienced a loosening of the wound then, in tincture, it is possible for the rest. At another level it simply means that the individual experience of transformation is not sufficient to effect the wider restoration. The process has begun but is far from complete. This incompleteness is symbolized for us by the way in several of the Grail stories the Grail chalice itself, even after it has been found, tends to later disappear from view. Manessier's continuation of Chrétien de Troyes's unfinished "Perceval" has the hero leave Arthur's court again to return to Castle Corbiere (the Grail Castle) after his uncle (the fisher king) has died. There he reigns in peace for seven years, after which he follows a hermit into the wilderness, along with the Grail and lance. There he serves the Lord for ten years, and when he dies, the Grail and lance must have been carried up to heaven, since from that day nobody has seen them. In the "Queste del Saint Graal," one year after following the Grail to the holy city of Sarras, Galahad's soul leaves his body, and a hand from heaven takes the Grail.

We need the Grail chalice on earth; we need it brought back to our ordinary worlds; we need to *finish* the myth. But it seems that in order for this to happen, more than one individual has to be involved. So this incomplete ending of the Grail story, of the individual, inner journey is the juncture at which we reenter the larger world and rejoin the collective story to find out how this wider restoration is going to be made possible—and how the quest is to be finished. I have said that the two threads of the King Arthur and Grail quest myth are intertwined, the one in the background of the other. The Grail story is concerned primarily with the individual process; the King Arthur story is about our collective destiny as a community and as a planet. Our individual stories are not separate from the events of the larger world: the two impinge on one another—and so it is in the myths.

What we find, of course, back in Arthur's court, is that twin troubles are brewing—Guinevere's love for Lancelot and Mordred's hatred of his father—that will eventually lead to the downfall of Camelot and the close of Arthur's reign. We find in fact that *both* strands of the myth, the Grail story and that of King Arthur, hang unfinished, unresolved yet with the tantalizing promise of future fulfillment. The promise inherent in the Grail story lies in the fact that the Grail has after all been found, while written on Arthur's grave is the inscription "the Once and future King," as if his reign of greatness and peace will one day come again.

9

OUT OF STONE INTO WATER

Now is the time to understand
That all your ideas of right and wrong
Were just a child's training wheels
To be laid aside
When you can finally live
With veracity
And love.
                    —HAFIZ, "NOW IS THE TIME,"
            TRANSLATED BY DANIEL LADINSKY

Woman is the circle
man comes into:

the cup, the sword
the nought, the one.

Nought and one make one—
a globe—
in which the child forms.

Make ten, commandments
in the ark.

And the chromosomes join
in pairs within the ark,
within the dark, till

ten centimetres
dilation and the
rough seas of birth
push the baby out.
                    —DIANA DURHAM,
                "ANTE-NATAL CIRCLE"

THE GRAIL STORY with its incomplete ending shows that while the individual path to wholeness will impact the wasteland condition of the larger society to some degree, the full restoration of that wider world is going to take more than just ourselves. In this chapter, then, I begin to move away from the individual process in order to examine the collective dynamics of the times we are living in. This means turning attention away from the inner landscape of the Grail quest and returning to the court of King Arthur, for it is in these stories that we find encoded the prophecy of how the wider restoration is destined to come about.

Now there are of course innumerable tales about the exploits of Arthur and all the many characters that people his court of Camelot, some of the most famous being Merlin, Guinevere, Lancelot, Morgana, and Mordred. Broadly speaking, we can divide all the tales into three chronological segments: the "early days" of uniting the kingdom, setting up Camelot, the marriage of Arthur and Guinevere, establishing the knights of the Round Table, and the arrival of Lancelot; the middle section, which includes the setting off en masse of the knights of the Round Table on the quest for the Grail; and the last part, in which the love affair between Lancelot and Guinevere and all the other twists and turns of the plot lead to the downfall of Camelot and the demise of Arthur.

I am mainly concerned here with this last part, for in a mysterious way, it is as if once the Grail quest is over, so too is Arthur's kingdom. I will briefly review the story in more detail.

Early on in his kingship, before he is married to Guinevere, Arthur sleeps with Morgana without realizing who she is. Mordred is the offspring of their union. Guinevere fails to produce an heir for Arthur, making Mordred the only claimant, and she falls in love with Lancelot, Arthur's closest friend and best knight. Mordred, who has been trained by his mother to hate his father, catches Guinevere and Lancelot together while Arthur is away and accuses them both of treachery. The result is a public split between Arthur and Lancelot. Guinevere is condemned to be burnt at the stake, and when Lancelot rescues her, as everybody expects him to do, he unwittingly kills Gareth and Gaheris, brothers of Gawain. This intensifies the feud, because Gawain will never forgive Lancelot, and the situation deteriorates into a series of in-decisive battles between the two factions. Gawain insists that Lancelot be banished forever from Britain, and Lancelot returns sorrowfully to his lands in France. There he is pursued by a reluctant Arthur and the ever-vengeful Gawain. Further battles and jousts continue, until news comes from England that Mordred, left as ruler in Arthur's place, has spread word that Arthur is slain and had himself crowned in his place. In addition, he is threatening to take Guinevere as his wife. Arthur returns to Britain, but without Lancelot his forces are not as strong, and Arthur is mortally wounded in battle by Mordred (who in turn is killed by Arthur).

Tennyson in his poetic version of the "Morte D'Arthur" evokes the poignancy of those closing moments of Arthur's reign, when, as he lies dying, he commands Sir Bedivere to throw the sword Excalibur into the lake. So painful is the thought of losing the sword that twice this most loyal knight disobeys Arthur and hides it instead. Finally, after incurring Arthur's great wrath, the third time he obeys.

> Then quickly rose Sir Bedivere, and ran,
> And, leaping down the ridges lightly, plunged
> Among the bulrush-beds, and clutch'd the sword,
> And strongly wheel'd and threw it. The great brand
> Made lightnings in the splendour of the moon,
> And flashing round and round, and whirl'd in an arch,
> Shot like a streamer of the northern morn,
> Seen where the moving isles of winter shock
> By night, with noises of the northern sea.
> So flash'd and fell the brand Excalibur.

Everything seems to be lost: the knights of the Round Table are scattered or killed, Arthur is mortally wounded, and now the sword has gone too.

The events surrounding the demise of Arthur and the fall of Camelot are some of the best known and most often told in the history of storytelling. Why do we never tire of hearing them? Because there is something that swirls around them—an aura, a mist, a meaning—that resonates deep within us but eludes understanding. What is this elusive shiver in the air? There is loss, yes, but there is also prophecy, a sense of destiny, for as the sorrowing Sir Bedivere watches, an arm rises out of the surface of the lake and catches the sword:

> But ere he dipt the surface, rose an arm
> Clothed in white samite, mystic, wonderful,
> And caught him by the hilt, and brandish'd him
> Three times, and drew him under in the mere.

What does this mysterious piece of symbolism mean? Is the sword Excalibur lost forever—or not? It is a woman's arm that catches the sword. A woman, the feminine.

The lake represents the deep feminine, the subconscious mind, the waters of truth. When Arthur first pulled the sword out of the stone, he was representing the great spiritual avatar who releases the truth from structured tradition and turns it back into a living experience. Arthur had no heir, and Camelot is no more; there is no bloodline or tradition to which Excalibur is entrusted. Instead the sword of power will rest in the collective deep of humankind's future where it awaits fulfillment in the lives and actions of the generations to come. The sword has been released from the hard, barren structured world, the wasteland of an arid human consciousness that is cut off from its source, and has returned to the well of power, the cistern of sparkling water that the Grail itself also symbolizes. Out of stone into water; released from form and returned to spirit.

By first drawing the sword out of the stone at the commencement of his reign and consigning it to the Lady of the Lake at the close of his reign, Arthur not only reenergizes the patterns of truth into living experience but makes it available to *all*. The waters of the lake symbolize the collective unconscious: that great shared pool of power and memory. The energized patterns of truth, the living experience of spiritual alignment, have been reimprinted onto the vibrational archives of the collective human psyche and are ready and available to nourish everyone and anyone who is willing to do the work to access them.

This is the work of the long line of great patriarchs and prophets, from Abraham to Jesus, from Buddha to Mohammed. It was the work as well of the two founders of my spiritual network, and of other spiritual leaders active at a similar time frame in other parts of the world such as Sotaeson in Korea, who founded the Won Buddhist movement, Meher Baba and his followers and Rajah Yoga, who started the Brahma Kumaris, in India, and Mokichi Okada in Japan, the originator of Jo Re Aikido.

Something that is difficult to miss here of course is that all these teachers and leaders were men. This fact tends to catalyze familiar reactions and precipitate overly simple conclusions: the dearth of women leaders is evidence of their oppression by the social structures imposed by a controlling patriarchy, or women just aren't good enough—they are inherently less emotionally stable than men and therefore not equipped to play the role of mentor. Putting these issues aside for a moment and thinking in purely symbolic terms, the moment when the sword goes into the lake is marking the end of the time when authority was located in a handful of male "greats"—when Excalibur was wielded on our behalf, in *representation* of our own authority. The sword, the masculine, of course is still present, but it is configured differently. It has become in fact the sword that is given to Perceval on his first visit to the Grail Castle. It is held now by each person who has embarked on the quest to find the Grail and heal the wound. In this sense, this episode is symbolizing the end of the sword's *isolation,* the end of the sword without its partnering symbol of Grail chalice. Fundamentally the absence of women is not so much a function of their being victims of an unfair social system but *a function of the wound itself.* Their silence and their nonappearance is symbolic of the wounded heart—of the Grail chalice that must be found.

The sword flung into the lake and being caught is also ushering in a new opportunity, the opportunity for collective leadership. The sword of leadership is held now by each person who has embarked on the quest. It becomes the *individual* version of that sword—the individual version of authority. There comes a point when we must relinquish our dependency on those leaders who wielded that sword and who played the role of spiritual mentor for us. As the angel says in Revelation: "See thou do it not." Don't worship the messenger anymore;

don't worship the sword that has been wielded on your behalf. "Worship God"—connect with your own source of authority. Be yourself; be the one you are looking for.

If we do this, instead of being dependent on the spiritual mentor we come into a position to offer partnership and support. Instead of "servants" we can be called friends. The idea of the collective, its roundness, round like the chalice, is also the feminine, as are the waters of the lake. So here is another way in which the sword of spiritual mentorship is no longer isolated but "clothed" in the responsive understanding of those who have done the work of completing the Grail quest.

After Sir Bedivere has thrown Excalibur into the lake, Arthur further commands his knight to carry him to the water's edge. When they get there, a dark barge sails into view:

> Then saw they how there hove a dusky barge,
> Dark as a funeral scarf from stern to stern,
> Beneath them; and descending they were ware
> That all the decks were dense with stately forms
> Black-stoled, black-hooded, like a dream—by these
> Three Queens with crowns of gold—and from them rose
> A cry that shivr'd to the tingling stars,
> And, as it were one voice an agony
> Of lamentation, like a wind, that shrills
> All night in a waste land, where no one comes,
> Or hath come, since the making of the world.
> Then murmur's Arthur, "Place me in the barge."

Sir Bedivere does so, and then, left alone and forsaken on the bank, cries out to Arthur as the barge moves away, asking him what will become of him now Arthur is leaving and he is left all alone among his enemies. Arthur replies that he is going to the Vale of Avalon to be healed of his wound. That night Sir Bedivere spends in the forest, lamenting the loss of his beloved king. In the morning, he comes upon a hermitage and a chapel. Inside the chapel he finds a hermit lying face down before a newly dug tomb. Bedivere asks who is buried there that he prays for so intently. In Malory's "Morte D'Arthur" the hermit replies:

> "I wot not verily but by deeming. But this same night, at midnight, here came a number of ladies and brought here a dead corse and prayed me to inter him. And here they offered an hundred tapers, and gave me a thousand besants."
>
> "Alas," said Sir Bedivere, "that was my lord King Arthur who lieth here graven in this chapel."

A little bit further on Malory tells us:

> Thus of Arthur I find no more written in books that had been authorized, neither more of the very certainty of his death heard I never read, but thus was he led away in a ship wherein were three queens; that one was King Arthur's sister, Queen Morgan le Fay, the second was the queen of North Galis; and the third was the Queen of the Waste Lands.
>
> Now more of the death of King Arthur could I never find, but that these ladies brought him to his grave, and such one was interred there which the hermit bare witness that sometime Bishop of Canterbury. But yet the hermit knew not in certain that he was verily the body of King Arthur; for this tale Sir Bedivere, a knight of the Table Round, made it to be written.
>
> Yet some men say in many parts of England that King Arthur is not dead, but had by the will of our Lord Jesus into another place; and men say that he shall come again, and he shall win the Holy Cross. Yet I will not say that it shall be so; but rather I would say that here in this world he changed his life. And many men say that there is written upon the tomb this:
>
> HIC IACET ARTHURUS REX QUONDAM REXQUE FUTURUS.

Malory thus leaves the ending of Arthur deliberately ambiguous. He may be buried in the ground, or he may be in Avalon, awaiting his return. Either way, his tomb is inscribed with the promise: "Here lies Arthur once and future king."

Here is the famous prophecy of return that swirls around the figure and era of King Arthur. But how can he and his time of fellowship and greatness come again? Because the sword is *not* lost, only resting in the deeps of our own subconscious. It's unbending principles of steel are merely dissolved temporarily into the fluid waters of memory, awaiting the time when they become formed once more into a blade of understanding within the conscious mind. So the return of Arthur is not going to be the return anymore of one lone, great patriarch who will save us all—much as we might like that idea. The return of Arthur is the return of true leadership embodied in many individuals who have accessed the sword of power for themselves. The return is a collective return, an era of collective leadership. A time when instead of one king wielding Excalibur, many wield their own individual and tempered swords of moral and spiritual authority.

However, if we recall, the individual sword is earned by going on a quest for and by finding the Grail chalice. This means that the era of collective leadership represented by many individuals graduating into the sense of their authentic selves and thus carrying the sword of individual authority is dependent on the finding of the Grail chalice. Why is this and what are the implications of it?

We remember that when Perceval is given the sword on his first visit to the Grail Castle, it is new and untried and represents the dawning conscious awareness of and alignment with both the Grail King energy and the wisdom of Merlin. However, this sword is not yet tried, and it will be broken and reforged by the work of the quest—meaning that the mind's knowing will not become assured experience without the heart's knowing.

The heart realm either obscures or makes possible a sense of connection to the divine energy source within us that I have called the presence of the Grail King. When the Grail or heart has been freed from the guardianship of the wound, it means that our heart realm is sufficiently clear to allow the sense of connection, of oneness with source, with God, to be known. The wound of separation has been healed. It is this sense of oneness with God that gives one one's authority, that enables one to wield one's individual sword of power. Without this sense of direct connection to God that the healed heart realm permits, one would still be dependent for one's orientation and identity on the presence of a King Arthur, and one would still be vulnerable to the machinations of a Wounded Fisher King leader.

This is one reason why one cannot wield one's individual sword of power or configure the collective return of Arthur without finding the Grail—or healing the heart.

At the same time, however, we know that the heart cannot be healed without the understanding of the mind. The sword assists us on the quest. What this means is that the conscious understanding of the mind can help us align with the Grail King energy even before the Grail itself is found. This is the meaning of the sword being gifted to Perceval on his first visit to the Grail Castle. We can, through the adoption of certain spiritual principles and practices, begin to deliberately align ourselves with the highest in us, even if, to begin with, it is not yet the true potency of the reforged sword because the heart itself is not yet fully engaged in the process. So the sword/mind assists us in the process of becoming entrained to the true nature of ourselves, even if this is still slightly brittle and not completely authentic.

The symbol of the sword depicts this alignment with the heavenly king. It is a single, vertical line—literally, "a-lined"—representing the consciousness that is oriented in something "higher," the energy of the heavenly king. The sword can also be seen in terms of the numeral 1. Oneness with the One God: the oneness of God and human being.

The circular rim of the Grail cup also symbolizes oneness, only this is more the oneness between one another, and can be seen in terms of the numeral 0, or zero, meaning also without end and without separation—one thing. The heart realm is where we know a sense of connection, a sense of being a part of one another and of God, not as an idea but as an experience.

If we put the two numerals one and zero together, we have of course the numeral 10. Then the symbolism gets very interesting because there were 10 commandments placed in the Ark of the Covenant of Old Testament times, signifying the agreement or union (i.e. oneness) between God and humanity.

The requirement to be aligned with God is what lay behind those 10 commandments given to Moses: "Thou shalt have no other gods before me" (Exodus 20:3). Several thousand years later Jesus rephrased the first commandment in the positive rather than the negative and added a new second:

> Thou shalt love the Lord thy God with all thy heart, and with all thy soul, and with all thy mind. This is the first and great commandment.
>
> And the second is like unto it, Thou shalt love thy neighbor as thyself.
>
> On these commandments hang all the law and the prophets. (Matthew 22:37–39)

The condition of "oneness with" God, or source, brings with it a sense of "oneness with" other people as well. This is something quite automatic; we do not have to try to bring it about. As the healing in the heart realm takes place because the sense of connection to the divine source fills in, the heart is healed not only of its sense of separation from source but from whatever conflicts, fears, and resentments may have been held toward other people. We are no longer subject to our reactions to others and instead are in position to extend a blessing. If we know oneness with God, we know oneness, wholeness, in ourselves, and we also know oneness with others, with our "neighbors," because we can recognize that they share the same, common spiritual heritage whether they experience it or not. This is how the second commandment follows naturally on the first and is "like unto it."

At times, when the heart feels safe and open, it is possible, as I have said, to experience this oneness directly, not theoretically, with others. Perhaps most people have known deep feelings of oneness with an individual—a child, a spouse, a close friend—but it can occur in larger groupings. Two such instances remain in my memory. One was at a large inspirational conference of about six hundred people. We were all asked to stand, take the hands of the people on either side of us, and sing together. My hand was held on one side by someone I knew, but was not close to, and on the other by a stranger. As we all began to sing, I suddenly knew the oneness. It was as if the two hands in mine were conduits that led through those two people to the others linked to them, and on into the whole hall of people. This was not a sentiment or even an emotion; it was like becoming aware, subtly and with a sense of recognition or familiarity, of a deeper ocean out of which we all arose and that contained us and was us, with all our differences and potential conflicts, and with all the distances between us. In other words, I felt no need to get to know the stranger or to draw closer to my acquaintance. The distances, the relationships, were just fine, appropriate to the patterning of that moment. They might change over time— some might draw closer to one another, others move away—but it didn't alter this great heritage of oneness between us.

On another occasion I was visiting one of the larger spiritual communities mentioned earlier. I had attended a regular midweek meeting and was walking back up the pathway from the meeting hall along with the many others who had also been at the meeting. People were walking singly, in pairs or in small groups, some talking, others silent. I was on my own, enjoying both the stillness of the evening and the quiet murmur of people's voices, when again I felt our oneness together, something that undergirded us, whether we knew it or not.

We begin to have not just an idea about but an actual experience of the fact that we are all parts of one whole. The sense of oneness is just that: one thing. No separation. Usually the only way any sense of connection between people can be sustained is when they find agreement in a point of leadership outside of themselves. At best, the agreement with the leader can ignite a sense of shared purpose; at worst, it simply prevents or suppresses the underlying conflicts. A classic example of the latter was demonstrated when after the death of Tito in the former Yugoslavia complex and bitter conflicts erupted between the different ethnic groups of the region.

So here is another reason why the configuration of collective leadership is dependent on finding the Grail: without this sense of oneness with others, which is signified by the circular Grail cup, we would remain dependent on a leader to hold our agreement together.

Oneness is the basis of morality. That is why Christ said "On these commandments hang all the law and the prophets." In other words, once this consciousness of oneness, wholeness, is operational, you can forget all your lists of rules and regulations, because you can be trusted to do what is right in circumstances as they arise. You can be trusted, furthermore, to think for yourself and not be conditioned or pressured into atrocities, large or small. An outer morality, one based on rules and regulations, can break down and cannot ultimately be trusted. The ordinary, decent law-abiding German citizens who participated in the hounding of the Jews had this kind of morality. This is the sword that will break. As initiates, as beginners, we align with the authority of King Arthur, who wields the sword of power, Excalibur. We align with someone or something, or some principle that is external to ourselves, in order to learn how eventually to know the inner alignment with spiritual source—which is the Grail.

The morality of oneness represents a marriage of Eastern and Western philosophies. The latter has long been concerned with rules and regulations, in an attempt to form a coherent system of behavior that would make functioning in the here and now a more just and graceful affair. The former gives less weight to the temporal world, as nothing matters in the face of nirvana, the mystical state of union underlying all things. Only a marriage of these two approaches makes life both bearable and meaningful. We need ethical behavior, or social life becomes untenable. It does matter what we do, how we treat others; it is important to challenge corruption, to make a stand. It is not good enough to put it all down to fate and turn away. But at the same time, we have to understand the deep ground of oneness out of which we and others arise, and we have to have a sense of processes that are not always understandable by our system of logic and law.

Does oneness mean a state of Pollyanna homogeneity? Again, it might if people *tried* to achieve such oneness, but in fact when something of the underlying connection is felt and known between people, the very opposite of homogeneity appears. It becomes safe enough for peoples' differences to show. Not just superficial differences, such as race, nationality, and sex, but inner differences of all kinds—of character, outlook, opinion, ambition, experience. This is very liberating—and very creative too, because instead of gingerly stalking around one another we can begin to engage robustly and honestly. Out of such interaction new insight and direction always emerges. We can allow each other to be complex beyond comparison.

Suddenly we realize that we've been on a subsistence diet of relationship, lacking the nourishment that full-blooded human contact brings, straitjacketed by social convention and mistrust. It is a subsistence diet because this multiplicity of difference exists not only in the collective but in the individual as well. We are many-faceted creatures, of many interests, moods, phases, insights, tastes, and spiritual essences. Generally speaking, we are much vaster internally than we usually ever allow ourselves to experience. Most of these parts of ourselves exist dormant or uneasily denied, floating around half-glimpsed in the unfathomable depths that we are. Often it takes other people to help integrate or understand these pieces of ourselves. While one is locked away in one's partial consciousness, one is separated both from those around one and from one's deeper selves, and only a small section of the spectrum of one's being is ever allowed to manifest. We are xenophobic and distrustful, accumulating material goods and slowly dying from the pain of isolation. In the Gnostic Gospel of Thomas, Jesus makes these very interesting comments: "If you bring forth what is within you, what you have will save you. If you do not have that within you, what you do not have within you [will] kill you" (Thomas 70).

Can we feel oneness with those who have betrayed or harmed us? This question seems to be answered by what Jesus said at the time of his crucifixion: "Father, forgive them for they know not what they do." The implication is that those who operate from a partial identity are not in a position to fully understand what they are doing. They are committing an atrocity, yes. Somewhere inside, they know that. They are responsible. But somewhere, again, they do not realize the full import of what they do. They have forgotten who they are; they have forgotten about the oneness, the sacredness. To suggest that we offer forgiveness is not therefore an admonition to be either superhuman or wimpish but is a reminder to stay aligned ourselves. As Billy Joel sings in his song "The Great Wall of China," "You only beat me when you get me to hate."

If someone does us wrong, and we start to hate them, we are "beaten" because it means we have come down to the same level as the violator. We have succumbed to his or her attempts to vibrationally ensnare us, because when someone "wrongs" us there are actually two actions going on at the same time. There is the "wrong" itself, causing mental, emotional, and sometimes physical pain in us, and there is also a challenge as to whether or not we are going to "lose it"—spin into emotional reaction and literally "lose" our connection to source and therefore at some level "agree" with the protagonist. The Wounded Fisher King energy often works this way. If a person cannot get one's power, one's response, by normal means, he or she will often attempt to do something that is calculated to make one react in fury or outrage (we call this having our buttons pressed), thus ensuring that he or she gets one's energy and attention by a kind of devious, backdoor method instead. This was why it was important in the movie *Star Wars* for Darth Vader to try to get Luke to hate him. If this happens to us, we will have forgotten the first commandment, and the second that goes with it, and instead of giving our response to the radiant energy of being at the center of ourselves, we give it instead to the Wounded Fisher King. Thus we can find ourselves locked in a kind of diabolic union with someone we despise. This could be described as a kind of "energy rape." But if we keep our alignment and remain "negative" to God instead of becoming "negative," that is, responsive, to the protagonist, we become "untouchable" at a vibrational level, because the violating positive has less potency than the true positive and will be repelled.

Rape is a crime because it is a violation of the sacred: the sacredness of the body, the sacredness of the sexual act, and most of all the sacredness of the already existing state of oneness. The word *sacred* means "dedicated to divinity" or "made holy." *Holy* relates to *wholeness,* so *sacred* also means "to make whole," to recognize that spirit and form are one. Immorality consists of violating the oneness that we are. This is of course why it is also a crime to murder or to steal. All these actions, recognized as primary crimes under most judicial systems, are violations of both our oneness and the sacred space between us. They are also violations of the collective presence of God. Viktor Frankl has an interesting comment: "What we need is not only the belief in the one God but also awareness of the one mankind, the awareness of the unity of humanity."

It's all about oneness. Oneness with God and oneness with one another, the first and second commandments, the alignment of the mind and the connection of the heart, the union of sword and cup.

About 35 miles northwest of Dublin, the River Boyne flows in a final curve before emptying into the Irish Sea. This curve encloses a hilly area dominated by the massive, quartz-faced, six-thousand-year-old chambered mound called Newgrange. Above the capstone of the entrance into the mound is a small rectangular opening. At midwinter sunrise the sun's rays are funneled through this "light box" and travel down a 70-foot-long stone passage to hit the far wall of a 20-foot-high inner chamber. This dark stone womb is then illuminated with golden light; the stone takes on the appearance of living gold. The sun god fertilizes with his seed the womb of Mother Earth—the pouring of blessing into the world at the new beginning of the year. The sun's rays symbolize both seed and phallus; the inner chamber, with its long passageway, is womb and vagina. This eternal imagery of phallus and womb, sword and chalice, plays throughout the Grail and Arthur myths. The knight with his sword, seeking the Grail, is seeking in fact union with the Grail. The maidens are not seeking in the same way: they stay within the Grail Castle, bearing the Grail. A woman has the womb, the Grail, already within her body, which suggests a further meaning. If the Grail is not sought and found by the questing knight, union and the consequent fertilizing of the earth—symbolized by the ending of the wasteland—is not achieved. Here again we see why the sexual maiming of the fisher king is so significant: an impotent king cannot find union with the Grail and allow the fertilization to take place. He wishes to benefit from the blessings of the Grail but not provide the blessing himself.

When Arthur commands the sword to be thrown into the lake, this sexual imagery is at work again. The sword of truth, of power, fertilizes the cup, the womb of the Mother, the waters of the subconscious. What is born out of that union will be the consciousness of oneness. As I have mentioned, both sword and cup are symbols in their own right of oneness: the numeral 1 and the circle of the 0—the oneness of alignment and the oneness of connection. (Together they form the 10, like the 10 centimeters that the womb must dilate to release the new life out into the world.) Their *union* means that the consciousness of oneness that they parent will include both the oneness of alignment and the oneness of connection.

When the ovum and sperm come together in the physical womb, they fuse into one large cell before drawing apart again (briefly forming the vesica shape) and beginning the miraculous process of division and multiplication that forms a new living body. We could call this the multiplication of oneness. The union of sword and chalice likewise gives birth to the *multiplication* of oneness—the multiplication of the union of the two aspects of oneness to form one body. But this time, it is not just one person, one king, who is born but a body of people, who share and know a consciousness of oneness, both oneness with God and oneness with each other.

The era when authority was located in the one leader, the single patriarch *who alone held the connection to source or God,* has come to an end. Now, because the Grail has been found, because the heart realm is healing, a sufficient sense of oneness with God and oneness with others is emerging to allow this singular point of authority to expand and be expressed collectively. From now on, the consciousness of the oneness with God and the consciousness of the one God will reside not in one great leader—King Arthur, Jesus, my spiritual mentor—but in the one body, a *collective* body.

The Grail was found, yet the myth remained unfinished. This was because the individual experience of healed identity does not have enough impact on the rest of humanity to bring about the wider restoration of the wasteland. This will require the presence of many individuals who know their own sense of connection to source and therefore a sense of oneness with others. If the era of singular leadership was represented by the sword, this plurality of leadership is represented by the Grail itself, whose round rim symbolizes well the collective circle of oneness. Therefore, the finding of the Grail signifies not only the healing of the individual heart through a sense of union with inner spiritual source but also the emergence of what might be called collective sovereignty.

10

GUINEVERE'S GIFT

And all you can answer is heart,
The one word you speak until you hear it
The one syllabled flight, breath and soul of it;
As you say your quest is to the heart of life.
—Jay Ramsay, "Parsifal"

EXCALIBUR HAS BEEN CAUGHT and drawn under the surface of the water by the Lady of the Lake; its submersion will fertilize the possibility of a new era of collective leadership. To poor Sir Bedivere, however, who has had to throw the precious sword into the lake and watch as his beloved king is borne away from him, this philosophical truth conveys little comfort. Tennyson marvelously conveys the bereft knight's heartbreaking sense of loss and the cold empty world that he now finds himself a stranger in.

> Then loudly cried the bold Sir Bedivere,
> "Ah! My Lord Arthur, whither shall I go?
> Where shall I hide my forehead and my eyes?
> For now I see the true old times are dead,
> When every morning brought a noble chance,
> And every chance brought out a noble knight.
> Such times have not been since the light that lead

The holy Elders with the gift of myrrh.
But now the whole ROUND TABLE is dissolved
Which was an image of the mighty world;
And I, the last, go forth companionless,
And the days darken round me, and the years,
Among new men, strange faces, other minds."

This experience of dissolution and desolation, terrible though it is, seems to be a part of the process of growth, both individual and collective. We have seen and been a part of something so perfect, so enthralling, that nothing else will ever hold meaning or pleasure again for us.

Who has not had an experience like this? Even if it is only growing up, and leaving the strange, passionate loyalties of teenage friendships behind. Or perhaps it was a college experience, a team at work, a community or group of some kind, a spiritual discipline. For me it was the dissolution that followed the death of the founder of the spiritual communities—the man who had played the role of the King Arthur spiritual mentor for me and many others.

There is nothing unusual about a movement or a community, even a corporation, starting to founder when the person who initiated and led it is no longer around. It is almost predictable that this will happen. The sudden absence of the leader tends to expose all the underlying weaknesses that before were covered up by the presence of his charisma. For some in our network, their own sense of direction and purpose seemed to evaporate—as if the leader had embodied this for them, and it could not exist when he was no longer around. Others set about looking for someone else to replace him so that they could continue in their dependency. Still others demanded radical change, wanted to call into question all the old structures and ways of doing things. Many felt abandoned and disoriented by the changes that did come. They had grown so dependent on leadership and so acculturated to a certain way of thinking and acting that they were thrown into confusion. The leader's son had taken on the overall leadership, although, wisely, he tried to stress that he would not be playing the same father-figure role for us but would act more as a peer and coordinator. He worked to let a system of shared leadership emerge, one that would allow a fuller expression of other people's leadership potential to be expressed. However, he also had to handle something of a polarization between those who wanted radical change and those who represented the old orthodoxies. When he eventually stepped down from a leadership role, there were many who found this a source of further destabilization. In the meantime, at a practical level, things were also chaotic. The communities had relied for a large part of their income on donations from the wider network of supporters. This flow of money dried up as people tended to their own individual lives or became disillusioned with what was happening. Thus the communities were forced to become financially independent, which again shook up many fixed patterns of attitude and behavior.

For me personally these changes, which were working out over a few years, formed the cataclysmic backdrop to a few cataclysms of my own. My partner and I had moved from London to New York, after having had a baby, sold our house, and got married—all within a few months. We made the move for my husband's work. What this meant was that he immediately had colleagues, a routine, an office, a project—a whole continuation of his identity—while I had just myself and a new baby and nothing else. All my friends and community, almost my whole identity, had been left behind in one six-hour flight across the Atlantic. I was now simply the wife of someone and the mother of someone else. While the magic of a beautiful new baby got me through this period, I had never felt so lonely and disoriented in my life. Difficult though this was, the situation deteriorated further and became very frightening when the documentary film project we had come over for went up in smoke, due mainly to the incompetence and corruption of the producer and commissioning editor. Now we found ourselves without income or even reason to be in America, in an expensive apartment, with few friends or resources. Added to this was the onset of summer temperatures, climbing to 95 degrees Fahrenheit and up, with humidity to match (new to my thick English blood), and no air conditioning in our top-floor brownstone home!

The unravelling of both our personal lives and the spiritual network seemed to me to be related. It felt as if some holding or safety net had been slashed, spilling many of us out into rough waters, for I was not the only one who had painful circumstances to handle around that time. Many friends were going through upheaval, marriages were breaking up and lives were coming apart, whether it was a matter of career moves or their roles within the communities. One friend was even killed during this period in a road accident.

I found myself facing a darkness that was more than personal. Above and beyond the anguish of my homesickness and the fear that my husband's career was over, I was looking at the possibility of failure. Failure not just of my own ability to handle what was happening from a place of genuine spiritual assurance, but—far worse—the failure of the whole spiritual enterprise.

The extent of corruption revealed to me through our dealings with the producer and cable company, as well as the betrayal of us by two men involved in the project (whom we had counted good friends for several years), were profoundly shocking to me. However, accompanying these revelations was the corresponding exposure in myself of an equally profound naivete. I got to see the extent to which I had looked at the world through rose-tinted "spiritual" glasses, assuming that our "friends" had the same spiritual frame of reference as me, that they wanted to make a contribution to the world and were fundamentally motivated by the desire to come into a greater awareness of their spiritual core and purpose. But they weren't. They were frightened, wounded people out for their own gain—happy to go along with our schemes if they could benefit from them, deeply suspicious of my husband's apparent success, and ready without a flicker of compunction to stab him in the back at the first opportunity and advance their own cause.

Under this layer of realization lay another one. I saw that not only had I been naive but I had deliberately *chosen* to be so. The naivete had suited me. In fact, in essence it wasn't so much even naivete as a subtle dishonesty. My stance had meant that I could move along through life paying a kind of lip service to my spiritual framework and values but not have to take a cold hard look at the reality either of myself or where people who had never received spiritual mentoring were really coming from. I could have my cake and eat it—dabble in the glamorous world of filmmaking and writing, live in a stylish way, and hold it all in the self-justifying context of a partially digested spiritual formula. It was a way of avoiding the work, the real hard work of completing the quest.

How many others of our spiritual network had done the same? Coasted along, hidden perhaps by the organizational momentum, or the genuine spiritual stature of others (most particularly the overall leader), but not really doing the inner work of grounding spiritual vision in the tougher areas of living. Had we failed? Now that the King Arthur leader was gone, was Camelot and its promise forever lost?

At the same time that all this change and upheaval was flooding in upon us, many of us were becoming aware of the extent to which we had failed to integrate the deeper, more challenging aspects of our emotional and sexual natures while so single-mindedly pursuing spiritual enlightenment. We could call this side of ourselves the dark or moon face of the feminine, represented in the tales by Morgana. Not realizing who she is, Arthur sleeps with Morgana (before he is married to Guinevere). While it is not spelled out in Malory's version of the story, the implication is that Morgana knows who Arthur is—knows he is her half-brother—and therefore may have deliberately tricked him. The son she conceives by their union grows up hating his father and helps lead to his downfall. It appears that Morgana is furious that her own lineage is not recognized, particularly by Arthur, and that therefore she seeks to undermine him. Only after the event does Arthur realize that he has committed incest. The incest and its progeny, Mordred, has a twofold meaning. Arthur is not aware of what he is doing—and for the most part we do remain unconscious of the flaw lines, the patterns of stuck energy, that run through our characters. Jung called these parts of ourselves the "shadow"—unclaimed forces and impulses that, unless brought into the light and integrated as valid parts of who we are, remain to dog our actions and undermine our achievements. Morgana and her offspring thus could be said to represent that which is spurned, those parts of ourselves, often the deeper emotional and sexual aspects, that are so often unacceptable to our rational minds and spiritual aspirations. If these spurned parts of ourselves are not ultimately included and valued, they will tend to manifest themselves in a more extreme and apparently destructive manner, breaking down whatever structures have refused to acknowledge them. In Euripides' tragedy *The Bacchae,* the god Dionysus says:

> Like it or not, this city must learn its lesson:
> it lacks initiation in my mysteries.

It became quite painfully obvious to many of us in the years of chaos that followed the death of the founder that we had done a lot of spurning of parts of ourselves, assuming that suppression of difficult emotions was the same as mastery of them or that a serene appearance was as good as the actual experience of spiritual wholeness. As a result, there followed something of the other extreme. People threw themselves into emotional therapies of all kinds; and the processes of disintegration already underway were then exacerbated when they wounded others in their new-found directness and desire to give vent to all the emotions of anger and grief and resentment that they might have formerly covered over.

Ten years after the founder's death, a mailing list of several thousand had dropped to a few hundred; four of the twelve communities were sold; all were ailing from lack of funds and attrition of members; people who had worked together for decades were alienated from each other; and others were stung and wounded by criticism or outraged by new practices. Things that I would have thought impossible had happened— betrayal, conflict, denial, and patterns of dependency exposed. What had been our Round Table—an ordered world and a noble purpose, perceived collectively—was found to change and slowly fall apart.

Looking again at the tales of King Arthur, we find of course that Morgana was not the only cause of Camelot's downfall. Another primary cause was Guinevere. Morgana and Guinevere might be said to represent the two faces of the heart. Morgana is the dark, magical wisdom that when not acknowledged and included works its power in a destructive or extreme way. Guinevere is the wisdom of the heart expressed as the compulsion of passionate desire. Neither one of them acts according to what is expected or to tradition, rules, or social acceptability.

Guinevere loves her husband Arthur and respects his greatness and his role. However, she is unable to bear him an heir, and she falls deeply in love with Lancelot. Lancelot loves Arthur above all men, and it is his greatest happiness to serve him. Arthur loves them both deeply. Yet an irresistible passion springs up between Lancelot and Guinevere, which they are unable to either ignore or override, even though it means the betrayal not only of the king whom they love as a man, but of the kingdom which they believe in and serve. This is the painful quandary that both Lancelot and Guinevere face, and we feel its terror and its ecstasy wearing them down all through the tale.

What does it mean when what you most desire appears to betray—even destroy—what you most love? I have experienced a parallel, albeit not so intense, situation in my own life, and it took me a long time to understand it. After living for about two years in the sister community in England, I met and fell in love with a man whose home base was in London and whose career made it impossible for him to leave his home and move into the community. I found myself inevitably pulled by my desire to be with him and in conflict over my loyalty to the community. It felt like I was deserting the others who lived there and, worse, that by so doing I was betraying the deep spiritual purpose that my life was most centrally about. Moreover, some members of the community shared the same doubts (albeit unexpressed for the most part), so I was in conflict not just with myself but with a culture of expectation of which I had been a part. However, the truth was that although I was conflicted, at some deeper level the choice had been made, and I left to go and live in London.

The parting was painful, yet somewhere I breathed a deep sigh of relief. Nevertheless, it was not for several years that I came to understand what this life-change had been about. All I did at the time was follow my heart—and by that I do not mean simple emotion or feeling but the deep, beating signal and conviction of the heart, of the feminine. Looking back with the benefit of hindsight, it is quite obvious that this move was about more than just being with the man I loved. It was about getting out, growing up; it was the next step that in fact had to be taken if I was going to grow and develop in a way that would better allow me to fulfill my spiritual purpose. In a way, there hadn't really been a choice; I was just doing what was inevitable.

In other words, the deep desire of my heart had never actually been in conflict with what I most loved. And deep down Guinevere was never in conflict with Arthur and the core purposes of his kingdom. Just as King Arthur and Lancelot were never really in conflict. How could the best knight in the world be in conflict with the noblest king? They are naturally in accord at the deeper level of things. It would be in fact an impossibility for the longings of the heart to contravene what we love the most—and this is why it is so important never to override the deep urgings of our desires. Even though they may appear to take us in a different, even a contradictory, direction to the *current manifestation* of what we love—in my case the community, in Guinevere's and Lancelot's Arthur and his court—in actual fact, they are simply guiding us away from attempting to serve that purpose and manifestation in ways that are destined to become institutionalized, rigid, and cultic.

Trusting our deepest desires is another way in which we draw the sword from the stone: cease investing our energy and inspiration in old, structured ways that will in the end destroy—just as surely as our enemies—what we most love. Spirit manifests itself in form, but it is not that form *alone*. Sometimes, if we are not yet skilled in the dance of dualities, in tying the worlds together, we will come to forget about the spirit and worship the form only. Then it will be necessary for the forces of life to break up that form in order to release the energy trapped within it and to set free again the ever-changing aspect of the divine from structures in consciousness that tend to harden over with rules and dogma, belief structures, and systems of righteousness and exclusiveness. The sword is pulled out of stone and thrown into water in a process of eternal renewal: the power of spirit freed up from crystallization and renewed in the waters of truth.

This was Guinevere's gift—that deep feminine urging of the heart. Nothing happened the way it should have, the way it was expected to. She fell in love with Lancelot. She failed to provide an heir for Arthur. His heritage was destined not to rest in a mere bloodline, in form, or to be carried forward by an institution; instead it rested in the air of the spirit and the waters of the deep subconscious, symbolized by the sword submerged in the waters of the lake.

My new life nourished me and allowed me to mature. Although I never lived in the community again, I served on its board, I organized events that were enriching for the community and those who attended, and, most important, I always held the community, its purpose, and its members in great respect and love. I found I was able to approach what was going on there with perspective and compassion, seeing the blind spots, sometimes throwing light on them, but always blessing because I could see the core value of what was provided. In other words, by following the desire of my heart I found ways to serve what I loved in ways that renewed that purpose.

After Sir Bedivere's despairing cry, Tennyson's poem continues:

> And slowly answered Arthur from the barge:
> "The old order changeth, yielding place to new,
> And God fulfills himself in many ways,
> Lest one good custom should corrupt the world."

Here Tennyson is explaining the need for renewal: "Lest one good custom should corrupt the world"—lest the current form of the spiritual reality come to obscure that reality. As Joseph Campbell writes, "The problem of the theologian [or spiritual leader] is to keep his symbol translucent, so that it may not block out the very light it is supposed to convey." I had a personal experience of how this spiritual translucency can become obscured when I lived for 18 months at another of the 12 spiritual communities that were associated together. Here it gradually became obvious that the local culture of the place that had temporarily given flesh and form to a spiritual truth had come to obscure it. The spirit had gone out of the place, and interestingly, in its stead was an obsession with its physical form: the complexities of boiler maintenance, whether the grass was cut. The physical form of the community had started to be reverenced rather than what had once given rise to that form. This community, not surprisingly, eventually failed, and the property was put up for sale.

The close of this community was just one of the changes that came thick and fast following the founder's death. However, the "heart wisdom" that had compelled me to move out and change direction had happened long before his death. Up until that change, I had more or less seen my life in terms of the community. My life was about sustaining and being a part of that larger life. By being drawn into a relationship and a new life that took me away from the community it looked as though I was betraying what I loved. But in reality by following the desires of my heart I started to take on my own individual differentiation of that larger life, and to face the challenges of growth and development that finishing the quest would require. To fulfil the quest, I had to leave King Arthur's court. And this compulsion was not unique to me. There were many others who had begun to feel the winds of change, who pondered in their own hearts whether differentiation of purpose meant betrayal of Camelot, but who nevertheless, out of the same compulsion, started to find their way out into the last, lonely stretches of the Grail quest journey.

And this brings me to the third cause of the downfall of Arthur's court, and that is the quest for the Grail itself. Perceval's journey delineates for us the inner landscape of the individual quest. But this journey has to be undertaken by all the knights, not just Perceval. The Grail quest is a journey that everyone must undertake, whether consciously or unconsciously. And this is symbolized by that moment when the Grail, covered in white samite, appears mysteriously during a great banquet at Camelot and passes around the room offering each one what his or her heart most desires. After tasting the delights that the Grail offers, each knight gets up in turn and vows to go on a quest to find the Grail and view it directly, that is, no longer covered by the cloth of white samite. This mysterious incident thus marks the beginning of the quest as undertaken by the knights of the Round Table. Alone of all the company, Arthur realizes that something else is also signified by this event. While the others are taken up in their zeal and excitement, he laments because he knows that the departure of his knights will also mean the dissolution of the Round Table:

> "No Christian king ever had so many good knights or men of rank and wisdom at his table as I have had this day, nor will again when these are gone, nor shall I ever see them reunited round my table as before." ("Queste del Saint Graal")

When Arthur and his knights are seated at the Round Table, they form the Fellowship or Knights of the Round Table, and they represent the very core of the (newly) United Kingdom of Britain. The Round Table was Guinevere's gift. Tradition has it that it was made by Merlin and kept safe by Guinevere's father, King Leodogran of Wales. On her marriage to Arthur, Guinevere brought with her the Round Table as a dowry. A wedding gift: a symbol of what would be born of the marriage between herself and Arthur—the unified kingdom with the Fellowship of the Round Table at its heart.

There is something revolutionary about the round shape of this table and the nature of this kingdom, because even though the king is present unlike the Wounded Fisher King he has not placed himself at the center of them. Something else is at the center of Camelot. Several fourteenth- and fifteenth-century manuscript illustrations depict the Round Table as doughnut shaped with a hollow in the middle. So we could say that at the core of Camelot, at the very center of the united kingdom, there is a hollow circle, and each knight seated at the table has equal access to that open, round center. This open, empty center represents the invisible, indescribable presence of God. The fact that each knight has equal access to the hub of the circle means that each one has the potential to be connected directly to—and also therefore the authority to represent—this presence.

There exist at least two fifteenth-century illustrations of the "Queste del Saint Graal" depicting that moment when the Grail, covered in white samite, appears at the banquet and inspires the knights to go off on the quest to view it directly. As I have already noted, this appearance of the Grail has a twofold significance, marking as it does both the beginning of the quest by *all* the knights (not just Perceval) and (therefore) the dissolution of the Round Table. In these illustrations the Grail chalice is shown *hovering in the hollow center of the table,* in the space where God is to be found.

To succeed on the quest for the Grail means that each knight must transfer his primary allegiance from King Arthur to that central presence symbolized by the hollow center of the table. We go on the quest to achieve our own direct relationship to God, and we do this by finding the Grail, by healing the heart realm from its wound of separation from that central, inner presence. The heart realm either acts as a veil that separates us or the connection that joins us to that presence of love. When the Grail appears at Camelot it is covered in white samite, a rich silk material often interwoven with gold (symbolizing the presence of love). This cloth represents that veil of separation, and the knights vow to go on a quest to view the Grail directly—to remove the veil of separation between their own beings and the presence of love.

The roundness of the table and its hollow center clearly echoes the symbol of the Grail chalice with its round rim and hollow cavity. The illustration of the Grail hovering in the open circle of the Round Table corroborates this parallel symbolism. It is as if the Round Table and the Grail chalice are synonymous, or are destined to *become* one and the same thing. We could say, then, that Guinevere's gift both of the Round Table as her dowry and of her own heart's compulsion was the *promise* of the Grail. This is Guinevere's deeper gift—the gift of the heart's wisdom itself, the gift of the Grail.

Before the knights embark on the quest, they sit at the table as a company united into their circle because of their love for and allegiance to King Arthur. In other words, they are still dependent for their sense of unity on a leader, on a point of reference external to themselves. Those of us who made up the spiritual network were—at least initially—united into a community because of our love for and allegiance to the founder, the man who had played the role of spiritual mentor, the King Arthur leader, for us. When he died, we got to find out to what extent we were united into a body of people because of our love for him, or whether—and how thoroughly—we had undertaken the work of the quest and had come to know directly, and not via the leader, a sense of oneness with inner source and therefore, as well, a sense of oneness with each other that was not dependent on an external point of leadership. This was a crucial difference, because one of the discoveries we made is how different we all were and how differently we understood our spiritual mission. When the consciousness of oneness is operative, these differences become differentiations of that oneness; when it is not, they become conflicts.

THE ROUND TABLE AND THE HOLY GRAIL, GAULTIER MAP, 1470
(Credit: Bibliotheque Nationale, Paris/The Bridgeman Art Library International Ltd.)

The work of the quest cannot be undertaken as a community; it has to be done individually. When the knights embark on the quest, they go alone:

Then they rode out from the castle and separated as they had decided amongst themselves, striking out into the forest one here,
one there, wherever they saw it thickest and wherever path or track
was absent. ("Queste del Saint Graal")

Each one chooses the place where the forest is thickest and where there
is no path for that individual. In other words, once one is on the quest
it is one's own subconscious process through which one has to find a
way whose thickets of fear and untrodden ways are unique to oneself.
We go alone. By embarking on the quest for the Grail, which is the
quest for their own direct connection to the heavenly king energy, the
knights are to undergo the transition from a company of initiates (which
means beginners) brought together as a community by their adherence
to an outer leader, Arthur, into a collective consciousness whose connection and sense of oneness is inherent, because the allegiance is no
longer to some person or some cause outside of themselves.

What was the amazing substance that was served from the Grail to
each of the knights and that caused every one of them to set off immediately on the quest? Something that was different, incidentally, for
each one. We could describe it as a taste of one's authentic self, of one's
tonally accurate voice. Something extraordinarily beautiful; something
unconditioned, large, loving; something from the heart, from the center of ourselves. The Grail chalice hovering there in the center of the
Round Table symbolizes the center and heart of ourselves, which,
when opened to and filled with the magical substance of God's love,
can "serve" us the full or unconditioned essence of ourselves.

The knights get only a taste of their authentic selves. It is a fleeting
experience. But the merest taste of what the Grail has to offer is so satisfying, so wonderful, that immediately they all stand and swear they
will never rest until they view it directly, without the covering of fine
cloth. They will never rest until they know this extraordinary experience of fulfilment permanently, fully, and completely.

The Grail chalice hovered in the center of the table. And to find the
chalice, which means to taste its blessings permanently instead of mo-
mentarily, we have to journey to the center: to the place where God is,
represented by the empty center of the Round Table. That journey is

the quest, signifying the process that will change the *model* of collective leadership into the *experience.* The journey to the center—the center where the Grail hovers—means the journey to the center of oneself to find the source of one's authority.

What is interesting about this incident in the story is that the moment of epiphany happens within the collective space and story. The Grail appears at Camelot, at the Round Table, whereas in Perceval's story it appears in the Grail Castle. In Chrétien de Troyes's story of Perceval, the whole court sets off on the quest after the dreadful hag has appeared and accuses Perceval of failing to ask the question. In both stories, the collective quest is undertaken after the individual quest is underway. The larger momentum of the collective opportunity snowballs gradually out of the individual strands and beginnings. We can also read this episode as symbolizing the way the collective presence can summon up for us an experience of ourselves. The collective presence can evoke the truth of brotherhood (and sisterhood), of oneness, and in that oneness of connection with others we sense the truth of our own oneness with source. The heart space has this kind of magical quality. Once we step into it, the boundaries of separation dissolve.

The table exists initially only as a promise of what it symbolizes and not yet as an experienced reality. When Arthur and his knights are gathered around the table they symbolize the possibility of shared government *by reason of access to and relationship with the center.* Until the knights journey to the center of themselves, they cannot have a relationship with or represent that center. If one's authentic self is not yet voiced, one can sit at the table, but one cannot share in governing, because one is not yet interacting with and representing the center.

In a paradoxical way, the Round Table cannot be fulfilled until it is dissolved. The knights must leave on the quest or they will not be transmuted from a company or community into the consciousness of oneness. The very design of the table signifies this for us. As this journey and work is undertaken, the presence of collective leadership begins to be configured—collective because now each one *does* have a sense of connection to what is symbolized by that hollow center.

The exit en masse of the knights on the quest and the sword arcing down into the lake and being caught by the mysterious woman's hand are two rather dramatic episodes that parallel, even comment on, each other. The die is cast. The Round Table has come to an end; the knights have left to find the Grail; the great potency of the sword of truth has impregnated the waters of the collective unconscious. In chapter 8 I discussed how the story of the individual Grail quest is essentially unfinished and can only be finished as the story of one person's journey is multiplied by many others to become the collective story. Now these two incidents of the collective quest and the sword submerged in the lake show us that the story of Arthur and the Round Table, the collective story, is also unfinished. Both myths lie unfinished but with an aura of prophecy and promise hanging over them. The finishing of the myth is now up to us, individually and collectively. The reconfiguring of the Round Table can only happen as each individual embarks on the journey and the process to earn the individual sword and find the Grail.

Even though on the surface it can look as though things have fallen apart, there is a healing aspect to this dissolution because in a sense, by embarking on the quest, or the last stages of the quest, we are also beginning the journey that will bring us back to rejoin the larger world— the world we had to leave for a season. While it was a necessary part of my process to be separated out from that world, there was also pain involved for both myself, in my relative isolation, and in the sense of abandonment in those whom I "left." My family and many of my friends, for instance, were perplexed at what I was doing when I went to live on the community, and I know the families of other friends in my network felt their children were somehow "lost" to them.

In a way, we could think of the symbol of the Round Table as a seedpod that appears to fall apart but is in fact opening to the cycles of growth, releasing the seeds that hold the promise of the multiplication and expansion of its essence. The change from the stasis and potential of the seed to the flux and growth cycles of the plant is life-bringing.

I remember having an intimation of the requirement for such a transition one summer evening during an extended stay on one of the major communities in North America. It was dinnertime, and we were all (maybe 150 or more) eating together in a special celebratory dinner outdoors. I cannot remember now the reason for the special occasion, but high ceremonial "banquets" of this kind were not unusual as ways to be together. So there we all were: it was high summer, and the court was in session, with Arthur—the leader of the network—present in our midst and with many others represented through all the connections. Yet as I looked out on our glorious company I suddenly felt that there was something inherently static about it all. As if the traditions of this "court" were a little too self-involved and overdependent for their meaning on serving the "king." Funnily enough, even though at the time I was not thinking about the Arthurian myth, the analogy that did come to mind was that the world of the community was like a medieval court that had a static quality to it. The baker was always the baker, the wine taster was always the wine taster, the king was always the king, and everything centered around him—the pattern never developed past its archetype. And a curious sense of claustrophobia came over me. When I left the community in England to move back to London with my boyfriend, my apprehension and ambivalence was mixed with a strong sense of joy at "rejoining" the world. And I think that, as well as anguish, many of my friends experienced a similar sense of freedom as the "medieval" structures of community broke apart with the growth and challenges of individual new beginnings.

At this point, then, in a sense, the myth comes to an end and our lives take over. Whether we succeed individually and collectively on the quest is our choice. The myth, in this sense, is completely real. It is the question and challenge that forms the backdrop and deepest context of our lives. Our response to the challenges of the quest, our ability to ask and understand the question, is what will determine whether our lives are ultimately meaningful or not.

In the end no one person organized our network back into coherence. It happened—and is still happening—spontaneously, as bit by bit, almost one by one, different individuals have emerged out of the waters of chaos and confusion, having sufficiently completed the internal, individual work that the spiritual quest entails. We were drawn by love—for one another; love for the reality of core being that we knew; and a compulsion to configure the new collective emergence. We knew the quality of being that was formerly held by the leader, the man who played the role of King Arthur to us, needed to be held as tangibly and radiantly, in an expanded way, not by one individual anymore but by many—by a *collective* of us. No one quite knew how to achieve this. Different ones had different ideas, and sometimes these ideas clashed and caused conflict; nevertheless, the compulsion to oneness and the networks of friendship have kept working. The leadership of the network has been reconfigured collectively, so that a small grouping share the leadership. Moreover, the nature of that leadership is no longer that of spiritual parent to child but of peer to peer. And we find ourselves forming not so much a physical community anymore but what might be called a field of oneness, an experience, still new, of functioning as different aspects of the one consciousness.

The spiritual reality of the Grail is not a form, a community, an idea, or even an ideal. It is the consciousness of oneness. Oneness with God and oneness with one another, a condition that is both individually and collectively configured. This is how the Round Table will be transmuted from a symbol into a living reality. The Round Table and the Grail chalice are to become the same thing; the promise of collective leadership is the full emergence of the Grail. The Grail is the heart that is once more in connection with God, with the nameless, invisible presence at the center of both the table—of us all—and of each one of us. It is the Grail, both individually—each one seated has equal access—*and* collectively: the company of knights together, the consciousness of oneness.

In the end, what was born out of Guinevere and Arthur's marriage was not only the Fellowship of the Round Table and the united kingdom but the Grail itself—the consciousness of oneness, of which both the one kingdom and the Round Table were but forerunners. This was more precious than a son and heir; this was more precious than the continuation of Camelot in ways that would sooner or later have crusted over into tradition and custom without ever igniting the experience of truth that lay behind them. This is what was discerned so long ago by Merlin, staring into the mists of the future. Something crucial to the destiny of all humankind.

Why is the Grail so significant? We remember that in the myths, King Arthur's court and the wasteland kingdom of the Wounded Fisher King *coexist*. This means that the existence of King Arthur and his reign of greatness—Camelot, the Round Table, and the rest—was not able to heal the wounded king and restore the wasteland. Instead, they provided the conditions in which the knights could undertake the quest for the Grail. It is the finding of the Grail—not the founding of Camelot—that carries the promise of healing both wound and wasteland.

In my explorations of the Grail's symbolic meanings, I have already shown that its primary meaning is the heart, healed from its wound of separation from the core energy of being. I also looked at the fact that one person's completion of the quest does not have sufficient impact on the larger world to restore the wasteland brought about by the controlling consciousness of the wounded king. Not just one but many individuals are required to complete the quest for wholeness. To the extent that this multiple emergence of whole individuals starts to be configured, they could be said to represent a collective Grail. When oneness is known with inner source, there follows a sense of oneness with others. This is the Grail in its aspect of collective leadership: a circle of peers knowing the connection with the central presence of God, and knowing the connection at the rim. This circle then becomes the *container* of God's presence. This cup serves the purposes of that central and collective presence. It cannot be used for anything else.

11

THE CHALICE OF
COLLECTIVE SOVEREIGNTY

*I hear people everywhere saying that the trouble with our time is
that we have no great leaders any more. If we look back we always
had them. But to me it seems that there is a very profound reason
why there are no great leaders anymore. It is because they are no
longer needed. The message is clear. You no longer want to be led
from the outside. Every man must be his own leader. He now
knows enough not to follow other people. He must follow the light
that's within himself, and through this light he will create a new
community. You see, wherever I go in the world, this to me is a
general trend. I am aware of the fact that there are already people
in existence today—take us—who really belong to a community
which does not yet exist. That is, we are the bridge between the
community we've left and the community which doesn't
exist yet.* —LAURENS VAN DER POST, *A Walk with a White Bushman*

THERE IS A great fear of losing the sword—a fear of losing the tradition and forms that have embodied the truth
for us, and a desire to try to preserve them in some way—
to disobey Arthur's command. Twice Sir Bedivere, that most loyal
and trusted knight, tries to hide Excalibur before finally obeying
Arthur and throwing the sword into the lake. After all, if we don't
preserve the sword, we might lose everything.

> And if indeed I cast the brand away,
> Surely a precious thing, one worthy note,
> Should thus be lost for ever from the earth, . . .
> What record, or what relic of my lord

> Should be to aftertime, but empty breath
> And rumours of a doubt?

Very often this is the way. The injection of spiritual reality brought by the great avatar, like Jesus or Buddha, one who is able to pull the sword of power, of spiritual authority, back out of the stone of fixed belief and tradition and wield it as a living reality, is turned after their death into a religion, a series of beliefs, a tradition. And people warm themselves on the little spark that still glows in the embers of that tradition, but they don't inherit the mantle of spiritual radiance. They have not become entrained into the understanding of what it really means to "Worship God"; they have not completed the quest.

In the aftermath of the death of my spiritual mentor I got to see firsthand just how strong this instinct to preserve the sword is. It was the fear of losing the sword that caused some people to try to cast the new leader in the old, patriarchal King Arthur role or made them cling to outmoded but familiar structures of thought and ways of doing things and rendered them unable to view changes as anything but heresy. The strength and grip of this preservation instinct was a revelation to me.

Nevertheless, even though I and others knew that to attempt a re-run of the past was a futile endeavor, we still experienced some of Sir Bedivere's anguish as events unravelled around us and so many left not only the communities but the circle of connection and seemed to have forgotten its potency and sacredness. Were we alone now? Had we lost our sense of communion and purpose, and—worst of all—was the truth that we had known lost? Had the sword been cast away forever, and had it all been for nothing? Once again, the question arose for us individually and collectively—had we failed?

In retrospect now, I can see that the most telling thing of all about our experience, both as individuals and as a grouping—to the extent we still constituted a grouping—was that we realized we had left the map. There was no rule book now, just as there was no singular leader around whom to configure. Even though we felt that there was still a purpose and a need to sustain an association together, and even though we even used the phrase *collective leadership,* we didn't know how to get there. All we could do was follow step-by-step as individuals what the compulsion of our hearts led us to do. We learned that we had to trust the direction of our hearts—and that there wasn't any other direction. In actual fact, in so doing we were really only continuing a process that had begun before the founder's death when gradually more and more individuals were beginning to act from their own sense of compulsion and to override the—almost equally strong—loyalty to preserving the sword. The leader's death simply helped accelerate a sea change in our organization that was already underway and that needed to happen if we weren't to just stagnate and ultimately lose momentum.

So by following the heart's compulsion and desire, we came to the heart—came to the Grail, the sense of direct connection to inner authority. And in the process we made sure that the sword was not preserved as an outer tradition but accessed from within. Thanks to Guinevere and Morgana (the heart's wisdom), Excalibur is not destined to become a sacred relic of a past glory "stored in some treasure-house of mighty kings." The heart's instinctual knowing of what is right has overridden the fears and the structures of the mind, thus ensuring that Arthur's true legacy—the legacy of potency, of truth, as represented by his sword—has become a living possibility available within the subconscious mind for us all to draw on. It has not fossilized into a tradition for the elite to fight over—whether a political elite or a priestly elite; it is beyond the reach of corruption, and can only be accessed by the innocent and the true. Thanks to the quest for the Grail, thanks to the heart's compulsion to take on one's individual path and authority, the Round Table could become what it was a promise of. Our network could be transmuted from a community into a new and potent consciousness of oneness.

This is why no matter which thread of the plot we retrace to uncover the cause of Camelot's downfall, we find ourselves staring into the face of the feminine, whether it be the actions of Guinevere and Morgana or the quest for the Grail itself. Only the heart's wisdom knows how to take us from symbol to reality and carries the passion and assurance that will allow the "old order" to change and find renewal.

So we can begin to approach the meaning of the fulfilment of the Grail quest from a number of different—but related—angles. First of all, the finding of the Grail (and the asking of the question) means that the sense of personal separation from inner source—which I have also called the Grail King energy, love, or God—is healed. Once this happens, our dependence on a King Arthur mentor figure ceases, and we begin to live our lives from a direct sense of what fits, of what is ours to do. We can trust the compulsion of our heart because the heart realm is now operating as a direct "transmitter" of our own inner being and purpose. In this way, the heart realm is the place of connection, or oneness, with God or spiritual source, and once that consciousness of union with source is a grounded reality within us—once the ego that thinks of itself as the center of the universe is no longer dominant—then there is a basis for connecting deeply with others. The heart realm becomes the means of connection with others, with one's "neighbors." Therefore, we also begin to share a sense of oneness with one another, and a sense of being—hologram-like—parts of a whole that also contain in miniature the design of that whole.

The sense of oneness with others, combined with the ability to discern direction for ourselves, enables the other meaning of the Grail to emerge, which is the aspect of collective leadership: the circle of many individuals forming one body.

Collective leadership is not possible while we are still dependent on a mentor figure both for our own sense of spiritual alignment and for a sense of direction. Nor is it possible unless there is the sense of oneness to bind us together—as well as the ability to discern for ourselves (as opposed to being subject to "peer pressure") what our actions need to be.

We remember that the individual sword—or sense of authority—is earned by going on a quest for the Grail. Perceval is given the sword on his first visit to the Grail Castle. The return of Arthur in the form of the return of many individuals wielding their individual swords—in other words, the condition of collective leadership—cannot come about until the Grail is found and this collective consciousness is formed.

So far I have tried to illustrate the meaning of the momentous closing moments of Arthur's reign in general terms, or in terms of the network of communities and friends that I was associated with. However, that is not the only context in which the dynamics of the transition from singular to collective leadership can be discerned. I believe that the demise of what I have termed the era of the sword can be seen in the larger world of which we are all a part. The closure of what has sometimes also been called the patriarchy and the emergence of a condition of collective leadership is what lies behind much of what on the surface appears to be confusing or troubling symptoms of our modern global society. In fact, everywhere we look today, we see the "old order" changing and the new putting in an appearance.

As that sword arcs down toward the surface of the water and the Lady of the Lake catches it and draws it under, we are in fact witnessing not only the closing of one era but the emergence of another. This is the era of the Grail, of the feminine, of collective leadership. This new era of the chalice has been emerging for some time. The emergence of women that has been going on for well over a century, the women's movement and, allied with it, the civil rights movement in America; the feminist reevaluation of literature and history are all aspects of the emergence of the Grail. The rise of the feminine and the era of collective leadership—which demands an inherent recognition that all people share the same rights—are one and the same. The roundness of the chalice cup symbolizes this circle of oneness: it is without hierarchy; it contains all.

Both the women's and civil rights movements gave inspiration to and derived massive impetus from the youth movements of the 1960s and 1970s, the huge wave of energy that buoyed up or was created by the baby boomer generation. Perhaps the overriding characteristic of this whole generation—whether expressed in the explosive new music, drug experimentation, or political protest—was discontent. Discontent with the old order and a determination to fashion a new one. What ultimately has evolved out of this determination is a quality of self-knowledge or spiritual wisdom that I believe forms the apex or core achievement of this whole generation.

The baby boomer generation grew up in the aftermath of World War II. Fed by the conversations of my parents and their friends, and by the war movies we watched on Sunday afternoons, my own imagination formed a collage of impressions of the war that was like a backdrop to my childhood. I pictured it as predominantly black and gray, splattered with gunfire and riven by the white rods of arc lights. Tiny gray figures spilled and milled about across darkened nations. Huge aircraft carriers swung slowly through metallic seas, radars sieved the invisible air; big guns jerked and rebounded, tanks tipped up and over across vast anonymous battlefields. There were jazz bands, women in uniform, starlit bombers waiting for the alert, sirens, cigarettes, Saint Paul's Cathedral outlined against a blitz-filled sky. The overall impression I had was exciting rather than dreadful, heroic rather than insane.

The war was always referred to by my parents as an experience against which all else was measured. But they were ambivalent about it. The war years had been the best years of their lives: a time of excitement and the camaraderie of shared purpose. Yet at the same time, the stress and upheaval of living through it had led to an overwhelming desire for security, for the material comfort of an ordinary life.

I was quite a bit older when I saw for the first time on TV archival footage shot by the allied troops that had liberated Dachau and Auschwitz: pile on pile of flesh-covered skeletons, brittle and dead, faces so craven and desperate it was hard to recognize them as human, pictures of the ovens built to burn human bodies, samples of lampshades made from human skin. These images—whose power to shock has never dimmed—seemed to both justify the flurry of war and destruction and at the same time deflate it all. They said: "Look, this is about something else entirely. Here is a poison, it has always been with you, it cannot be fought with tanks."

The death camps, and finally the mushroom clouds of Hiroshima and Nagasaki—destroying as they did not only two entire cities but the whole notion of heroism—arose like giant question marks over my growing up. How could these things have happened? What did they tell us about ourselves? What were the changes needed in us as human beings to make sure this could never happen again?

I found that my parents and their peers were unable to help me answer such questions. It was as if underlying their lives of quiet security was an unspoken decision to cease evolving, and to avoid the questions the war had raised. This silence about matters of import, combined with the very ordinary but nonetheless at times acute unhappiness of their lives—manifested itself to me as a kind of madness from which I wished to escape. All I ever wanted to do was get away from my house, away from that atmosphere of mad, sad security. I took refuge in friends' homes as often as I could, but I discovered after a while that their parents were "mad" as well. So I joined the ranks of so many of my generation in rebelling against the carefully guarded security of my parent's lives.

I call us the window generation. We were born into and, by our sheer numbers, created a unique window in history (at least in the Western world), a window of both security and opportunity to bring change. It was a time of the ascendancy of the middle classes; we were all well fed and looked after and offered good education and the opportunity to go on to college. No conventional war and no major diseases threatened our well-being. What we did have hanging over us, of course—the legacy of the war—was the possibility of nuclear Armageddon, which was even given the official name of Mutually Assured Destruction. And this large-scale MADness, combined with the small-scale madness that we saw in the suffocating misery and tangled neuroses of many of our parents' lives, caused us to vehemently reject such a heritage and such a world, which we blamed our parents and their peers for creating. We would have none of it.

Indeed, as the hippy and peace movements gained momentum in the 1960s and 1970s, my generation wasn't content with this world at all; we were determined to storm heaven itself. Whatever it took—drugs, free love, endless pilgrimage, frenzied music:

> We're gonna fly so high
> and never gonna die.
> —STEPPENWOLF, "BORN TO BE WILD"

We were going to break through into another state. No secure suburban box for us. The same determination fed the political protests of the sixties in France and the peace movement in the United States as the government became mired in the Vietnam war.

Although I felt some of the impact of these trends, my rebellion essentially took a quieter form. Partly I was too young to be caught up fully in them, but also it seemed to me that the answer to the questions raised by both the horrors of World War II and the claustrophobic unhappiness of my parents' lives lay in a different direction. Ultimately these questions led me along the so-called less-travelled path of spiritual understanding.

Looking back with the wisdom and compassion of hindsight, the fact was that the tools of insight and mentorship that might have shed light on both my parents' lives and the larger issues of their times were by and large simply not available to their generation. Psychoanalysis and marriage guidance counselling of course existed, but at that time quite a stigma was attached to seeking help in this way. The plethora of emotional/spiritual/therapeutic approaches that exist today were not yet developed, mainly because it was our generation who would evolve these tools, and we were still in our childhood or teenage years. Small surprise then, that they were ill equipped to mentor me. Ironically, the gift they did give was the very thing against which we rebelled: a "window" of relative stability in which such tools of insight could be forged. Had we been brought up in deprivation, instability, and anxiety, the boldness to go psychically adventuring would not have been ours.

The eighties brought a new materialism, but by now the streams created by the impetus of the 1960s and 1970s youth movements were deepening and maturing, as people started to see that they were bound as much by their own conditioning as by the edicts of the old order, and protest was gradually replaced by self-exploration. This attempt to eradicate the old order from within oneself, to become more fully alive, earned baby boomers the title of the "me" generation; all those experiments in therapy and spiritual disciplines continued to develop as an alternative momentum alongside the resurgent orthodoxy of the 1980s.

When I began associating with the network of spiritual communities first introduced to me by my long-lost cousin, it was the mid-1970s, and at that time we appeared to be a tiny seed in a teeming and largely oblivious world. The quest was the journey away from that world, away from the mainstream, and toward the spiritual source of oneself. But about a decade later, our grouping and community in England played host to and organized an event called the Human Unity Conference, which was attended by over six hundred people and brought speakers representing a huge diversity and number of spiritual groupings and initiatives from around the world. Almost overnight I became aware of just how many people (because we realized that even this was only a small sampling) there were exploring the nature of their inner selves. Suddenly the so-called less-travelled path had become quite crowded.

Where had this stream of spiritual adventurers come from? The energy, protests, and experimentation of the youth movements had been refined into multiple developments in what have been termed the New Age and "alternative" fields, all exploring essentially the spiritual/healing/emotional dimensions of being. The path to the heart is the spiritual path. The quest. The heart cannot be healed until identity is made whole, rooted in the spiritual source of oneself.

It is among the ranks of that "alternative" stream—birthed out of the rock concerts, the breaking of taboos, the all-or-nothing attempt to storm heaven; out of gestalt therapy, New Age philosophies, "channellers," the men's movement, and the Buddhist retreat; in other words, out of that collective motion of consciousness that has broken with the materialist orthodoxy and embraced as vital and necessary the spiritual dimension of humanity—that we find today a multitude of pilgrims and mentors. Nowadays I believe it is possible for anyone to reach out and connect with a network of people and ideas within which somewhere and somehow they will find responsible mentoring—whether it be the man leading an "Inner King" workshop or a healer, a shaman who sets up a vision quest, or a religious philosopher like Matthew Fox or a spiritual therapist like Thomas Moore. So nowadays we have many people playing the role of the spiritual mentor, as well as increasing numbers of individuals who are learning to "take up" their own swords, their own authority. Here is a collective configuration of mentorship.

This is the "spiritual revolution" that the renowned mystic Madame Blavatsky, writing over one hundred years ago, predicted would take place during the last quarter of the twentieth century. This revolution, she said, would be led by ordinary people, not by those in power. What does *spiritual* mean? The first definition of the word "spirit" given in my *Shorter Oxford Dictionary* is: "the animating or vital principle in man . . . that which gives life to the physical organism, in contrast to its purely material elements; the breath of life." The second definition is: "the soul of a person." Thus *spiritual* means: "of, pertaining to, affecting, or concerning" the spirit. *Revolution* means literally a rotation, a turning around, and in social/historical contexts has come to mean an overthrow of or change in the existing order. A *spiritual revolution* means, then, a change in identity, a turning away from a former sense of identity based predominantly on personality, culture, background, race, and so on and a turning toward the spiritual source of identity: the change in polarity that the Grail quest brings about. Sometimes the phrase *spiritual revolution* is used to describe the substitution of one set of spiritual or religious beliefs for another set. But this is to confuse the map with the territory. A spiritual revolution is not about a change of maps but is about exploring the territory, the reality of spiritual identity. It is about shifting into an awareness of a deeper dimension of ourselves.

Revolutions always involve upheaval, and the chaos and confusion of today's global society could be seen in part as the result of such a revolution. Fortunately, though, this is a "bloodless" revolution. It is not being brought about by a group of people seizing political or military power but by a critical mass of individuals undergoing a shift in their own identities. When this shift happens, the so-called mainstream of our society begins to falter, because it starts to seem irrelevant to our vision and aims. This may be why so few people vote nowadays in elections, and why the TV and cable networks have to maintain a constant struggle to shore up their ever-slipping ratings.

On the surface it can look as if we are lost and leaderless, and many pundits today bemoan the breakdown of families and the loss of traditional values and role models. However, what is really happening is that leadership is landing in another place—or rather places—as power seeps away from its traditional repositories and is taken up by the individual.

In other words, it is the revolution in identity that is bringing the changes in our global society, and in this way power and authority are relocating in "ordinary people." There exist, still, of course, governmental, legislative, and judicial structures that continue to exert an executive power that is backed up and enforceable by law. But although we may still acknowledge the power that these institutions and the individuals appointed to them wield, I do not think that we view the same people and institutions as vested any longer with authority—particularly moral authority. The same is true of our attitude toward the "professions." A simple example is the change in attitude that has taken place in Britain over one generation toward doctors and teachers. (I do not think the same shift is as clearly evident yet in the United States.) My mother still has an unquestioning reverence for medical doctors; and when I was in school she had a similar, albeit not quite so marked, respect for my teachers. Indeed, professionals of any sort—university professors, lawyers, and so on—evoked in her a mild and semiconscious awe. My generation has a very different approach. Doctors are questioned, criticized, and compared one to another. Their opinions and diagnoses are not regarded as holy writ. Nor do teachers benefit any longer from unquestioned accreditation with what is right. A friend of mine who is a teacher in a British high school complained to me about the almost constant barrage of inquiry and interference from the pupils' parents. When we were at school, such intervention by parents was unheard of.

I think a big blow was struck to the moral authority of the United States Supreme Court when its five-to-four decision put a stop to counting votes in Florida toward the end of the 2000 election and went against the Florida supreme court's decision to allow the count; the decision appeared to be blatantly partisan in favor of the Republican Party. It is as if the mask had come off. There is a modern cameo scene that symbolizes this for me, and that was at the end of a televised debate between George Bush Senior and Bill Clinton during the 1992 election campaign. Clinton did well, coming out from behind his lectern and talking directly and conversationally, as a peer, to the audience. The debate was in its closing stages when suddenly Bush started looking irritatedly at his watch, as if to say he was really too busy and important to humor this child's play any longer. That one gesture instantly shattered Bush's public persona: his statesmanship and his gravitas were suddenly exposed as illusions.

On a wider screen, one can ask: Does authority lie with the United States, as the last "superpower" and world leader? Again, it is generally acknowledged that power lies with the United States: it is the world's richest and largest economy and it possesses the most powerful military force. However, there has been an attempt to invest *authority* in the collective presence of the United Nations, even though it doesn't always work very well. This was quite clearly demonstrated prior to the 1991

Gulf War when the allied forces brought together by George Bush Sr. sought authority from the UN to take military action against Iraq.

The United Nations is an example of leadership being held and configured in a collective: and the sanction of this circle was needed in order give the United States and its allies moral validity in pursuing the war. In other words, the era of collective leadership means not only that authority is shifting away from the former patriarchal structures but also that leadership will increasingly be configured in a collective way.

Of course in the 2003 war in Iraq, this seeking of authority from the UN and the attempt to play out a course of action within a pattern of collective agreement was reversed by the George Bush Junior administration. However, I think it is true to say that while this administration's actions are all about the use of power, the longer term results may be to widen the gap between that power and any authority that might be invested in its brand of leadership.

Surveying the world scene today, I see only one great King Arthur leader still living: Nelson Mandela. No doubt, someone of his stature was still required to help guide the process of transition and resolution of conflict in South Africa. An extremely wise man, Mandela has said that when a tall tree falls in the forest, many new ones can grow in the space and light that is created. He is aware that a leader of King Arthur's stature necessarily blocks the light from us, as much as he may inspire growth, and Mandela has been at pains to nurture and invest power in others who must follow after him. I can certainly remember at times feeling pygmy-like in comparison to my own spiritual mentor.

Of course, there is still a deep nostalgia in us for an old-style hero. I think this explains the eagerness there was in many for Colin Powell to run for president in 1996. Here, apparently, is a man of genuine integrity and accomplishment. Let us vote him in as our leader and bask in his reflected glory. This again can be seen as the preserve-the-sword energy at work. Colin Powell, it seems, was sensible enough to acknowledge that he really did not have the required motivation to run for president. Perhaps he was also wise enough to sense that the time of heroes and patriarchs is over.

The shift that is taking place in the nature of leadership could be likened to the sword emerging in us individually. We have to access this sword in ourselves now; we are not going to find it somewhere else, in some institution or group of experts. The sword of power is beginning to rise up from the waters of the lake, from the collective unconscious, and is surfacing in the consciousness of many people.

I have also noticed the collective nature of our times operating in the field of literature, particularly in the United States. Having studied English literature, I was brought up on the notion of there being in each generation a handful of "greats" who articulated themes and insights necessary to that generation. But not anymore. Now there are hundreds of "named" poets, novelists, and playwrights. And very often a writer in any field succeeds as much because he or she is representing some new strand of humanity or the local culture as because of the quality of his or her writing. A pluralistic society is thus collectively articulated not by a handful of mainstream greats but by a veritable army of writers. This does not mean that all these writers are good; indeed, in the United States in particular, quality will sometimes suffer in the rush to represent some new point of view or section of society. However, what it does mean is that much of the force of current has left the "mainstream," reducing its flow considerably (which it of course pretends is not happening). I believe the massive consolidation of the large publishing houses is symptomatic of this trend. The market has become so unpredictable that only very very big fish can survive in it, but even they are vulnerable to the changes that new developments in technology—particularly to do with publishing and the Internet—may bring. I have also felt at times that the works produced by those who are considered current mainstream greats, though marvelous in many respects, seem curiously irrelevant—as if the writer is writing about a world, and a way of seeing that world, that has passed away or that belongs to a literary tradition of the past, not of the present; or at least to a tradition that is not aware of the other currents now taking shape in the world. Works are considered great if they add to or take forward the established literary mode rather than—as in the past, and this is what actually created the "great"ness of the tradition—because they are groundbreaking in some radical way.

The river has broadened out and is represented no longer by an elite few but by many voices. It thus becomes harder to perceive who are the real artists but also harder for the establishments used to arbitrating such claims to maintain their exclusive pedigree. The aristocratic (in literary terms) publishing houses, the *Times Literary Supplement,* the *New York Times Book Review,* and the academic institutions may still try to claim authority for creating and framing the emerging "greats," but they find themselves undermined by thousands of other voices, showcases, publications, and institutions.

A similar explosion of outlets is happening within the television and motion picture industry, as well as a parallel process of consolidation of the bigger fish. None of this is completely under anyone's control—at least not yet—and no one can quite figure out how it will all shake down.

The Internet of course is one of the most obvious manifestations of this new collective state. There is no hierarchy controlling access to this system, and no preimposed set of values and beliefs govern it. And it is a symbol of the potential interconnectedness (oneness?) between all people.

Another arena in which the sense of collective leadership is beginning to configure is in the corporate world. Over the past decade, many corporations have been busy employing squadrons of business consultants with the basic aim of changing the structure of their company from one large and often unwieldy hierarchy, with long chains of command, to a collection of smaller "team"-based units. Studies have shown that greater efficiency comes when people work in smaller, more team-oriented structures and when communication and feedback travel shorter distances, that is, when higher management is more accessible. Thus middle management has been largely removed, and responsibility and initiative are more collectively held. The consultants advise on everything from restructuring the company to techniques for empowering individual employees. The aim of all this consultancy is twofold. The corporations wish to operate more efficiently within a competitive market. Downsizing and removing middle management saves them an enormous amount of money and, according to the newest theories of management, achieves greater motivation and efficiency within the remaining workforce. At the same time, by supposedly "empowering" the employee, the aim is to foster not only better performance but also independence. In this way the corporations can shift away from their perceived role as the paternal employer who provides everything the employee needs (including health benefits and retirement funds) and change the "job for life" attitude with its attendant qualities of dependency and inertia. In other words, the corporations themselves are embracing the idea that the company should operate in a more collective fashion, whereby individuals take greater responsibility for decisions, initiative, and communication, working with patterns of leadership but more as peers than followers.

Collective leadership means sharing the responsibilities of leading; it does not mean having no more leaders. Leadership and coordination are always needed. But the nature of the relationship with leadership is different: there is no longer any need to either worship or kill the king. The challenge of our modern era is to allow the king to die as *king* and receive the human person back as peer, or perhaps as elder statesperson. This means we have to let the *way we have viewed the leader* die. Collective leadership, in which all individuals carry responsibility, means that we move out of the cult mentality with its dependence on a leader or dogma. The king must be allowed to die to his or her role of absolute authority but still be retained as leader and peer. We prove, by needing neither to adulate nor undermine him, that we have been weaned onto our own authority.

This new relationship with the leader is a fine balance. It requires of course that we never, like the fawning courtiers of old, fall in with the leader's own delusions and compliment him on his fine new clothes when he is in fact naked. We must honor our loyalty to the leader, but our loyalty to God comes first—that is to say, our own insight and sense of what is right. The leader depends on our ability to do this, and calamity can result if we fail. In his book *In Retrospect,* the former U.S. defense secretary Robert McNamara examines "the tragedy and lessons of Vietnam," meaning of course the Vietnam war. On assuming the presidency, Lyndon Johnson, according to McNamara, made it clear that he wanted "to win the war." Bit by bit, support and training of the South Vietnamese was augmented first by covert operations, next by bombing North Vietnam, and then by sending in ground troops, until finally the United States was embroiled in a major conflict. Time and again throughout the book McNamara says that he and his peers should have analyzed more thoroughly the consequences of what they were doing, but failed to do so:

> Looking back, I clearly erred by not forcing—then or later, in either Saigon or Washington—a knock-down, drag-out debate over the loose assumptions, unasked questions, and thin analyses underlying our military strategy in Vietnam. I had spent twenty years as a manager identifying problems and forcing organizations—often against their will—to think deeply and realistically about alternative courses of action and their consequences. I doubt I will ever fully understand why I did not do so here.

But was it not because the "king" had said that he wanted to win the war, and McNamara could not bring himself to disappoint that expectation by stating clearly much earlier on his own fundamental conviction that the administration was escalating a war that could not be won on any acceptable terms?

The actions and decisions of leadership relative to the Vietnam war, along with the Watergate scandal, stand out as perhaps some of the most glaring instances in the twentieth century when leadership was out of touch and out of step. The violent protests against the war that so shook America at the time and undermined its war policy were, as I have said, one of the strands of the youth movements of the 1960s and 1970s, which themselves were allied on many fronts with the two other great popular reforming currents of the women's and civil rights movements. While these movements had their great leaders, they were all essentially grassroots movements that ended up changing the face of society. They were not legislated from above. In this era of the chalice, we see direction and understanding emerging out of the whole, out of the center of the circle, and no longer so much out of the leadership. Leadership today is no longer primarily about inspiring others or laying down a policy that others must follow but is about drawing out and orchestrating what we are collectively authoring.

Michael Sandel, a professor of political philosophy at Harvard, has written about the need for collective leadership, arguing that coherent involvement in democracy and therefore in self-government can only happen if sovereignty is dispersed among the communities and individuals of a nation. The time of pushing sovereignty "up" on to "big government" is over—and has not worked very well in encouraging participation. Nor, he says, will it work to somehow create global governing bodies if there is not a connection felt between these institutions and individuals in their immediate, local settings: "The hope for self-government today lies not in relocating sovereignty but in dispersing it." This use of the word *sovereignty* is pleasing: it contains connotations of power, authority, and responsibility as well as evoking qualities of character that border on the transcendent. Sandel goes on: "America was born of the conviction that sovereignty need not exist in one place." (This was and is a great promise, and may be the reason why the United States is today the world leader. It is another way of describing the collective return of the spirit of Arthur. It is a promise that has not yet been fulfilled.) "From the start the Constitution divided power among branches and levels of government. Over time, however, we, too, have pushed sovereignty and citizenship upward, in the direction of the nation." Sandel summarizes the new complexities that undermine national sovereignty today:

> National sovereignty is eroded from above by the mobility of capital, goods, and information across national boundaries, the integration of world financial markets, and the transnational character of industrial production. And national sovereignty is challenged from below by the resurgent aspirations of subnational groups for autonomy and self-rule.

In other words, authority is no longer found in one place but in many:

> Self-government today . . . requires a politics that plays itself out in a multiplicity of settings, from neighborhoods to nations to the world as a whole. Such a politics requires citizens who can abide the ambiguity associated with divided sovereignty, who can think and act as multiply situated selves. The civic virtue distinctive to our time is the capacity to negotiate our way among the sometimes

overlapping and sometimes conflicting obligations that claim us, and to live with the tension to which multiple loyalties give rise.

What this analysis does not take into account is the state of the individual himself or herself. How can someone learn to function in this complex and interdependent fashion, as a "multiply situated self," if there is only a two-dimensional sense of self to begin with? We can only function outwardly as "multiply situated selves," with all the understanding, tolerance, and vision that requires, if we have accessed the multiplicity of our interior worlds. And this we can only do if we have undertaken the quest of purifying our hearts, so that the vaster inheritance of spiritual identity can cross over into the world of form, and the fundamental oneness of all things can be understood:

> When the soul lies down
> in that grass,
> the world is too full to talk about—
> ideas, languages,
> even the phrase each other
> don't make any sense.
>
> —RUMI

"Even the phrase each other" doesn't make sense when we relax into the deep underlying ground of oneness. We have made the journey to the center where God resides and where the Grail was hovering, which turns out to be the center of ourselves, and have found the connection—the Grail—to the heavenly king and to one another.

The changes in our individual hearts that our inward journey entails and the paralleling changes that are swirling around in the social and political landscapes we find ourselves in can be seen as evidences of the fulfilment of the prophecy of the once and future king. The "spiritual revolution" prophesied by Madame Blavatsky, the changes and new thinking about the structures of leadership in and between nations and within corporations, the meltdown of the traditional mainstream hold of the media, the power of grassroots movements, and the disenchantment with the system of democracry as it currently operates are all evidences of the ongoing emergence of a condition of collective leadership or collective sovereignty. The promised return of Arthur does not mean the reappearance of one great hero or messiah but a collective return of the spirit of leadership that the figure of Arthur symbolizes for us.

When the sword is cast out over the waters of the lake, it is caught and brandished by a Lady of the Lake. It is not lost. The sword and the lake, sword and collective chalice, have become one thing. The sword has fertilized the new possibility of collective leadership. We could say that in this sense, a new era of union between sword and chalice, male and female, is now open to us. The word *collective* suggests the roundness and the inclusiveness of the feminine; the word *leadership* suggests the one-pointedness and absoluteness of the masculine. Together these symbols delineate the opportunity awaiting all of us today: our story—which is also each person's individual story.

Is this collective return an inevitability? Is fulfilment of the prophecy assured? These questions are related to the issue of whether or not Camelot failed, and whether or not my spiritual network failed. In the end the answer cannot be made on behalf of the whole. It can only be made individually. Have I followed through in the work of the quest, am I emerging as a point of authentic spiritual leadership for my world or not? It is really the same question and answer that Perceval has to understand and make real for himself in the story of the quest.

This is how the individual and collective stories become woven into one. The question as to how and whether the quest is finished and how the promise of the collective Grail can emerge is an individual choice. The work of "King Arthur," of Jesus, of my spiritual mentors and others who emerged around a similar time frame in the early years of the twentieth century have played their part. The sword has gone into the lake. The positive, healing current of truth is alive within the collective unconscious. The individual version of that sword, that truth, awaits us in the Grail Castle, just as it did Perceval, if we go on the quest and if we do the work of making that sword strong and authentic.

In the "Queste del Saint Graal" it is described how the Round Table was originally set up on the advice of Merlin—Merlin, who discerns the patterns of the future, the shape of things to come:

Afterwards the Round Table was set up on Merlin's advice, and its establishment was not without significance, for it was called the Round Table to signify the roundness of the world. And the situation of the planets and the elements in the firmament, and in the circumstances of the firmament can be seen the stars and many other things; so that one could say that the world is rightly signified by the Round Table.

The Round Table then symbolized not just Camelot or the united kingdom of Britain but the whole world, indeed the whole visible cosmos. The whole. The One place. In the same way, the Grail chalice comes to mean the collective chalice of our oneness, our connectedness (which is perceived or known directly in the heart). This is really the meaning of the apparent dissolution of the Fellowship of the Round Table: not failure but transition into a reality that includes the whole world.

The Round Table expands to become the whole world; the Grail chalice expands to become the consciousness of oneness. The forming of the collective chalice is how the quest is finished.

The opportunity is here; there are places at the table. But one has to do the work required to earn one's seat there. The path through to collective leadership is the quest. The ingredient that makes collective sovereignty work is true emotional and spiritual maturity, the reality of identity grounded in the deeper level of being. Nothing else will qualify us in the end to navigate the requirements of being "multiply situated selves" in a multifaceted and intensely interdependent world.

The expanded Round Table, the collective chalice of oneness, symbolizes the state that has been described as being "with one accord in one place." The one place is large—it is the planet, the cosmos. And the one accord is the oneness known in the heart both with our inner source and with one another. Then the power that "overflows" from this collective cup, the power of blessing, is available to water the wasteland. First it waters the parched places in human hearts, then it waters the land round about, and at last our great wound is healed, and we feel instead the waters of renewal, the waters of life.

12

DAUGHTER OF GOD

But in Dorothea's mind there was a current into which all thought and feeling were apt sooner or later to flow—the reaching forward of the whole consciousness towards the fullest truth, the least partial good. —George Eliot, *Middlemarch*

The heart is the instrument of the Father, the mind is the instrument of the Mother.
—Lloyd Meeker, "Cycles of Creative Forces"

THE CHALICE of collective sovereignty began to form, I believe, with the transformation in women's experience that has been termed the women's movement. Beginning in the mid–nineteenth century with the demand for voting rights, this feminist wave gained momentum throughout the twentieth century, building into the fight for equal rights, education, and equal opportunity and pay. By the latter part of the century this movement had developed and proliferated still further, with the feminist reevaluation of literature and history, the reimagining of mythology from a feminist point of view—including new findings about and interest in the importance of goddess worship— and the campaign for women to play the role of priest or minister. This great opening up of the feminine consciousness has been fundamental to the emergence of collective leadership. In fact, we could say that the women's movement was not only a crucial aspect of but a prerequisite to this new possibility. I have already shown how the feminist movement, predating by more than half a century the civil rights and youth movements, helped loosen the cogs in consciousness to give impetus and life to those other, allied reforming currents. But more than this, the women's movement was a prerequisite to the collective chalice because the feminine has an essential role to play in its collective dynamics.

As I mentioned in the previous chapter, in his analysis of the new complexity of societies in the global age, the philosopher Michael Sandel has described the need for "citizens who can abide the ambiguity associated with divided sovereignty, who can think and act as multiply situated selves." Who are better qualified and uniquely evolved to act as "multiply situated selves" than women? During the course of a century or more, women have been engaged in both an external political and an internal emotional struggle first to be integrated more fully into society and then to integrate their new roles within themselves. The campaign was fought on both fronts, as it were, because as the opportunities for women opened up and they found themselves able to play the roles not only of wife and mother but of career professional or artist, they have had to deal with the conflicting demands that the different roles inevitably bring. As women we are familiar with the role of the career woman who feels an emptiness if she finds it is too late to start a family; the role of the mother-at-home who feels smothered and frustrated as her life energy is poured into the repetitious routine of childcare and housekeeping; the role of the mother who has no choice but to go out to work and hand over her children to someone else when she would prefer to stay and look after them herself in their tender years.

The balancing act that this multiplicity of roles requires has led to some marvelous insights into the range of inner roles or essences that are part of women's makeup. One such "map" of our interior selves was developed by Jean Shinoda Bolen, a clinical professor of psychiatry, who in her book *Goddesses in Everywoman* uses the seven goddesses of the Greek pantheon to describe seven archetypes that play out in women. Bolen's work emerged directly out of her own attempts to resolve the conflict she felt in being both a psychiatrist and a mother. There are many "goddesses" in any individual woman, and the more complicated the woman the more likely it is that many are active within her and that what is fulfilling to one part of her may be meaningless to another. The goddess archetypes Bolen describes can enable us to accept and be at peace with the many different aspects and moods of ourselves, rather than trying to batten down and get rid of one side of us that seems to threaten the security of another side, or feeling confused and in conflict. Cycles of time also come into play, both long term and short term. Obviously a woman who has young children is wise to enjoy that time, to cultivate the quality of Demeter the mother goddess. Yet at the same time, she need not feel that Artemis, the independent, self-motivated campaigner/creator, or Aphrodite, the artist/lover, have to be completely banished. These different parts can stay alive within us, perhaps not center stage for the time being, without having to spoil our enjoyment of what is currently a dominant role. There are shorter cycles too. At times, for instance, I am completely content to float in the sea of home and children. To take care of all the little tasks: setting out cereal bowls, watering the flowers, picking up my daughter's coat, sharing a joke with my three-year-old. The ambience of family and home are enough—my children are divine beings, and we exist together in the magical world of my home, whose details I see and savor anew: the way the kettle shines on the stove, the ornamental plaque on the wall, the sun filling the window framed with plants and flowers. It's all as gauzy as those soft-focus, light-filled TV ads. Yet the next day, even the next hour, I am in another space altogether. Gone is the diffuse glow of Demeter, and instead the intensely focused beam of Artemis has been switched on as I concentrate my attention on finding the exact phrase in a newly forming poem. The three-year-old is asleep; the older daughter is playing outside. The world has changed completely; a different archetype has taken over.

There are other models or maps of our invisible sides too. There are what have been termed the four archetypes of sovereign, warrior, magician, and lover, as delineated by Robert Moore and Douglas Gillette in their book *King, Warrior, Magician, Lover* and developed by Cliff Barry and Mary Ellen Blandford in the four quarters of Shadow Work, in which the repressed energies of each archetype are explored and released. Here, too, different aspects of ourselves are in focus at different times, often depending on the role we are playing. When I am deep in the realms of thought, grappling with and birthing the invisible patterns of insight and ideas, I am the magician. My body is sitting at my desk, but I am primarily active at another level. A few hours later, I am more sovereign, when I convene my women's group and reach out to include and help create a sense of community. Or I might be accessing the warrior energy in setting up a workshop, assessing the costs, finding the right location, connecting with potential participants, following through on 101 administrative details. In the evening I connect with my body and with lover energy as I do yoga, make a meal, have a glass of wine, and, after the children are in bed, take a bath perfumed with essential oil of sandalwood. Like the "goddesses," one of these four archetypes might be more dominant at different times of our lives. Perhaps the sovereign is more dominant in later years and the magician when we are studying or apprenticing for a profession, and it may be that one of them is just naturally more dominant in one's essence.

One of the maps that can guide one through the invisible part of onself, then, is the realm of archetypes, but there are many other maps. A well-trained and intuitive astrologer, for instance, can outline, often with extraordinary accuracy, forces and tendencies that come to play in our lives. Or a psychic can place us within a whole new vocabulary of cosmology that will help explain some of the "knotted" areas of our lives. Then there are the different mythologies, some of which we are exploring in this book, that can help throw light on our interior architecture and processes.

So one of the results of the the opening up of the outer roles for women has been a kind of moving up into an awareness of more subtle or invisible roles and "maps" that then can help us to synthesize and be effective in the outer roles we play. But how to synthesize and manage the conflicting demands of these inner aspects of ourselves? And who in the end is looking at all this? My experience has been that the complexity of inner essence pushes me further up again—forces me to source identity, the core sense of myself, in a place that is still higher or more essential. In the end we find that none of these roles, archetypes, or patternings is who we are. Even though one or all of them seem to go some way toward defining us, ultimately the territory that we are is not fully captured in the maps. There is always a point beyond which the maps fail to find us. What we discover is that all these roles and patternings that I am calling maps are really just facets; facets of a gem; and inside that gem there is a light—a light that is refracted in a multitude of ways through the facets of ourselves. In other words, the roles or facets are not who we ultimately are but are the many ways through which who we are can be expressed. This is the inner light of our being which we are becoming aware of when we find ourselves in the Grail Castle.

There is a paradox here. Until the outer roles were opened up to women, their inner roles remained obscure and confusing. As the multiplicity of outer and therefore also inner roles and essences started to be understood and explored, so the sense of identity could in one sense move back away from the roles, or shift from the roles to the center— from the facets to the light. The roles helped reveal the essence. In this way, the feminine experience could be said to carry within it an inherent understanding of the interaction between the whole and its parts, or between the circle and the individuals who compose it. This includes an understanding that all the parts are necessary to give expression to the whole but no one part defines the whole, that the functioning of the whole is determined by the complexities of the interrelationship of its parts and by cycles of evolutionary change, and at the same time an awareness of the mystery that the whole is greater than the sum of its parts, and that the presence of the whole also conditions and affects the parts, or the individuals.

In chapter 9 I spoke about the way people's differences are allowed to show up more when an underlying sense of oneness and kinship is experienced. These differences, far from separating us, are found to be ways the oneness is differentiated.

This easy relationship between the whole and its parts and between one and another could all be described as the dynamics of the chalice— of collective leadership—in which direction no longer emerges from the "top" down but out of the center of the collective presence and out of the relationship between its parts. This is something akin to systems theory, or the dynamics of quantum theory, in which the universe takes shape according to cycles of energy and the interrelationship of particles and the particles are affected by their connections to the whole.

David Bohm suggested that not only the material universe but our very consciousness is linked in this way. Bohm's idea was to look at all matter, including consciousness, which he calls a subtle level of matter, as constantly unfolding from what he termed the implicate to the explicate order. In the unfolded, or explicate, order things might look separate in space and time, but in the implicate realm they are all connected, all one:

> In the nonmanifest order, all is one. You see, there is no separation in space and time. In ordinary matter, this is so and it's equally so or even more so for this subtle matter which is consciousness. Therefore, if we are separate it is because we are sticking largely to the manifest world as the basic reality, where the whole point of the manifest world is to *have* separate units. I mean relatively so anyway, separate but interacting and so on. Now, in nonmanifest reality it's all inter-penetrating, interconnected in one. So we say deep down the consciousness of man is one.

You may have to be a physicist to understand conceptually how to arrive at this conclusion, but you don't have to be a physicist to have the experience. The experience is known in the heart. The heart could be said to hold the feminine intelligence, which includes an understanding of the cosmic dance of oneness, which is also the dynamics of the era of the chalice. Women naturally have a feel for these dynamics because they hold the focus for the feminine, obviously, and because of the evolution in consciousness that they have so recently undertaken. The dynamics of the chalice are different from those of the sword, when matters had to be conceptually or mentally understood and when direction came from the leader and was repeated to or arbitrarily overlaid on the "followers," or when the universe was still perceived as being made up of separate parts, locally related, and mechanistic in its essential nature.

Bohm suggested that all humankind's problems stem from a way of thinking that is itself fragmented and not deeply aware of the essential web of oneness that is the reality at the quantum level. We could call this the wound of the separated consciousness. This habit of fragmented thought has gone on for literally ages and has caused a buildup of "pollution" in that shared consciousness.

> We could call that the corruption of mankind, that the brain and the consciousness and the deeper levels, not only in the manifest levels of the brain but also in the nonmanifest, that there has been left this pollution, which is this whole view which leads to all this violence, corruption, disorder, self-deception, which momentarily relieves pressures arising from this way of thinking, of being separate.

Out of his work as a physicist, Bohm evolved and initiated the idea of dialogue and dialogue groups as a way of helping to expose and erase this pollution and access the deeper consciousness of oneness.

Bohm's idea was that if a group of people can stay together or meet regularly for long enough to "dialogue" together, that is, talk together without an agenda or overheavy leadership, these patterns of flawed thought begin to be exposed and new meanings take their place—and ultimately a "one-mindedness."

So the process of dialogue in a grouping of people, if allowed to go deep enough, can permit someone to come into the presence of the collective king or oneness and get in touch with his or her own pollution. The group presence plays the role of King Arthur in catalyzing a process of clarification—the exposure and suspension of fixed positions and their attendant emotions (which arise from childhood experiences/deep pollution, etc). This can then go on to free up consciousness back to a sense of its own unpolluted source. Of course, such a scenario is still dependent, at least in its opening stages, on a leader/facilitator figure to hold a safe place and to help keep the process moving and "unhook" people gracefully from their reactions. However, ultimately the leader becomes simply another peer in the circle.

The possibility of initiation by the group or collective rather than one person is also borne out by my experience of spiritual community. The "classic" pattern, and one that my own experience followed, was that one individual or maybe one or two would play the role of King Arthur, blessing and healing at first and then catalyzing the quest of purification and the ultimate return to the round table as a whole and mature peer. However, as time went on, this pattern changed for those who were newer to things. There were many for whom no one person represented Arthur but for whom the community itself, the circle of many people, provided the blessing and catalyst of the king. Different individuals in the grouping would provide blessing and acceptance; other experiences would catalyze the deeper work of self-transfiguration. Here was the reality of collective sovereignty at work, just as potently as in an individual figurehead.

If the process of dialogue is allowed to build and go deep enough, the condition of "one-mindedness" starts to be experienced by the individuals in the group. Bohm again: "People are no longer primarily in opposition, nor can they be said to be interacting; rather, they are participating in this pool of common meaning which is capable of constant development and change." William Isaacs, who has developed the art of dialogue within a wide range of corporate and institutional contexts, calls this the fourth phase of dialogue. He describes it as a space in which the people in the group experience a new level of alignment and connection among themselves: "when someone speaks from this experience, their words have a thunder behind them that is greater than if they were simply speaking on their own or for themselves." In my own experience in dialogue group and other gatherings, not only does the sense of this one-mindedness "add thunder" to my words but also it conditions what I think and what I say, in the sense of modifying or refining it, making it more accurate, more whole, less partial. One of the ways that my spiritual network has reordered itself is by having twice-yearly gatherings of about 60 or so people. The collective presence that is convened in this way is extremely potent, and there is a clear sensing that what is formed is larger than the sum of its parts. The circle or the Grail itself will not only help my own thought fill out but will hone and align my own expression. It is as if an aperture is formed, a transparency, and ultimately one is listening for what comes out of that transparency, what is to emerge from it, via oneself and the contributions of others. At the same time, the whole is affected and created by the interaction of the individuals who form it. As we interact within the circle, or one-on-one, it is as if we are completing, filling out, the expression of the whole. Leadership is still needed in this context: to convene the circle, hold an overview, and, at first anyway, to "activate" the container or circle by offering initiatory direction. To the extent, however, that there is an attempt to dominate, censor, or overstructure what emerges, this feels like a discordant note. In other words, once the collective process is underway, the role of leadership is more to receive and guide than direct.

The reality of the way this all happens is not some wonderful, immaculate process. It is or can be quite messy and quite confusing, because no one individual has emerged into a complete and flawless expression yet of himself or herself. As I have already mentioned, the individual work of centering in the inner realm or in the Grail King energy is ongoing. Something fundamental may have shifted in our minds and hearts; nevertheless, we do not transform overnight into perfect beings with all our ego wounds and blind spots suddenly erased. We have to learn the subtle art of bringing our perspective and "piece" without an underlying Wounded Fisher King demand that the collective Grail of the group presence serve our particular agenda.

If we look again at the great arc of the women's movement, we could say that what started with the demand for women to be allowed the same opportunities and value in society as men culminated in the great flooding into awareness of the need for the feminine to be understood as a part of God. Phrases like "the rise of the feminine" or the "return of the Goddess" are ways of articulating not only the social ascent of women but the emergence or reemergence of an awareness that deity must have a feminine, and not an exclusively masculine, face.

This issue, while in some ways the last to emerge, nevertheless seems to me to be the most crucial and fundamental concern of the whole feminist emergence.

So why were God and "his" affairs deemed to be mainly if not exclusively masculine?

God is always referred to as "he" in the ancient texts of the Bible that have been the source of both the Jewish and Christian religious traditions. In his book *The Hebrew Goddess* Raphael Patai points out that it was a linguistic factor only that caused God to be referred to as a masculine deity:

> Yet one factor, a linguistic one, defied all theological repugnance to the attribution of bodily qualities to God. It is in the nature of the Hebrew language that every noun has either the masculine or the feminine gender (except a very few which can take either). The two Biblical names of God, *Yahweh* (pronounced, out of reverence for its great holiness, as "Adonai" and usually translated as "the Lord") and *Elohim* (or briefly *El,* translated as "God") are masculine. When a pronoun is used to refer to God, it is the masculine "He"; when a verb describes that He did something or when an adjective qualified Him, they appear in the masculine form (in Hebrew there are male and female forms for verbs and adjectives). Thus, every verbal statement about God conveyed the idea that He was masculine.

This is very helpful and revealing information, yet a mere linguistical throw of the dice does not seem to be sufficient reason to explain the almost complete absence of the feminine from the spiritual stage. And it seems even less likely to be the full explanation when we read the description of the creation of man that is found in the very first chapter of Genesis:

> And God said, Let us make man in our image, after our likeness, and let *them* have dominion over the fish in the sea and over the fowl of the Earth and over the cattle and over all the Earth and over every creeping thing that creepeth upon the Earth. So God created man in his own image, in the image of God created he him; male and female created he them. (Genesis 1:26)

Given that in the English language the pronouns that refer to living, sentient beings are either male or female (while the genderless pronoun *it* usually designates either an animal an inanimate object or has a pejorative connotation if used about a person—or deity), so that God, when not plural, in this passage ("our") is referred to once more by "his" and "he" and "him"—what we have here is as clear a statement as it is possible to have that God is *both* male and female. How otherwise would "man" (meaning humankind, male and female) be created "male and female" in God's image and after God's likeness? If humankind is created in God's image and after "his" likeness, and humankind is male and female, then it stands to reason that God is also male and female.

Clearly God is and has always been male and female; and the representation or extension of God in the form of humankind, man and woman, made in God's image, has always been and is also male and female. What then happened to the feminine representation of God, and that aspect of divinity that "she" represents? Why was it that the long line of patriarchs and prophets—who represented God in a specific way—were all men? Why were women, until relatively recently, marginalized in Western culture and why are they still overtly suppressed in certain other cultures?

If we go back to the first chapter of Genesis, man, male and female, is created; in the second chapter man is created again "of the dust of the ground." This man is called Adam, and Eve is formed out of his rib. First man is formed in God's image, male and female, and then Adam is formed of the dust of the ground and Eve from his rib. We could say that the first creation of man, male and female, was the spirit aspect, and the second creation, of Adam and Eve, was the form aspect—the "dust of the ground." Spirit and then form.

This inner and outer doubling up of the masculine and feminine aspects of God is embodied in one of God's names: YHWH. This name is regarded in the Kabbala as an abbreviated symbol of the divine tetrad or family of God, namely Father, Mother, Son, Daughter. They are also seen as symbolizing four divine elements—wisdom, understanding, beauty, and kingship—that characterize and form the deity. Wisdom correlates with the Father and understanding with the Mother, and—perhaps surprisingly—beauty correlates with the Son and kingship with the Daughter. In this Kabbalistic symbolism, then, the male and female nature of God is once again underscored. God is first Father and Mother and then Son and Daughter. YH is itself a short form of the name of God, so *God* repeated is the full name: YHWH. This correlates with the way YHWH is sometimes translated: I AM THAT I AM. A repetition of identity but at a different level.

If we write it this way:

Y	H	I	AM
		THAT	
W	H	I	AM

we could say that Father and Mother, YH, the first I AM, parallel the first chapter of Genesis, as the origin and spirit; and then the Son and Daughter, WH, the second I AM, parallel the second chapter, emerging into form—Adam and Eve in the garden. In the inner realm, the realm of spirit, the two aspects of God are Father and Mother; in the outer realm, at the level of form, the two aspects of God are Son and Daughter. The fourth aspect of God—the fourth aspect of consciousness—is the Daughter of God. So the female representative of God in the outer realm of form, using this symbolism from the Kabbala, correlates with the Daughter and with kingship.

So another way to phrase our inquiry about the absence of the feminine representation of God, is to say: What happened to the Daughter of God? Interestingly, this question also leads us to ask—because the fourth aspect of God represents kingship as well—what happened to the kingdom of God?

To return for a moment to the symbolism of the Arthur and Grail myths—at the beginning of Arthur's reign, the sword was taken out of the stone; and at the end, it was thrown into water—into the lake. The sword is a symbol of the truth: something fixed, unbending, the absolute principle of life's blueprint. The sword is the symbol of the masculine principle. Water is also a symbol of truth: eternally fluid, renewing, nourishing, always different, always the same. The water is a symbol of the feminine.

The sword is the symbol of the conscious mind and conscious alignment with divinity. The water symbolizes the subconscious mind and memory, the purified cistern of sparkling waters. So here are two symbols of the truth—let us name them Son and Mother. In the spelling of the name of God "YHWH" they are next to each other—the first *H* and the *W.* The Son, the third aspect of the name of God, has this beautiful relationship of truth with Mother, the second aspect of the name of God. Like the water and the sword—both symbols of truth— they are completely different and exactly the same.

When Sir Bedivere hurls Excalibur out over the waters of the lake, it is a woman's hand that reaches up to take it. The sword of power, of conscious understanding of the truth, is returned to the Mother for safekeeping. That is where the sword belongs—in the subconscious realm—because Mother and Son, subconscious and conscious, share the same nature.

The Mother, the second face of God, correlates with the subconscious realm, or the water; the Son, the third aspect, correlates with the conscious mind, or the sword. We can begin to see here that our own consciousness is patterned after the name of God—this makes sense after all, if we are fashioned in the image and likeness of God, doesn't it?

So what about the Father and the Daughter? Here is a passage from the Zohar, or "Book of Splendor," written circa 1286 by Moses de Leon but attributed by him to Shimeon ben Yohai, a second-century Palestinian teacher and mystic:

> Wisdom spread out and brought forth Understanding, and they were found to be male and female, Wisdom the Father, and Understanding the Mother. . . . Then these two united, and lighted up each other, and the H [i.e. the Mother] conceived and gave birth to a Son. Through the birth of the Son the Father and the Mother found their perfection, and this led to the *completion* of everything, the *inclusion* of everything: Father, Mother, Son and Daughter. (My italics.)

In other words, the Daughter completes the manifestation of God. She represents the completion of the work of manifestation that the Father initiated. This is why Daughter is associated with kingship: she represents the *kingdom* of God.

Referring back once more to the Grail myth, consider Perceval's first visit to the Grail Castle and the symbolism of that banqueting hall and the two inner rooms. In a sense what we have here is the anatomy of our consciousness laid out, and we can diagram it as the vesica:

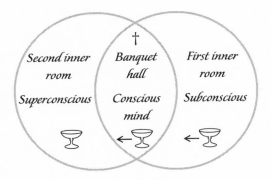

Here the vesica shape is the conscious mind illuminated by epiphany, the banqueting hall filled with light. The first inner room from out of which the Grail and other objects emerge is the realm of the subconscious, the waters of the deep, and the place where Merlin resides. The sword is brought into the banqueting hall, into the conscious mind, and stays there—it belongs there because it is a symbol of the conscious mind. But the Grail traverses the whole range of consciousness—from the subconscious, through the conscious, and into the superconscious, the realm of spirit where the Grail King lives. The Grail represents the heart, and the heart interpenetrates all the levels of our being. The vesica piscis symbol as a whole, as I have already discussed, is a symbol itself of the Grail and therefore of the heart. If we remember, it has also been described as the vulva of the Mother Goddess. A fascinating insight here is that the physical organ of the human heart itself has been described as looking not really like the traditional heart shape at all but much more like the vulva. There are sexual implications here of course, which I will explore further in the last chapter, but for now the significance of the human heart actually looking like the vulva/vesica piscis is that the whole thing, the whole design of consciousness, is also somehow the heart. Or, to put it another way, when we have the heart/vesica activated or healed, we have the physical whole—the kingdom!

The Grail is kept in the Grail Castle, and strangely enough, although the Grail King has lived for many years in his inner room, the Grail Castle is the home of the Wounded Fisher King. In fact, this king is guardian of the Grail. So the heart has been in the keep of the wound. Our house of being has been dominated by, and our hearts have been held hostage by, the wound of separation from spiritual source, even though that source is always present. When Perceval fails to ask about the Grail, he demonstrates the fact that he does not yet understand the meaning of his epiphany, which is the need to consciously orient in the inner spiritual source of one's being, symbolized by the Grail King. We go on the inner work of the quest, enlisting the understanding of the—properly aligned—conscious mind (or sword) in order to heal the heart from its wound of separation so that it is once again open to the spiritual source of ourselves. After all, where else is pain and fear felt but in the heart?

The Grail chalice is carried by a maiden out of one inner room of the Grail Castle and into another. Inside that second inner room lives the Grail King, who symbolizes for us God the Father. Moreover, the myth tells us, the Grail King is *served* by the Grail: it is what sustains him.

Once again many meanings overlap here. I have already considered one of them: the idea of reversed polarity addressed by the question: Whom does the Grail serve? The Grail as cornucopia spilling out the fruit of creation symbolizes creation and its fruits, which are there to serve God, or serve a consciousness that is aligned with a presence larger than its own ego. The "Grail wound" is when we try to get satisfaction from the material realm without an understanding of our deeper source of identity.

Now we have emerging a more literal meaning. The heart that is pure and open to God, or to a deeper sourcing of identity, "feeds" that source (with the refined wafer from the cup)—enriches it and *gives it body*. This body or container for the love of God makes it possible for that spiritual current to then flood into the world and change it from a wasteland into a garden—the cup that "runneth over." The heart/Grail is the body of God, the kingdom—the Daughter.

In chapter 9 I said that the silence, the absence of women, was deep down a function not of them as victims but of the wound itself. The missing Daughter, the silence of women, and their exclusion from the

realm of the sacred are reflections of the wounded heart. The heart—
which gives body to the Father, to the masculine aspect of God, and at
the same time represents the feminine aspect of God at the outer
level—was wounded. This is why Perceval and we have to go on a quest
for it! Until the heart/Grail is found, the name of God cannot be
spelled in its entirety; therefore, the presence of God, the kingdom of
God, cannot be completed.

We remember that the shape of the chalice

equates with the diagram depicting the seven dimensions of being.

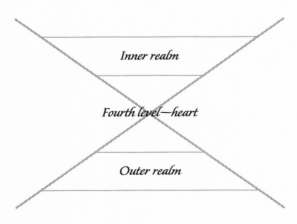

The fourth level is the heart, which, when purified, connects inner and outer. The seven candlesticks of Revelation give us a parallel symbolism.

"And in the midst of the seven candlesticks one like unto the Son of man" (Revelation 1:13). In other words, the Christ consciousness, the consciousness that is one with God, is symbolized by the fourth candlestick, the connecting level between the three inner and the three outer. Then there are the seven days of Creation in the opening chapters of Genesis; and on the fourth day the lights in the firmament appeared, and so here we have fire, the fire of love, that is known in the heart, associated with the fourth. All these fours—the fourth level of being, the fourth candlestick, the fourth day of Creation, and the fourth letter in the name of God—correlate with Daughter and heart, with the aspect of being that leads to oneness with the source of being, the Father. Completion.

Here we have, then, the completion of the name of God as patterned in our consciousness: the Father is the fire of love, the superconscious, and is symbolized in the myths by the Grail King; and the Daughter is the heart that is the container of that fire. Mother and Son have a special relationship to do with truth/water; Father and Daughter have a special relationship to do with love/fire. At the same time, the Son, the masculine, represents the Father at the level of consciousness, and the Daughter represents the Mother at the conscious level. This would mean that wisdom is present in the conscious mind and understanding is present in the heart. Another way of understanding this is to say that when the spirit of King Arthur is represented by the individual, or when the individual sword has been accessed, the magical powers of the subconscious mind, or of Merlin, are freed up from the crystal cave and are once more available. Wherever there is Arthur, there is Merlin. Wherever there is wisdom, there is understanding.

So we have:

Y	Father	Wisdom	Love/fire	Superconscious	Sovereign
H	Mother	Understanding	Truth/water	Subconscious	Magician
W	Son	Beauty	Sword/air	Conscious mind	Warrior
H	Daughter	Kingship	Chalice/earth	Heart/intuition	Lover

If we draw a square and place on it the names Father, Mother, Son, Daughter, and their correlations in our consciousness, as in the illustration, we have a simple diagram of the divine tetrad laid out, with the Son representing Father at the level of form or consciousness and the Daughter representing Mother (the repetition of the *H*) at the level of form or consciousness. If we next draw a diagonal line from Son to Mother, representing their special relationship of truth, and another diagonal from Daughter to Father representing their special relationship of love, as in the illustration, we have the design of the seven levels again, and also if we picture it in three dimensions, we have the pyramid—four sides of three—yet another symbolic portrayal of completion.

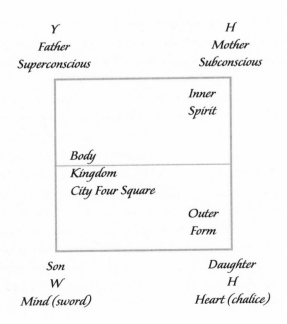

Y
Father
Superconscious

H
Mother
Subconscious

Inner
Spirit

Body
Kingdom
City Four Square

Outer
Form

Son
W
Mind (sword)

Daughter
H
Heart (chalice)

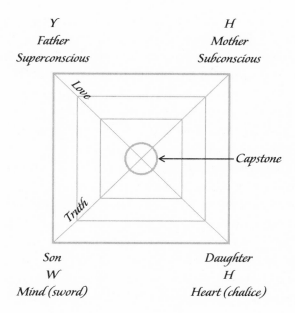

The pyramid of course is yet another enormously rich symbol. The Great Pyramid in Gizeh has its capstone missing. This missing capstone might correlate with the fourth level, the heart level, which brings union. This missing capstone is what we need to get back in ourselves.

Why was Arthur so important? He united the kingdom. The kingdom of Britain was brought into oneness for the first time under him because he represented the capstone, the capstone of understanding that had its open connection to God. Here is this heart consciousness, the connecting level, the middle candlestick—whatever symbol we choose— all relating to the capstone of understanding, the all-encompassing love that understands and so is able to heal the factions of ourselves—or of the larger world or kingdom.

This capstone consciousness, the Daughter consciousness, is not the domain of women alone, but women know more acutely than most men that the many parts of us can only be unified by locating consciousness in this invisible capstone place. If I lose my sense of what I'm calling the capstone, I become a mess. I don't know if I'm a mother, wife, writer, housekeeper, or harrassed, cross person. I don't know whether I should be gardening or working on a new poem; I don't know whether I should be living in America or in England—all these factions, all these parts of me, go into disarray. When the capstone is present, they all fit together. In fact they are needed to allow all the different aspects of my expression. In this sense the reality of spiritual identity is not an option but a sheer necessity if I am going to survive or live with any grace and sense of fulfilment.

When the heart is healed and open to the inner source of being, the name of God is completed in ourselves, and, as this work is undertaken by increasing numbers of people, so the name of God begins to be spelled out collectively too. Our consciousness is patterned after the name of God—after the consciousness of divinity. We actually are made in the image and likeness of God, just as it says in the first chapter of Genesis, and we are supposed to be God at this level of creation. Sometimes when terrible acts are committed by people—the atrocities of genocide, war, or terrorism—we ponder as to why or how God could allow them to happen. This to me is like standing in front of a mirror with our eyes closed, and wondering where we are. If we care to open our eyes and stare into the reflection, we are gazing in fact on the face of God, on the mechanism that is designed to bring the expression of the divine right here on Planet Earth, which is how the wasteland—in all its many aspects—will be healed.

The momentous significance of our times is that thanks to the opening up of the feminine consciousness and experience, and the spiritual revolution that developed out of the youth movements, the element that completes this collective body of God, that most precious object—the Grail—has been and is being found by increasing numbers of people. For not only have women needed to understand divinity in terms of the feminine, of Mother God, but deity itself has needed the feminine, specifically the aspect of the heart symbolized by the Daughter, in order to be fully manifested. The Daughter of God, the fourth face of God, the healed heart realm is once more operational, and because it is, the collective Grail can begin to form. The process of forming this collective Grail is far from complete, but it is under way. The forming of the Grail is not the creation of some huge unwieldy organization; the circle of the collective chalice forms whenever or wherever there exists a sense of oneness and inclusiveness. This could be in the thousands of women's groups that have formed spontaneously all over the world, or in church communities, or in grassroots networks of all kinds. Any circle that is drawn together on the basis of the conscious-ness of oneness is part of the one circle of the Grail. This is very different of course from banding together on the basis of a cultic consciousness that shores up the individual ego by making it feel that it belongs to a group that is supreme or special, a mentality that in its more extreme forms becomes bigoted or racist. In times of war or conflict, too, people will be drawn together because they are all against someone else. But this is not real oneness; this is a temporary coming together because of a common enemy. The sense of unity soon breaks down when the conflict is over or the situation changes in other unforeseen ways. The hallmark of the Grail circle of oneness is that it cannot be used for pur-poses that violate its nature.

The answer to the question is the same, whether it is the collective or individual heart in question. The collective Grail serves and sustains the purposes and presence of the Grail King. It cannot be used for any-thing other than the purposes of love, because it is neither controlled nor called into being by any one person or any one group's agenda. The consciousness of oneness can neither violate nor be violated.

13

THE DANCE

*'The Woman in me kneels and weeps in tender rapture;
the Man in me rushes forth but only to be baffled. Yet
the time will come when, from the union of this tragic
king and queeen, shall be born a radiant sovereign self.'*
—MARGARET FULLER

*Out of the arc of meeting—
hands paired in prayer—
out of the spun tension
of opposites—
the drawn bow readied
with its arrow—
and from the parted lips
comes
the spell of making
love.*
—DIANA DURHAM, "THE ARC"

SOME YEARS AGO the BBC made a sumptuous, six-part dramatization of Jane Austen's most beloved novel, *Pride and Prejudice.* Having grown up on Jane Austen's writing, it was something of a shock and at the same time a delight to take in the translation of a few brief paragraphs of descriptive prose into a full-blown colored moving picture, detailed and textured, of the houses, the parlors, the ballrooms, the gowns, the uniforms and—what struck me most of all—the no-holds-barred recreation of the dances.

These dances were very formal; they were made up of a series of couples dancing with one another and in interchange, forming together a collective patterning of couples. It was almost the only time that men and women who were not married to one another could touch at all, and then it was only a hand held or an arm taken; and it was also one of the few times an unmarried man and woman could talk together in relative isolation.

If a man was attracted to a woman—or to her fortune—or wished to "press his suit" (meaning in this context wooing, not ironing his clothes!) then asking her to reserve a dance or, better still, more than one dance, for him could be an opening or a following move in a courtship ritual. The dance only happens as a man and a woman come together to dance it. They never dance alone.

Pride and Prejudice is of course a love story between the principal character Elizabeth Bennett and the aloof and handsome Darcy. These two characters are drawn together by social chance but kept apart by their individual myopias: Darcy's pride and Elizabeth's prejudice. At one juncture Darcy pays Elizabeth a huge compliment by singling her out to dance. She unwillingly agrees and their conversation during the dance is an illustration of how great the buildup of misunderstanding already is between them. So they are dancing outwardly, but not yet dancing in an inner sense. The plot's unfoldment creates a gradual change in both, to the point where they are able to join in the permanent dance of marriage.

In both the dances and the plot of *Pride and Prejudice* I see a kind of allegory about the way the two aspects of God—male and female, mind and heart—function and change in and through us. In fact I have sometimes thought that the best way to understand the dynamics of God is to think of them in terms of a love story. Or even, to turn that thought back around, that love stories are really about the way we function as the two poles of God.

Although long hailed as a literary classic, *Pride and Prejudice* is in some respects just a few steps away from a fairy story in which Darcy, the impossibly handsome, rich, and well-bred "prince" is won by the true-heartedness of the lowly-born maiden, who turns out in the end to be a princess because of her sensibility. These fairy stories in which the lovers are brought together against almost impossible or unlikely odds to live "happily ever after" are myths that foretell the way the union between the poles of God can only be achieved after the lost princess is found.

I have looked at how, historically, women were, in some kind of literal way, not present or at least not integrated into the workings of society. They were consigned to the "inner" realm of family and child rearing and denied voting rights and just about every other "right" to participate in the "outer" worlds of politics and the professions. At the same time, God was thought of always as God the Father, as *him*, as male. The role of the priest or minister could only be conferred on men, like all the other power roles in society. And particularly in the Catholic religion, nothing of the domain of God was to do with women. Not only were priests to be men, they were to be celibate, as if sex itself—as if women themselves and their bodies—were outside the circle of the sacred. To this day, if a woman seeks to enter Saint Paul's cathedral in Rome, she will be turned away if her shoulders or head are uncovered. So women were not part of the workings of the world outside the domestic scene; and they were not able to function within the domain of the sacred, because God was considered to be only male, and therefore how could this *he* be represented by a *she*?

We can think about these strange biases that existed for so long within rational and "progressive" society, and that still persist in some ways today, as evidences of the missing Daughter, the wounded heart realm. The Daughter was not present to represent the Mother, we could say. Interestingly, she was also not present to hold the presence of the Father, because both man and woman embody the essences of the divine, male and female, in different and complementary ways, and if one aspect is not functioning or is not present, then that embodiment cannot happen in a full way, and only certain limited dimensions of the inner powers are available.

Therefore, women, the feminine face of God, have not until relatively recently, at least in a certain way, been present. At the same time, the heart realm—in everyone, men and women—has been wounded and not functioning properly.

One of the most significant implications of what I have been terming the return of the Daughter, of the fourth aspect of God, is that the union of the poles of God that so many fairy stories encode is now possible. The fairy tale can become a reality. And what we might call the love affair of God, or the love affair between the poles of God, Son and Daughter, can be first healed—because there has been literal heartbreak here—and then consummated in a full way.

At first, Darcy and Elizabeth are "poles apart," in both social standing and understanding of one another. Slowly the two poles are brought together by the attractive and compelling force of love. This force is set spinning between them, catalyzing repulsion as well as attraction, and eventually brings about not only their union but also works the changes in each that are required for them to be able to unite. In this way, the plot can serve as a metaphor for the process of healing and renewing the dance between the poles of God that we find ourselves involved in at an individual, one-to-one, and collective level.

In chapter 6 I used the symbols of sword and cup to explore the way the work of the quest brings about a healing partnership between mind and heart. The brittleness of the sword is slowly reforged into potency as the cup of union is "found"; but equally, the cup cannot be found without the help of the sword. The two help each other. The two are made whole together.

I believe that as this process of healing—being made whole—gathers momentum within the individual, a parallel process of cohealing can start to work out between men and women and beyond that rung again, between the poles of God as they manifest in the way we function collectively.

In the first chapter of this book, I looked at the requirement to essentially reverse one's "polarity" so that we become "negative" to God, or to the "positive" current of radiance from the Grail King within, instead of being "negative" to the world around one and to one's own emotional reactions. This work of reversing polarity is the essential work of the quest. As we achieve this reversal, we become aligned with the radiant energy within and therefore become ourselves "positive" to our worlds—which means we are in position to offer blessing: "I was blessed, and could bless." In this way we have become the outer representative of the inner king. If we are "negative" to the outer world, we immediately become "positive" to God or the inner flow. Two positives repel, so we experience separation from that inner flow.

This kind of magical electrical analogy comes into play when we speak about how the poles of God configure in mind and heart and male and female. In both arenas we experience either a flow or "polarization"—depending on whether we are dancing or reacting. At first Elizabeth is attracted to Darcy because of his good looks; however, he declines the opportunity to dance with her because he does not consider her handsome enough to warrant his attention. His putdown of her causes her to react in disgust at his arrogance. After that, she becomes as disdainful of him as he was of her, and she remains unaware of his growing attraction to her.

To begin with, Darcy could be said to represent the false positive, the brittle sword full of ideas about its superiority but lacking the true potency of love. Darcy's attitude makes him unable at first to recognize the qualities of Elizabeth. Eventually as the story proceeds, his pride turns to humility and his real character comes out—the mended sword, the true gentleman. As this happens, Elizabeth finds herself falling in love in her turn—becoming "negative" to him—and having to let go of her own prejudices and reactions. Both come to know themselves better as a result of knowing one another. The true positive and the true negative can join together and of course live happily ever after.

Darcy's mind said one thing, his heart said another. His mind said: this woman is my social inferior and her family have appalling manners and I cannot possibly marry her. His heart said: I love her. In the end, his heart overcame his mind. Or, more accurately, the quality of love and character was shown to be of greater import than social traditions and expectations.

Inner conflict is what one knows when one's heart is saying one thing and one's mind another. If one holds an intention in one's mind but finds that one's "heart isn't in it," the intention probably won't become a reality, or if it does it will be a "halfhearted" pale excuse of a reality, a kind of sop to make the mind feel okay. Sometimes, though, we know in our minds that something is wrong even though in our hearts we want to do it. This could be as trivial as wanting another helping of dessert; we want it, but our mind knows it will put on weight, give us indigestion, cost more (if eating out) or leave less for others (if at home). Mind and heart can interact in both a true and a false—reactive—way, just as men and women can. There is a big difference between love winning out and passing emotional desire controlling us; just as there is a big difference between the censorship of our emotions by mental ideas of what is right and wrong and the proper control of our actions through discernment and a sense of responsibility for the overall context.

The poles of God have more often than not been "polarized" in conflict rather than engaged in an interplay. We see and experience this most commonly and clearly in ourselves and in the area of male/female relationships. However, we know that conflict exists at the collective level as well—between nations, groupings, races, and so on. So we might suspect something of the same dynamics are playing out there as well, whether that be the way a local residents' group interacts with a city council or the way whole nations or cultures interact and view one another, such as Iraq and the United States, or the Muslim world and Western secular society.

When we turn to the stories of King Arthur and the Round Table we find that virtually none of the passionate love tales swirling around the court end happily. I have already explored somewhat the meaning of the most famous of all these love stories, that between Lancelot and Guinevere, but there are many other implications to that tale, not least of which is the trail of broken hearts left by Lancelot's single-minded devotion to his queen. One "fair damosel"—among many—that Lancelot meets points this out to him:

> "But it is noised that ye love Queen Guenivere, that she hath ordained by enchantment that ye shall never love any other but her, and that no other damosel or lady shall ever rejoice you. Wherefore many in this land, of high estate and low, make great sorrow."

The two most notable among the broken-hearted both have (coincidentally?) the same name. The first Elaine is saved by Lancelot from a painful enchantment. Knowing she is to conceive Galahad with Lancelot, this Elaine tricks him into sleeping with her with the aid of a powerful enchantress, Dame Brysen, who convinces Lancelot that Elaine is in fact Guinevere. However, when he realizes his mistake, Lancelot is adamant that he cannot marry or love Elaine, who in turn spurns her admirer Sir Bromel, saying that her "love is set upon the best knight in the world."

The second lady's name is spelled *Elayne,* and she is also known more famously as the Fair Maid of Astolat. Elayne nurses Lancelot after he has been wounded, and she falls so deeply in love with him that she begs him to: "have mercy upon me and suffer me not to die for your love." Lancelot once again is unbending and will neither marry her or become her paramour as she asks, with the result that Elayne wastes away and dies. Her last request is to be placed in a barge covered in black samite, with a letter explaining what happened to her placed in one hand. And King Arthur and Guinevere witness this black barge floating past their window on the Thames.

The Fair Maid of Astolat was not the only woman to die of unrequited love for Lancelot. There was also Hellawes the Sorceress, who, knowing that she could never have him as her lover alive, had planned to kill Lancelot and keep his embalmed body to embrace and kiss. When her plans were foiled and Lancelot left her, she "made such sorrow that she died within a fortnight."

Morgana also loves Lancelot, and her jealousy of Guinevere makes the two enemies, further alienating Morgana from Camelot.

Then there is the long saga of the love affair between Tristram and Iseult, who is so beautiful that Arthur himself almost loses his head over her. Other knights also love Iseult, and she is married to the evil King Mark of Cornwall, so one way and another much anguish is experienced by various characters as the tale of the lovers' many unions and enforced separations untangles itself. Ultimately, of all the love stories, this one ends relatively happily, with the couple going off to live together in the Castle of Joyous Guard.

Various minor subplots of lovers who are betrayed or killed also weave themselves into the tapestry of the tales. One damosel, for instance, coming across the body of her lover Lanceor, dead at the hands of Balyn, runs herself through with Lanceor's own sword.

I have looked at the fact that at one level there is something true in the love between Guinevere and Lancelot. Arthur wished not to hear about it because, even though he suspected their love, he loved them both and was indebted to both. It was the hatred and envy of Mordred and Agravaine that finally exposed their love in such a way as to force a split between Arthur and Lancelot—a split that didn't really exist at a heart level. If we try to look at these stories through a moral lens (as Malory at times does himself) we will fail to understand their meaning. When Lancelot is called by Arthur and Guinevere to give an explanation of the death of the Fair Maid of Astolat, he says: "For, madame, I like not to be constrained by love; love must arise only from the heart and not by an constraint." To which Arthur replies: "'That is truth,' said the king. 'And for many a knight love is free in itself and will not be bound; where it is bound, it loses itself.'" Here is a beautiful recognition that the shape and design of love between people cannot be bound or fixed into arbitrary shapes, whether they be the moral shapes of Christianity, the customs of courtly love, or the individual's personal desires. Love has its own designs, and there has always been an uneasy relationship between those designs and the expectations and structures of human society.

Nevertheless, despite all this understanding, and despite the unwavering loyalty of Lancelot to Guinevere, neither of them are free in their love. Guinevere becomes increasingly irrational and demanding toward Lancelot. She drives him away by her jealous rage and accusations that he is unfaithful to her, causing him great anguish. Even though they love one another, somehow they never experience the oneness of their love; they never rest in the knowledge of their communion.

In Malory's "Morte D'Arthur" Lancelot is depicted as ultimately failing on the quest for the Grail, even though he is the best knight in the world. Drawing near to a chamber within the Castle of Corbenic (the Grail Castle of this version of the story) he can sense that the Grail is within, but as the door opens a voice warns him not to enter. Sadly, he draws back. Inside he can see a silver table with the holy vessel on it, but the Grail chalice is covered in red samite, and Lancelot is unable to view it directly without its covering. When he does enter, he is assailed by what feels like a breath of fire, and he falls into a swoon that lasts 24 days and nights.

The reason for Lancelot's partial success in finding the Grail is, as we are told over and over again, his "sin" of loving Guinevere. Beneath this rather heavy-handed Christian moralizing there can be discerned a spiritual truth. It is possible to fail in achieving one's direct sense of connection to spiritual source, and the reason for such failure, a failure to complete the quest, is always because some "pull," or addiction, cannot be let go of. So that instead of being controlled by the power of love, by the radiant outflowing presence of the Grail King, we are controlled by something else: a career, money—and perhaps strongest of all the pulls—a relationship. Underneath what we are really controlled by is fear—fear of loss of any of these three primary areas. And it is also the case that if the Grail union is not achieved, if we do not go all the way through and start to know our core reality, not just the theory of it, then the love affairs and relationships we have will not ultimately either stabilize or stay alive.

How many of us have ruined love when it appeared between us because we did not have the spiritual anchoring to trust in the process of that love's unfoldment and to hold the intensity of what we felt? How many times has love been lost because of fear, jealousies, doubts—mostly, or at least initially, groundless? It is as if love is too great a power to be contained in us and between us if that first centering in spirit is not in place, if we have not learned the reality of what it means to obey the first commandment, which is the work of finding the Grail.

So far in this book I have looked at the meaning of finding the Grail both individually and collectively. The collective Grail—the circle of oneness and emergent condition of collective leadership—puts in an appearance to the degree that we as individuals come to know union with the inner radiant spiritual source of ourselves. We experience that sense of connection with inner source and with one another in the heart. The heart opened in this way becomes the place of connection between the inner and outer realms and the means by which the currents of love and blessing flow out to replenish the wasteland.

The symbol of the vesica piscis is another symbol for the Grail, particularly in its sense of the connecting medium between inner and outer. The vesica piscis shape is formed by two equal circles, the circumference of each intersecting the center of each. As well as the many other ways this magical symbol can be read, we can also interpret it more simply as a beautiful image of a balanced relationship between two people. Each is whole in his or her own right—the circles are of equal size—but their union, created by the outer edge of each penetrating to the center of the other, creates something else again.

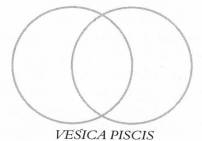

VESICA PISCIS

Thinking about the symbol this way, we see that the Grail is also formed by the union of man and woman, male and female. We have probably all seen at some point or other a drawing similar to the one shown here, which can look either like the profiles of two people looking at each other or a chalice cup:

If we assume that these two profiles represent a man and a woman, here is another symbolic depiction of how the Grail chalice—holding as it does the presence of God, of love—is formed by the mirroring partnership of man and woman. And if we remember that one primary meaning of the chalice cup is the heart, then we can also say that the heart space is both the connecting medium and the defining shape of relationship. This parallels yet again the vesica symbolism, in which the middle shape of the "vessel," or "fish," itself is read as the place of connection between inner and outer.

This is the balanced, whole state that we strive for in our relationships, but it is difficult to achieve unless we do the work of becoming whole as individuals first, or at least at the same time. We've already seen how one cannot have a balanced, peer relationship with leadership until one comes to know a direct connection with the spiritual reality—the radiance of the Grail King—that lies at one's own core. Until this happens, one remains dependent on spiritual leadership for one's sense of connection to that source. The quest for the Grail is the work of achieving this union, because the heart is no longer a veil of separation from that presence but the medium of connection to it. A similar process is involved in intimate relationships. It is difficult to achieve a balanced relationship of man and woman without first having in place our relationship to God. To the extent that we begin to experience that presence in us, we become whole people—symbolized by the equal circles that form the vesica. If we are not whole in this sense, we cannot form the vesica shape—cannot form the Grail together. What's more, we will seek to have the other person in the relationship serve us: feed our hunger, fill our emptiness. And we will find, just as those who try to fill themselves with the bounties of the Grail find, that without our own connection to the inner realm of source, we remain dependent on our partner while at the same time finding that we can never "get" satisfaction from him or her. When we "fall" in love with someone, it is similar to the positive transference we feel for the spiritual mentor. We are seeing the presence of God in our lover—just as we did in our spiritual mentor—and will try to connect to that presence *through them* in a vicarious attempt to join with that.

Ironically of course, we are *supposed* to see the presence of God in one another. "Blessed are the pure in heart, for they shall see God"— and primarily we see God in one another. Perceval's name means "to pierce the veil," to pierce the veil by purifying the heart/going on quest so that the heart changes from veil to connecting medium. We are supposed to see the presence of God in our partnerships—in fact we are supposed to complete the presence of God by coming together in relationship—but this cannot happen if the reality of spiritual grounding is not firmly in place in both individuals.

The difference between these two conditions is well depicted in the contrasting love affairs of Lancelot and Guinevere and Perceval and Blanchefleur. The agonizing inability of Guinevere to rest in the sense of communion and oneness with Lancelot is characteristic of a passionate relationship in which the individuals do not know a stable connection to their own spiritual source and seek to unite with that source through one another only. How different is the equal and delicate mirroring togetherness of Perceval and Blanchefleur, who all night "slept mouth to mouth in each other's arms until daybreak." Here is the sweet innocence of communion, spiritual and physical. There is no wrenching sense of loss when Perceval departs; instead the two carry on with what they each have to do, content in their pledged love for one another.

We begin to be made whole as we do the work of finding the Grail and asking the question—reversing our polarity. In the previous chapter I used symbolism from the Kabbala to explore the way the finding of the Grail/healing of the heart correlates with the return of the Daughter, or the fourth "consonant" of God's "name." So another way to describe the process of becoming whole (complete) is to say that we complete the spelling of the name of God in our own consciousness. I envisioned this name and this map of consciousness as a square with the consonants of God's name and the components of consciousness at its four corners, as shown in the illustration.

This fourfold aspect of consciousness has two sets of male and female aspects—one "pair,"—Father and Mother, in the inner realm, and another pair, Son and Daughter, in the outer realms. This is how the name of God is spelled, male and female repeated, I AM in the inner realm THAT I AM in the outer realm.

The return of the Daughter that allows for the complete spelling of the name of God correlates with the finding of the Grail. The parallel symbol of the Grail is the vesica piscis. What is fascinating is that the vesica symbol can also be used to "spell" the name of God, with two sets of male/female pairs, one in the inner realm and one in the outer. In the previous chapter I envisioned the vesica as laid out like the Grail

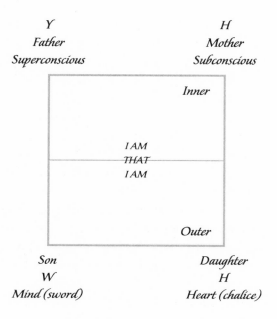

Y
Father
Superconscious

H
Mother
Subconscious

Inner

I AM
THAT
I AM

Outer

Son
W
Mind (sword)

Daughter
H
Heart (chalice)

Castle, with the first inner room being the subconcious realm, the second inner room the realm of spirit or the superconsciousness, and the "fish" shape in the middle, the banqueting hall, the place of conscious connection between the two.

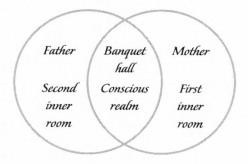

Father

Banquet hall

Mother

Second inner room

Conscious realm

First inner room

If we call one circle Father and the other Mother, we have the two aspects of God in the inner realm. The two arcs where they join form the banqueting hall, the place of conscious connection—the pair in the outer realm, which we can call Son and Daughter.

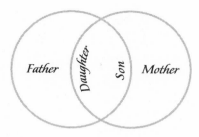

The full "spelling" of the name of God, Father, Mother, Son, and Daughter *is* the forming of the Grail.

According to Greg Braden, the two arcs that form the fish shape of the vesica symbol delineate the electrical and magnetic fields that are foundational to life on this planet. In sacred geometry, these two forces are expressed in the language of rotational and counterrotational movement and are perceived as positive (male) and negative (female). The rotation to the right, clockwise, is the rotation of the electrical, male current, and is frequently expressed in sacred geometry as an arc to the right:). The counterrotational movement, anticlockwise, is the magnetic, female field, expressed as an arc to the left:(. Combined, the two "opposing" arcs express a complete electromagnetic signal.

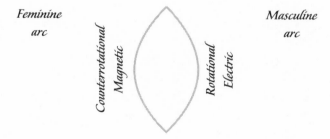

The language of sacred geometry symbolizes the way the union of the male and female poles, whether at the level of the electromagnetic field or within the consciousness of the individual or between men and women, is foundational to the way life works.

What happens if the two arcs cannot join and if the poles are not working properly at the individual level, in the individual consciousness? The illustration shows the vesica shape again, diagramed as the fourfold aspects of consciousness, but this time with the symbol turned on its head.

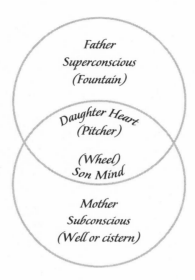

Father
Superconscious
(Fountain)

Daughter Heart
(Pitcher)

(Wheel)
Son Mind

Mother
Subconscious
(Well or cistern)

The "top" circle, the Father or superconscious, represents the realm of spiritual inspiration, of the invisible fountain of life force that animates us; the "bottom" circle represents the Mother, the subconscious, the realm of emotional power and the archives of memory and thought form. The two arcs of the "fish" shape symbolize the male and female aspects of consciousness—mind and heart—as they function in us at the consciously perceiving level. When we go to sleep at night, we rest primarily in the arms of Mother and Father. To the extent we can recall our dreams, we may know some awareness of their presence, but we are primarily unconscious. The awake state is the kingdom of the Son and Daughter, of consciousness.

Obviously this does not mean that the realm of the superconscious at the individual level is God the Father in the fullness of what those words mean, but that it is the place where as individuals we access this primary frequency of being. Likewise, when I speak of the subconscious realm as it wells up in the individual corresponding with Mother God, I do not mean the fullness of what God the Mother is, but the arena that energy or frequency of being *uses,* or *powers.* In some ways we run out of words here, or approach a territory that exists beyond both words and our conscious minds. When we talk about both the individual design of consciousness, and the collective, we could not say that here is the totality of what is meant by God; at the same time, there is another way of seeing that it is all One, that there is only one substance of consciousness, just differentiated—at least potentially differentiated, over and over again, inner and outer—and interacting in the myriad star systems and constellations of our interrelationships.

I have likened the subconscious mind to the waters of the lake in the Arthurian myths. Water is a symbol of spirit and of truth. Truth is not a series of principles or beliefs but a living presence in us, a fundamental energy of life. In the passage from Ecclesiastes quoted in chapter 5, there are these beautiful lines: "Or ever the silver cord be loosed, or the golden bowl be broken, or the pitcher be broken at the fountain, or the wheel broken at the cistern" (Ecclesiastes 12:6). Here is more water imagery: the fountain, the waters of truth that spring up and flow ever new, the spiritual source of being; and the cistern, the waters of truth that stay sparkling and still in the subconscious reservoir of power and understanding. The "pitcher" and the "wheel" are the means by which the flowing and the still waters of spirit are accessed and made available; we could call them heart and mind. The golden bowl is another container, a parallel symbol to the golden chalice, the container formed by heart and body. As I discussed in chapter 5, the passage from Ecclesiastes is describing the separation that occurs at death between the "flesh," or outer form, and the quickening spirit. If the body or conscious mind or heart cease functioning, death follows. But this passage can also be understood as signalling the way consciousness is designed to function, how it is the means by which the invisible flow of the waters of truth are made visible and available to the worlds we live in.

If the pitcher "is broken at the fountain" and the wheel "broken at the cistern," if the heart is broken and if the mind is isolated, the flow cannot work the way it is supposed to. One of the founders of my spiritual network, Lloyd Meeker, described the way the waters of the cistern, of the subconscious mind, are designed to be continually renewed by the flow of the water from the fountain. If the pitcher is broken, the connection from fountain to cistern is cut off. Standing water that has no flow becomes stagnant. The waters of the subconscious mind have become polluted, primarily with fear and shame. This leads to a further difficulty because the subconscious mind is the realm where the invisible spirit is given form before it rises into the conscious mind (the turning wheel). If there is only stagnant water, and distorted thought forms and emotion, then the invisible cannot be adequately clothed and known. In Lloyd Meeker's words:

> When the wheel begins to turn, the conscious mind to think, it picks up something out of the subconscious as the starting point, and if it does not pick up something from the subconscious as the starting point the inspiration from the Higher Source cannot find manifestation in form. Spirit, or Divine Intelligence, that which is of God, can have no meaning to human beings until it is allowed manifestation and function in form.

As I have said, the water I am talking about here is not literal water but the substance of truth, which is a magical, tangible presence. It is also the flow of love—truth and love, silver and gold, intermingled. The flow of this water of energy, with its powerful charge of blessing, is clothed in the forms—the ideas, concepts, and patternings of understanding in the archives of memory—that our mind and hearts are designed to convey into the outer realm. This is the "water" that brings life to the wasteland. If we remember, this was the intangible but very real flow of energy from the spiritual mentor that is felt at every level of one's being. This is very different from the regurgitation of prepackaged or partial thoughts and concepts or the twinging currents of fear and shame.

When the circuitry and flow of consciousness is not running as it is designed to do, we find ourselves living not in a garden of growing, fruit-bearing forms but in a wasteland—a dry, fearful, brittle place. Without the deep emotional flow from the heart, the mind knows no joy, and without the sense of inspiration from the higher dimensions of being, one's underlying experience is one of fear. Slowly, painstakingly, we set about building worlds that will be safe and, if we are lucky, bring at least some of what we want as well: five-year plans, insurance policies, career strategies. We exist in the small boxes of our relationships, too scared to admit to ourselves the dysfunctional patterns that bind us together. We wrestle certain images of the good life into place—whether it be small trivial items, like an ornament from a catalogue, or the so-called dream home—and proceed on our way in the hypnotized conviction that once every piece of our mind-made world is put together, we will know fulfilment.

As a child I remember noticing the succession of obsessional goals that punctuated the life of a family friend's wife. First it was a baby, then another baby, and then she had to try again to get a girl—which she did. Then it was the home, then it was the office extension on the home, and then the extension to the kitchen at the back. She achieved all these objectives and probably others I wasn't aware of, but the anticipated breakthrough into the golden glow of contentment never happened. In fact the larger her family and house grew, the more ragged and unhappy the atmosphere seemed to become when we visited there. Here was the Grail wound at work again: the attempt to make up for the absence of the flow of life by filling oneself up from outside.

The saying goes "You can't take it with you when you die," but we can't really take it with us when we're alive either. We can't actually get those things—tangible, intangible, goods and chattels, lovers and partners, even children—inside us. They just don't fit! They cannot take the place of the wellspring and the well.

An excacerbating factor in all this is the problem that the wasteland, materialist consciousness, has little or no ability to understand or—more important—give validity to any expression or person that tends to come more from the flow of the heart. I came upon this conundrum when studying English literature at university. Even though D. H. Lawrence was one of my favorite writers, I could not bring myself to take the course on him. The faculty at my college, like most faculties in most colleges no doubt (in the early 1970s at any rate) were for the most part left-wing or left-of-center intellectuals—very clever people, very buttoned-up people, deeply convinced of their own view of the world. I balked at the prospect of witnessing the passionate outpourings of Lawrence, visonary and poet, being subjected to the blind scrutiny of the rigorously rational and somewhat jaundiced mentality of those who, to use Joseph Campbell's phrase, "are fractions" but "imagine themselves to be complete."

Perhaps it was myself I was protecting as much as the legacy of D. H. Lawrence, because I had in a sense invested myself in—or taken refuge in—his works, as well as those of other novelists and poets, in order to escape the onslaught of just that kind of unseeing, mind-without-the-heart consciousness. There have always been visionaries, such as some of the great writers and poets, who have known and expressed something of the flow from the higher and deeper frequencies of insight and inspiration. We love their works because when we read them we feel a kind of entrainment into that flow ourselves. Often, however, as individuals these writers—or whoever else—tend to be more vision than action, and they do not always appear to be completely stable. Lawrence is a good example. He walked his talk by writing it and also by his controversial marriage. But on the whole there was no other way for him to ground his vision. He dabbled in various ill-founded utopian communities, railed against the materialist deadening of the world, and died early of tuberculosis—and anger.

The poet and artist William Blake is another example of someone who guarded vision in dark times. The times he lived in were petty and materialist, and almost singlehandedly he held the balance of another kind of world, which comes down to us in this verse:

> I will not cease from Mental Fight,
> Nor shall my sword sleep in my hand
> Till we have built Jerusalem
> In England's green & pleasant Land.

These words form the fourth stanza of a poem that, set to the music of Hubert Parry, has become virtually the national song of England, but in his time Blake, who conversed with spirits and continually heard voices (and made no secret about either) was dismissed as an eccentric or derided as a madman. His extraordinary spiritual view of the world was given expression in his poetry, paintings, and engravings but he was never acknowledged as the great artist and writer he was. The spiritual heart's insights are not taken seriously. What is more, the poet or prophet demonstrates, by the very absence of any mirroring reality in form, the nonvalidity of his or her vision. Such artists do not warrant being taken seriously, and the disregard for what they bring (maybe years later they are put up on the shelf of Literature) helps reentrench the materialist worldview.

The dismissal of the visionary by the rationalist is of course more complex than merely the desire to sustain the hegemony of a particular worldview. Irrational instincts underly the rational putdown of the heart. What is really going on is more of the attempt to build a world that will keep us safe. It's all about the attempt to have control over what we fear, and what we fear is our heart—both its wisdom and its wound.

While our heart is wounded and cut off from the flow of spirit, we cannot really trust ourselves. The mind may try to act in a rational manner, but it is enthralled by a subconscious that is polluted with fear and shame. We cannot rely on our emotional perceptions to be accurate. Our feelings often seem to betray us, cause us to make fools of ourselves, or inflict damage on our own or other people's lives. The mind wants to just keep this whole show under wraps, to control it at all costs. The flow and power of the deep heart current (which includes our sexuality) gets shamed and sublimated at the same time.

We sit on and silence the energy flow of the heart, but it still has to move. Instead of moving through the system of body, mind, and heart, the way it is designed to, it takes strange back routes and side passages. Suppressed, it moves into psychosis and shadow, both emotional and sexual; sublimated, it drives us to achieve goals that can seem either noble or self-centered but are somewhere unnatural or bought at too great a price. And as we learn all the ways to suppress the flow of ourselves, at the same time we recreate that suppression in the world around us. We learn to stifle in others what we have stifled in ourselves, and in this way we control them too.

In chapter 4 I touched on the cliché of the "stiff upper lip" that has come to characterize the British during the empire. This restraint was the other side of the sublimated energy of sentiment and passion on which the empire was largely built: a missionary zeal to spread democracy, a religious conviction that slavery was wrong, a sense of larger purpose, a huge upwelling of patriotic emotion for the green and mystic heartland of Britain. Deep currents of feeling were held in check, just as the swarming and exotic hordes of the Indian subcontinent and many other places were held in check. In fact the great panoply of the British Empire is a fascinating study of a whole cultural bias that tended to suppress in others that which had been suppressed in itself. Not only abroad but at home all that was feminine and of the heart was severely disciplined or suppressed. Sexuality was crushed and hemmed in by the bulwark of Victorian family morality: women were trussed up in masses and layers of clothes—even piano legs were to be covered up lest they titillate desire by reminding men of women's legs; adultery or premarital sex would banish a woman from society for life. These attitudes lingered long: copies of D. H. Lawrence's novel *Lady Chatterley's Lover* were banned, and it was not until the 1960s that the book ceased to be officially censored. Children were to be "seen and not heard"; they were looked after by wet nurses and nannies, kept away from their parents in nurseries and massive perambulators, and then, if boys, sent off to boarding school.

After World War II, as the empire ebbed away, the buttress of morality relaxed and the so-called modern world was gradually ushered in. But the wound did not go away. Now, feeling seemed to be deadened or was not permitted at all. The rise of communism in the East added weight to the intellectual/materialistic orthodoxies that held sway in western Europe, which scorned sentiment and intuition of any kind; while in America cynicism set in after the assassinations of the two Kennedys and of Martin Luther King Jr., and the scandals of Watergate. Perhaps the person who best articulated the mood of the times was another English poet, Philip Larkin:

> Life is first boredom, then fear.
> Whether or not we use it, it goes,
> And leaves what something hidden from us chose,
> And age, and then the only end of age.

Larkin surprises and shocks us—still—by beautifully and exactly evoking some of the very unbeautiful places of the inner wasteland, the sort of junkyard, dead-end, and deadened parts of the mind's landscape. The skill with which he did this tended once again to reinforce the mind's view of the world, of what we call "realism." When we tell someone to be "realistic," we really mean be a bit pessimistic, have a little iron in the soul, don't expect too much. "Life's a bitch and then you die" is a kind of summary of a realistic view of things. You could argue that Larkin merely gave us the gift of noticing, of not fooling ourselves about our experience. He may not necessarily have meant this is how it really is or has to be. This is how it is without the flow. In this sense, he played one aspect of the poet's role well: wrote poetry that told the truth and wrote it brilliantly. But the other aspect, what he largely failed to do, or never pretended he was able to do, would have been to bring not only the words but the Word, or the flow behind the words of life and vision, as Blake and Lawrence did. Words without honesty and accuracy are meaningless, but ultimately words without love are only words.

Writing at the same time as Larkin was Sylvia Plath, and in her all-too-famous collection of poems, *Ariel,* the prologue to her suicide, we have these words that could express perhaps the full agony of what it means to live in the landscape of fear and separation from the inner flow of blessing and love:

This is the light of the mind, cold and planetary.
The trees of the mind are black. The light is blue.
The grasses unload their griefs on my feet as if I were God,
Prickling my ankles and murmuring of their humility.
Fumy, spiritous mists inhabit this place
Separated from my house by a row of headstones.
I simply cannot see where there is to get to.

The moon is no door. It is a face in its own right,
White as a knuckle and terribly upset.
It drags the sea after it like a dark crime; it is quiet
With the O-gape of complete despair. I live here.

The moon is my mother. She is not sweet like Mary.
Her blue garments unloose small bats and owls.
How I would like to believe in tenderness—
The face of the effigy, gentled by candles,
Bending, on me in particular, its mild eyes.

I have fallen a long way. Clouds are flowering
Blue and mystical over the face of the stars.
Inside the church, the saints will be all blue,
Floating on their delicate feet over the cold pews,
Their hands and faces stiff with holiness.
The moon sees nothing of this. She is bald and wild.
And the message of the yew tree is blackness—blackness
   and silence.

It is the "light of the mind, cold and planetary," without the warmth of its companion, the heart. We are back to seeing how the wounded or "missing" heart creates a wasteland, the experience of death. In Sylvia Plath's case, this meant literal death.

This is why the prophet exhorted us to "remember now thy creator in the days of thy youth" before age (or despair) and death set in. Remember the creator, literally re-member, put back in place the parts of the creator's body, which is essentially one's own body, mind, and heart, so that the fourfold "technology" of consciousness is working again. Let the pitcher, the heart, and the mind, the wheel, be mended. Let the arc of their union be consummated so that the full name of God can be spelled.

To the extent we begin to spell out the full name of God, or to form the Grail/vesica within our own consciousness, we begin to be in position to form this Grail and spell this name in the contexts of our relationships. For just as the two outer "poles" of mind and heart represent the inner duality of superconscious and subconscious, so man and woman represent the inner duality of Father and Mother God, and are potentially in position to "magnify" the name of God in their union.

Unless at least some healing has occurred within the individual, the exact same patterning of polarization that is experienced between mind and heart gets constellated between men and women. Interestingly, these patternings reflect the same positive/negative charge of the currents of transference that get projected onto the spiritual mentor—the worship/kill the king instincts. Essentially in men, these patterns show up as alternately doting on or spurning/putting down women; and in women they take the form of alternately seeing the man as their rescuer or undermining/withholding—whatever it is: affections, bodies, cooperation, words—going silent, and so on. Both the negative and positive projections are symptoms of polarization rather than union.

The working of these negative poles are illustrated for us in the tales by some curious episodes concerning Excalibur's scabbard and Morgana's hatred of Arthur, her half-brother.

Arthur is given Excalibur after his first sword, the one he drew out of the stone, is broken in a fight with King Pellinore. (It is worth noting that this episode is another variation on the broken sword theme. Even Arthur's sword breaks; only this time instead of it being reforged, he is given another.) Without a sword, Arthur is at a disadvantage in the struggle, and Merlin has to overcome his opponent with magic to prevent him cutting off Arthur's head. After resting up for three days to mend his wounds, Arthur is setting off once more with Merlin, when Arthur says, "I have no sword." Merlin tells him not to worry, for he has plans to get him another. They ride until they come to a lake in the middle of which is raised an arm clothed in white samite and holding a beautiful sword. The Lady of the Lake comes walking along the shore and Merlin instructs Arthur to ask her if he might have the sword. She tells him that the sword belongs to her, but that he might have it if he will give her a gift when she asks him for one. He agrees, and she tells him to get in the barge that is moored nearby and row out to the sword and take both it and its scabbard. Arthur does so, and then goes on his way with Merlin. A little later, while Arthur is admiring the sword, Merlin asks him which pleases him better, the sword or the scabbard. Arthur replies that it is the sword that pleases him better. Arthur's reply provokes a warning from Merlin:

> "Ye are the more unwise," said Merlin, "for the scabbard is worth
> ten of the sword. While ye have the scabbard upon you, ye shall

never lose any blood, be ye ever so sorely wounded. Therefore always keep the scabbard with you."

The scabbard is of course something of a parallel symbol to the chalice cup. The sexual imagery of sword and scabbard is more explicit than sword and cup, making the scabbard an obvious symbol of the feminine, and particularly the feminine in its aspect of container. The linkage of the scabbard symbol with the chalice also designates the heart realm, particularly the conscious heart: the capacity of emotional perception that operates at the conscious level.

Merlin tells him that if he keeps the scabbard with him, he can never be wounded. Yet Arthur values the sword more. What does this mean? That he values the masculine over the feminine, the mind over the heart, the spirit over the form. It is the shadow blind spot of the patriarchal approach to the world. A slightly patronizing putdown and/or distrust of all things intuitive or "emotional." It could also be read as the way traditional religions have for centuries slanted their message, that heaven is "good" and earth is "bad," the ascetic's denial of the flesh, the Christian cross versus the pagan circle, and so on.

Merlin also warns Arthur to guard the sword and scabbard well because a woman "whom he most trusted" would steal it from him. This turns out to be his half-sister Morgana. Through enchantment Morgana imprisons Arthur in such a way that he will only be freed if he agrees to do battle with a knight on behalf of the lord of the castle where he finds himself. Arthur agrees. Meanwhile Morgana brings Excalibur and its sheath, which she has stolen, to her lover Accolon, whom she has waylaid under the same enchantment. Accolon is set up to fight Arthur, not knowing who he is, and Arthur is given a sword and scabbard that he thinks are his own but are in fact "counterfeit and brittle," having been made by more of Morgana's magic.

This elaborate setup, which is a plan to kill Arthur and place Accolon on the throne in his stead, goes awry due to the interference of Nymue (one of the Ladies of the Lake) who often looks after Arthur. During the fight Arthur is badly wounded and about to be defeated when Nymue causes Excalibur to fall out of Accolon's hand. Arthur, whose fake sword has broken, picks it up and instantly knows it is the true Excalibur. Then Arthur recognizes Accolon, and vice versa, and gradually the plot of Morgana's trickery comes out. Arthur spares Accolon because he realizes he has been duped; however, Accolon dies anyway of his wounds, and Arthur has his dead body sent back to Morgana at court. Morgana knows that Arthur will be after her own life and flees. She rides all day and almost all the night until she comes to the abbey of nuns where Arthur is recovering from his wounds. While he is asleep, she slips into his room, aiming to steal Excalibur once again. However, Arthur is holding it in his sleep, and she knows she cannot take it without waking him, so she takes the scabbard instead. When he awakes and realizes what has happened, Arthur sets off in furious pursuit. He is soon close on her trail, and when she sees that she cannot escape, Morgana rides up to a lake and says: "Whatsoever comes of me, my brother shall not have this scabbard." Then she throws the scabbard out into the deepest part of the lake, where it quickly sinks, being heavy with gold and precious stones. Morgana then rides into a valley of stones where she changes herself, her men, and the horses into great marble stones. Arthur fails therefore to find either his sister or his scabbard and returns to the abbey.

Why is Morgana so alienated from her brother? We have already named Morgana as representing the feminine of sexuality and the emotional power—and sometimes the irrationality—of the heart. All these elements are implicit in the symbol of the scabbard. The scabbard/sexuality connection also denotes the body—the body which is the container of the spirit. When Arthur values the spirit over the flesh, there is echoed that revulsion for the flesh body and its sexual appetites that to some degree has underlain Western society. However, whatever is banished will be in control. As much as we have denied the flesh and its appetites, we have been controlled by them. We are controlled by our repulsion/fascination with the body. The recent exposure of just how endemic sexual exploitation of parishioners has been by Catholic priests is a good example of this dual denial/control syndrome.

So when Arthur values the sword more, he is somewhere devaluing Morgana and her realm—all that she stands for, all that she can bring. As has already been pointed out, it is the area of sexuality and deep emotion that we often on the one hand suppress or spurn in ourselves and on the other are controlled by. Here is the doting/spurning pattern manifesting in ourselves as individuals; and in the story of Arthur and Morgana we can also read the way it works out between men and women. Morgana is the first woman Arthur sleeps with. He falls in love with her, or at least wants sexual union with her, not realizing who she is. Then he spurns her and her realm. Morgana's actions and attitudes are the result of such undervaluing: "Hell hath no fury like a woman spurned": like the feminine spurned. Her reaction is to steal the scabbard and cast it away so that it is lost. Here is the pattern of undermining and withholding protection from Arthur.

Arthur does not recognize who Morgana is and doesn't realize she is his half-sister—that she is his equal in some senses. At the same time, he does not understand how vital the sheath is. He cannot actually see what it is that Morgana brings.

This piece of the story is about the way that women find themselves subject to the same double bind as the visionary poet who finds no answering understanding in the rational world and is thereby discredited. Women bring up insights from the intuitive/emotional realm that men often cannot get their minds around. The insights may not take the shape of logical, linear conclusions or arguments. They are more like seeds, concentrated bundles of essence that need to be expanded in order to be understood. Quite often, because the man cannot relate to what is brought, he will decide that it isn't to be taken seriously. The woman's insights therefore find no answering reality in the man. She feels put down, spurned.

What is supposed to happen is partnership. The unformed concentrate of the insights needs to be decoded by the more logical perspective of the mind. The feeling perception from the inner realms has to be seen in the light of day—has to be translated in terms of space and time. The man can play the role of landing the seed in the earth, making the dream a reality. Interestingly, at the mental level, women are the ones who can fertilize the consciousness of the man with their seed of insight, and the man is the one who brings it to birth in form.

Again, before this partnership can work between men and women, both have to have some feeling of how it works inside themselves. Women have to do some work on unfolding and grounding their own perceptions, not just dropping them completely unformed at the feet of men and expecting them to get it and, what's more, act on it. Sometimes the insights of the woman take the form of a strong or even absolute conviction that a certain course of action is right or is wrong. Not much rational backup for the conviction is available, just an overwhelming hunch or feeling. Sometimes a man will act on this hunch, only to find later on down the path that it wasn't quite the thing. The insight had been "clothed" in form—in what to do, whatever it is, buy a house, have a baby, resign his position—prematurely. Nothing wrong with the insight, but its translation was faulty. The man then feels he's been "had" and is doubly suspicious next time around—will spurn even more. So men also have to get used to working and listening to their own intuitive realms, seeing how strong hunches actually need to play out, rather than being taken over by the energy and getting trapped into a limited translation of it.

If the woman feels put down, her response or support turns into undermining. Morgana threw the scabbard away. But even before she did that, she had already seduced her half-brother. He did not recognize her as an equal, so she hooked him through his sexual response to her. The son she conceives will be a big part of Arthur's undoing. This is a pretty classic way that women can wreak their revenge on men. If you don't recognize me as an equal, I'll make you subject to me sexually. And of course the very reason the man is vulnerable is because he hasn't recognized the partnership—the possibility of real union, true partnership—at whatever level. So again, he is controlled by what he has put down.

The sexual union of Arthur and Morgana was incestuous because they were half-brother and sister. Incest denotes wrong polarity—polarity in the form, without the reality of spiritual partnership that then embraces and includes the form.

Morgana is Arthur's half-sister and his equal. She is of royal birth in her own right, but while her brother is king and carries governmental responsibilities, she is more queen over the realms of magic. In some versions of these stories it is Morgana who is Merlin's apprentice in magic. She is also said to be one of the nine fairies of the Insula Pomorum, the Island of Apples, or Avalon, and Avalon itself in some ways parallels the enchanted land that lies under the magical lake that is the home of the Ladies of the Lake. She is the representative of this realm at the court, the conscious aspect of the unconscious power. Morgana represents the Daughter, the feminine aspect of God in the outer realm.

When Morgana turns her back on Camelot, and the scabbard sinks into the depths of the lake, into the depths of the subconscious, it is signalling to us that the capacity of emotional perception that operates at the conscious level is lost to the conscious realm, lost to Camelot. The Mother or the subconscious power loses its representative, the Daughter, at the conscious level. The Grail is lost, the heart is wounded.

Woven in and around the story of the scabbard and Morgana are two other rather disturbing episodes that also elaborate on the theme of the wounded heart or missing Daughter. The first is when the Lady of the Lake comes to Camelot to request the gift Arthur has promised in return for her sword and is part of a very complicated series of events involving people's heads (as in being decapitated) and swords. The Lady of the Lake appears just as a knight called Balyn is about to depart. Balyn has just won renown by being able to pull another sword out of its scabbard that was brought by a mysterious damosel. After he has done so, she asks for it back, but Balyn refuses. When Arthur asks the Lady of the Lake to name her desire, she asks for the head of the knight who has just won the sword brought by the damosel (i.e. Balyn) or else the head of the damosel. Better still, she would like both their heads, for the knight slew her brother, and the damosel was the cause of her father's death.

Taken aback, Arthur says that he cannot grant either request and entreats her to ask for something else. The Lady of the Lake, however, is adamant and says she will ask "no other thing." While this conversation is going on, Balyn catches sight of the Lady of the Lake, who, it turns out, was responsible for the death of his mother. When he hears that she has asked for his head, he goes straight up to her and says: "Evil be you found: ye would have my head, and therefore ye shall lose yours!" So saying he takes his new-found sword and cuts off her head. Arthur is aghast and banishes Balyn, and then has the Lady of the Lake buried.

The second episode takes place following the wedding of Arthur and Guinevere and the establishment of the Round Table. The first sentence of book 4 tells us that Merlin "fell into dotage" upon one of the damosels of the Lady of the Lake, whose name is Nymue. Nymue tolerates Merlin until she has learned from him much magic art. We are also told how Merlin foresees that he will "not endure long" but will be "put in the earth alive." Merlin tells Arthur of his coming fate; he also warns Arthur to guard well his sword and scabbard, saying that they would be stolen from him by a woman whom he most trusted. Merlin tells Arthur that he will miss him: "Rather than have all your lands ye will wish to have me back." Arthur asks if he cannot prepare for his fate and avoid it, but Merlin says, "Nay, it will not be."

Soon after this Merlin and Nymue travel to Cornwall, where Merlin shows Nymue a "great wonder wrought by enchantment under a huge stone." Nymue, who has grown both tired of Merlin's attentions and fearful of his power, then gets Merlin to go under the stone so that he can tell her about the marvels there. "But she so wrought there that he never came out, for all the craft he could exert." So Merlin is shut up within the earth, just as he foresaw.

The Lady of the Lake, who represents the deep magical subconscious powers (as does Merlin), loses her head at Camelot. We could say she loses her conscious capacity—the head. She dies, and the wisdom of the subconscious mind is no longer available to the court, to Arthur. The conscious heart is no longer available to represent the magical powers of the subconscious; the Daughter is lost to the Mother.

After the Lady of the Lake loses her head in a literal way, Merlin loses his head metaphorically over Nymue. This losing of his conscious rational faculty then leads directly to the embodiment of that condition, namely being shut up under the ground, no longer present on the surface of the earth and no longer accessible in the conscious realm.

Merlin is trapped by his subjection to his young apprentice. The deeper, magical powers of the subconscious mind get trapped there, underground, because of involvement with the more surface layers of the heart. The true power of the heart cannot get past the "lid" of the rock ceiling of the cavern. The wounded surface (younger) layers of the subconscious keep its power damped down and unavailable.

Merlin dotes on Nymue, and she—tired of his attentions and fearful of his power—uses his infatuation to control him. This is a fairly well-known scenario that can work out between men and women. The attention may be flattering but deep down it is really quite frightening. Nymue was frightened of Merlin. And deeper even than the fear, I know in myself there can be a sense of betrayal. As I have been left to hold it all on my own, the other pole has kind of caved in on me, and it's a lonely and ultimately irritating place to be. Certainly, no current can move of any intensity if only one of the poles is being held. Fundamentally, women don't want to be either worshipped or spurned. They want partnership. And so do men. The women longs for the man to hold steady, to be the sword; and the man longs for the opening of the woman, the chalice of protection, that is no longer tinged with fear and holdout. Unless both poles are functioning as they are designed to, the power between them cannot move, the arc of relationship cannot form.

The alienation of Morgana, the loss of the scabbard, the beheading of the Lady of the Lake, the imprisonment of Merlin, are all variations on the theme of the wounded heart, the missing Daughter. In essence they tell us that the wound—the wound in the heart, the separation from spiritual source—is still operating within men and women and the collective, despite the presence of Arthur and the formation of the Round Table. This is also the meaning of the unhappy love affairs. The promise is heralded but not yet actualized. The Grail of union has not yet been found. Camelot is a staging post on the way to something. It is a *model* of a reality but not yet the reality. The Round Table, with its empty center where God and the Grail chalice of connection to that presence reside, presages the coming of the Grail, of the sense of oneness with God and with one another, but is not yet that grounded consciousness of collective sovereignty. As already noted, this sense of Camelot being a part of a larger process rather than the end and aim of that process, is symbolized for us in other ways too. Camelot and the wasteland kingdom of the Wounded Fisher King coexist. The company of the Round Table and the great kingship of Arthur are not enough to dispel the wounded state. Only the Grail can do that.

The heart wound, whose cause and beginning lead us back far into the mists of time and of our own childhoods, is still operating in us as individuals and becomes reenacted and even reentrenched in the complex and often terrible and literally heartbreaking way that men and women wound and rewound themselves.

And this wound can only be healed by going on the quest for the Grail, the journey to heal the dark hurt places of the heart, so that the golden Grail cup encrusted with gems, the gold and jewel-encrusted scabbard, may be found once more and allowed to rise up from the depths of the lake, of the subconscious realm, just as the chalice cup is carried out of that first inner room of the Grail Castle.

When we speak about the wound in the heart and the absence of women, it can sound as if the wound has only operated in one aspect of the poles of God. But there has been pain in the heart *and* in the mind, pain in both women and men. The poles cannot really be separated because they are part of one thing.

When Perceval is sitting in the banqueting hall of the Grail Castle and the strange procession starts to pass before him, the very first precious object that is carried out is a bleeding lance. And later, when Perceval has left the castle and is being interrogated by the grieving maiden about where he has been and what he has seen, although her main concern is with the Grail, in fact the very first question she asks him is whether he saw the bleeding lance, and the second question is did he ask why it bled. When he says no to the second question, she tells him off:

> "And tell me whether, when you did sit next to him, you saw the lance whose tip bleeds without there being any flesh or vein there."—"Whether I saw it? Yes, certainly."—"And did you ask why it bled?"—"I didn't speak a word, so help me God."—"Let me tell you, then, that you've acted very badly."

Clearly this surreal, Salvador Dali–like image has a whole range of meanings. It is a painful symbol, and a male, phallic symbol and also calls to mind the spear that pierced the side of Christ on the cross.

All these connotations combine in the essential meaning of the pain of the true masculine presence without the protective surround of the chalice/sheath, of the true feminine. The mind finds itself brittle and full of fear without the understanding heart; men are isolated and made impotent by the undermining or the withhold of women. Arthur is ultimately mortally wounded by Mordred in the last battle of his kingdom. Mordred is the son conceived by sleeping with Morgana; and Arthur is without the protection of the scabbard. Merlin told Arthur that he would never lose any blood while the scabbard was with him— but without it he is seriously wounded and loses so much blood it seems a fatal blow. The lance is bleeding. Christ's body was pierced by the lance, and his blood is collected by Joseph of Arimathea in a chalice cup. The masculine principle of God needs the corresponding protection—completion—of and by the feminine principle of God. Christ was crucified because the male presence of God found no answering understanding and clothing in the creation he had come to bless. Until the Grail is found, God is vulnerable to our wound.

Part of the significance of the times we are living in is that this wound is healing over because of the work of many individuals pursuing the emotional/spiritual/healing path in themselves—the journey and work of the quest. As the individual wound in the heart is healing over, as the Grail or scabbard is found individually, it means that the wounded relationship between men and woman is also ripe for healing. And not only healing but making anew—because both poles, both men and women, have to change and be renewed in order to move beyond conflict to dance.

In *Pride and Prejudice* both Darcy and Elizabeth had to undergo a transformation in their convictions and characters before they could come together, and we could say that this is what is going to be needed now in male and female. And instead of the formal dances, in which each move was already laid down and known and each partner had only to follow the rules, now the dance has changed. It is no longer so formal, its rules no longer so clearly formulated, and its patterns and rhythms have to be discerned individually and together and collectively as they emerge in the moment. The dance no longer emerges out of precedent and tradition; women are no longer dancing to someone else's tune, and their active presence changes the nature of the dance.

This spontaneous dancing that is created out of the interchange of male and female was not possible while the Daughter was missing.

The return of the Daughter has huge implications for the experience of the Son. Again, we know that as women have emerged it has shifted the territory and roles around between men and women. As women's identity fills out and takes on other aspects, there has been an accompanying requirement that men also shift and grow in their identity. Men share more in childrearing; some even stay home and look after the children while the woman is the primary money-earner for the household. As men's roles have taken on some of the feminine territory, or as men have to deal with women in the workplace, they have had to face up more to their own emotional realms. Each begins to affect the other in this dance toward a new union.

Clearly the changeover of roles and the implications of women entering the workplace has brought up and continues to bring up emotional difficulties of all kinds for both men and women that have to be navigated. The union is far from achieved, and the transformation of attitudes in this arena is ongoing and often heavy going. Women may be able now to become doctors, but there is precious little support for them if they also wish to have children. One PBS documentary I watched about women holding down top banking jobs gave an insight into how their male colleagues—and competitors—resented them. When any of these women got pregnant and had a baby, their male counterparts watched them like hawks for any signs of slacking off—phone calls to the nanny, being a little bit late for work, or leaving early. To the point where at least one of the women gave it up, and resigned her position in order to be able to be with her child without the pressure.

Sometimes in the long unfoldment of the women's movement and in the struggle for women to integrate into a "man's" world, there has been the idea that men and women really are or should be no different. A confusion over gender identity has set in, and we have seen women attempting to become men and men women. This has had its painful side, as women have tried to ride roughshod over their own emotional sensibilities, and men have emasculated themselves in attempting to make up for centuries of patriarchal exploitation.

While men do have a feminine component to them and women a masculine (which in Jungian terms is called the anima and the animus), they are and are supposed to be different. If they weren't different, they couldn't fall in love. The love affair between the poles of God couldn't happen. They are two aspects of one thing; indeed their differences are the way in which oneness is made possible. This is literally true in love-making, in which the different sexual physiologies of men and women are what makes it possible for them to join at a physical level to become one.

These physical and sexual differences symbolize rather beautifully differences of essence and function at other levels, some of which we've been looking at in this chapter. The sword/phallus, and the chalice/womb. The male sex organs are on the outside of his body, the woman's on the inside. Both are mutually vulnerable to each other. The man's arena of action—particularly in the mental realm—is more the "outer" and the woman's the "inner." And by and large, even in today's society, women still bear the main load of childrearing and men of breadwinning.

The union of men and women finds its most intense and sacred form in the act of lovemaking, which at its fullest weaves the substance of body, mind, heart, and spirit together in an act of interchange and renewal. In the sexual coming together of man and woman there has to be more than just body parts involved. If there is no sexual "charge" it won't be very exciting or full; in fact the act of lovemaking becomes almost impossible without the arcing of the "positive" and "negative" currents between partners.

We remember that in the language of ancient sacred geometry the fish shape formed by the vesica piscis is a symbol of the electromagnetic field formed by the fused opposites of the positive/masculine rotational and the negative/feminine counterrotational arcs.

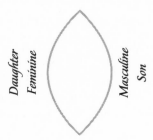

In Gregg Braden's book *Awakening to Zero Point* he further explains that the symbol of the vesica piscis is the *Egyptian glyph for the "mouth" and for the "creator."* The two arcs of positive and negative current join to form the mouthpiece of God. God "speaks" or creates through the joining of the male/female arcs. In physical sex this can of course take the form of a child being conceived—the creation of life because of the union.

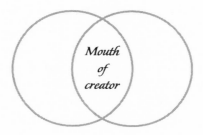

The fish shape of the vesica is also known as the vulva of the Mother Goddess, out of whose body all the forms of life come and all the shapes of sacred geometry are formed. The combined associations of vulva and mouth and creator are telling us something about the oneness and sacredness of sex. The vulva is a mouth itself, through which the deep currents of the female orgasm "speak"—and out of which the child is born. The sexual joining of man and woman is one of the ways in which God "speaks."

The creation of the vesica shape by the interpenetration of the two circles represents the way the Creator is differentiated. The Creator "speaks"—produces the life-bearing Word—through the mouthpiece formed by the union of the positive and negative poles, whether that be mind and heart, in the individual consciousness, or man and woman. The two "arcs" of Son and Daughter represent at the outer level the inner archetypes of Father and Mother: "in the *image of God* created he him; *male* and *female* created he *them*." This vesica symbolism builds on the meaning from the Kabbala because it demonstrates both how God is *configured* and how God *creates* through masculine and feminine. Even more significant, the symbolism also enacts that God is configured and creates not by the mere outer presence of male and female, of Son and

Daughter, but by their *union*. If the two circles don't join, the vesica shape is not formed; if the two "opposing" (different, positive and negative) poles don't unite, the mouth of God, the means by which the Word of God is spoken, is not formed.

The vesica/mouth/vulva is also a symbol of the Grail. One of the ways the Grail is formed/found is by the joining of male and female, and whenever the Grail appears that same question must be asked and its answer understood. What is the chalice of union for? Whom does it serve? And of course the answer is the same. This chalice of union serves God, serves the purposes of God, gives God body—"In the image and likeness made he *them*."

The body is sacred. Spirituality and sexuality are truly one and the same. This is what both Blake and D. H. Lawrence knew. They saw that the denigrating or shutting down of the sexual act and current was a kind of blasphemy, and the source of the deepest human pain and confusion.

The flow of energy that can move through heart and mind as the circuitry of consciousness—the pitcher and the wheel—begins to work, and true thinking starts to take place, has its counterpart in the body. The sexual current is designed to turn through the body, specifically through the loins but also the whole body, just as the flow of thought seems to focus primarily in our head and the emotional current in our heart. The flow of thought, of emotion and inspiration, and of the sexual current are all the ways the spirit of God is "embodied" and given form and expression.

Just as the cistern of the subconscious has to yield up its wounds and distortions at an emotional/mental level, so the cistern of our sexual function has to be purified and made holy again. There has been a kind of pollution of defilement here; the question has not been asked or its answer understood, and the chalice of sexual union has not been used for the purposes of God—so that the most popular but nonetheless potent swear word or curse is a word that means to copulate, with overtones of the coarsest kind. We constantly, in our very language, curse and defile the most central sacred union between men and women. Sex has been used as a weapon and a means of control. Rape is widespread and always has been. Prostitution sells it for money. The film *Last*

Tango in Paris was about the deliberate pollution of the currents of sex, to the point where the woman shoots and kills her lover, played by Marlon Brando, as a kind of revenge or self-defense.

A huge proportion of the secondary wounding in society is sexual wounding—from child abuse, other kinds of sexual exploitation, or rape. By secondary wounding I mean the wounds received, often but not solely in childhood, from others who are themselves already wounded. All secondary wounds, however they are caused, are fundamentally the result of—and then can re-create, particularly in a child—the primary wound, which is the sense of separation from the inner radiant source of being.

The Wounded Fisher King was said to be suffering from a wound in both thighs: "But he was wounded and indeed maimed in a battle, so that he has not been able to manage for himself since; for he was struck by a javelin right through both thighs." He can no longer mount a horse or take part in any sport—there are sexual overtones here. This wound in the thighs is a wound in the genitals—this king is impotent. Impotency implies a disconnect from the life source and the fear subsequent on the disconnect. It is said that a central motivation for the act of rape is not sexual drive nor a craving for union but a desire to dominate and control. The need to control stems from the fear that is itself engendered by the loss of connection to the life flow. Intimacy is not what we seek, in fact when we are in the grip of fear, separated from the flow of love, we have a deep fear of intimacy, because it means opening to someone, and in opening our own vulnerability will be exposed.

This is why the arena of sex is so terrifying, and why so often it is either abused or sat on and kind of ignored. We are terrified of the requirement for intimacy that sexual union implies because it means we cannot hide. In a way, we could say that it means we cannot hide from the presence of God—when He and She come calling in the cool of the evening, we feel the fear of taking off the fig leaves of coverup, composed primarily of fear and shame. This coverup can include the fig leaves of sexual competency and intense physical sensation, because even sexual abandon is not necessarily true intimacy and openness in the presence of God.

Sexual union is spiritual union. It is the gate of the garden, the most potent experience available to us in which we can come into the presence of God and embody that in and between us as the true poles of that expression. The seeds we plant in that garden and the fullness of the currents we are able to hold is how we create the wider garden of our lives and determines whether we live in a garden—or a wasteland.

God both is *configured* and God *creates* through masculine and feminine. It is both the presence and the *interaction* of the poles of God that creates life. In the previous chapter I discussed the assertion in Genesis that God is both male and female: "So God created man in his own image, in the image of God created he him; male and female created he them." But God was always the One God as well: "The Lord thy God is One God." And the first commandment given at that time was: "Thou shalt have no other gods before me"—there is only the oneness. What does this mean? That the masculine and feminine poles form the oneness that is God. They are the way the oneness works. If they weren't different, they couldn't join to become one.

The two poles of God, of positive and negative current, constellate in us as individuals and between us in our one-on-one relationships, and they also show up and get differentiated in the way we work in the collective. They are embodied in the very makeup and nature of our functioning together. In a recent neighborhood group meeting, for instance, these poles showed up as those for and against a proposed new development in the area. In a corporate setting the poles may already exist in the different views of management and workforce or unions. We can also think of North and South Korea, racial differences of all kinds, First World versus Third World politics, Conservative and Labour, Republican and Democratic, hard-liner and liberal, and so on and on. All of these examples can be seen as embodying the *two basic aspects of one process or entity,* a duality that is *necessary to the functioning of that entity* but that generally works through conflict rather than through creative and open partnership.

The two together form One. If we get into conflict with one another, we have forgotten the Oneness. The second commandment at that time was:

Thou shalt not make unto thee any graven image, or any likeness
of any thing that is in heaven above, or that is in the earth beneath,
or that is in the water under the earth:

Thou shalt not bow down thyself to them, nor serve them.
(Exodus 20:4)

I have already considered this from the standpoint of staying oriented
in spirit rather than in form, but it could also be read as an injunction
against forming images—the false ideas and ego projections—of one
another instead of seeing the oneness. There is a difference between an
image and a symbol. An image blocks rather than connects. An image
can misrepresent, or insert an incorrect idea between the reality it is
supposed to represent and those to whom it is representing that
reality—the golden calf was not a very adequate representation of the
One God, for instance. An image is like the human ego that has confused itself with the center of the universe and says in effect "I am as
God" instead of "I am an aspect of, have a connection to something
larger than myself." A symbol, on the other hand, is something than can
connect an essence to the unseen or larger reality. A symbol demonstrates that which it symbolizes. And the symbol of God was male and
female: "And God said, Let us make man in our image, after our likeness, and let *them* have dominion over . . . all the Earth." No other
graven images, because here was the image of God! The image of God,
the symbol of God, was and is male and female. Always was, always will
be. The two in partnership are *the way the Oneness of God is formed and
the way that Oneness functions.*

It is sometimes said that love makes the world go round, and in the
sacred act of love-"making" we see both a reality and a symbol of the
way God is formed and the way God functions at the individual and
male/female arenas and also in the collective. Collective leadership cannot work without the freed-up interchange and dance of the male and
female poles of God, because the latter fires and fuels the former.

In a sense, we could describe the wound—whether thinking of it
as the separation between our consciousness and our deeper spiritual
source or the conflict between mind and heart, men and women, or

the conflict between groups or nations—as the breaking of the One-ness, the oneness that is the two-in-one of God, of ourselves, individ-ually, one-on-one, and collectively.

The healing of the wound, the mending of the oneness, happens and is happening at many levels simultaneously. As the poles of God, masculine and feminine, begin to dance—within the individual, be-tween man and woman—so they begin to unlock from confrontation and conflict within the different ways (and ultimately the whole) the collective is configured.

One person's experience of healing, of finding the Grail, is not able to heal the wider wound and restore the wasteland. Nor is one truly loving relationship. Partly because the impact of one person (or two people) is not enough, and partly because we are all one. The conscious-ness of one person cannot be fully restored until the whole consciousness is healed. At the same time, the change and opening in the individual, and in many individuals, does affect the whole, and the experience of the collective blessing, to the extent it forms, can heal the individual. There is a coemergence and co-opening and healing between all three aspects of God—individual, male and female, and the collective—that is cumulative, building and accelerating in ways that are unquantifiable.

Healing and function happen together. We are both doing the work of healing our hearts and also learning the new dance together simul-taneously. This takes time and discernment, and the role of the Daugh-ter in this enterprise is essential. I learned this firsthand after having attended several of the twice-yearly gatherings of my newly reconfig-uring spiritual network.

On one of these occasions, the first evening that we gathered to-gether, I remember feeling how magical and potent our collective pres-ence was. It had been several years, for myself and quite a few others, since we had been together, in any significant numbers, and there was a great joy in the room at being reunited. This joy was intensified for me because it did not feel like a hopeful rerun of the past, nor was it inflated with naive euphoria. Instead there was that very familiar and precious sense of communion, of being in one place with one accord. It seemed to me that we had come through difficulty and confusion and were bringing our maturity to a new harvest of collective function.

However, as the next few days unfolded it appeared that the condition of one-heartedness that was so strong in my experience was not shared by all. Specifically, it did not seem to be experienced very strongly by those who were providing the leadership and structuring the ways to be together. It began to dawn on me that, to some degree at any rate, this aspect of the "masculine" pole was attempting to play out its role according to an old formula, an obsolete idea that leadership meant setting the tone for others to follow and laying down guidelines of how to proceed instead of opening the space for interaction. As this tendency made itself apparent, it set off corresponding reactions in myself and others who were sensing the same sense of discord. Here were the oppposite forces of the male/female "arcs" beginning to show themselves within the group dynamic, but as yet instead of understanding that there was a new dance to be had, they were "polarized" in reaction to one another.

These opposite forces did not just lie in what people were saying or thinking but in the very ground out of which they were experiencing reality. As these differences began to emerge in people's different approaches, thoughts, and emotional experiences they appeared to be so opposed that each seemed to threaten the other or to be somehow undermining of what the other felt needed to happen. This tended to set off currents of panic, anger, and distrust that further reinforced what appeared to be polarization rather than complementation. At another gathering, one old friend of mine was attending for the first time. In his enthusiasm for what was happening, and as was perhaps also somewhat habitual for him, he spoke quite often in the collective space and sometimes rather "eloquently." After a couple of days, however, I noticed that he had grown much quieter and seemed more "damped down." It turned out that he had been taken aside by the coordinators and asked to be more sensitive to the extent to which he was dominating the collective space. This caused more reaction in myself and others, which further exacerbated the already existing tension between the "poles." How could someone inhibit the flow to such a degree, censor and control the way that collective expresses itself through the spontaneous participation of its "parts"? But the other "arc" felt just as strongly that not to have acted as it did was to hinder the flow of the collective just as much.

Fundamentally, the "masculine" pole felt that it needed to control the situation quite heavily in order for a container of intensity to form, while the feminine pole wanted more spontaneity, felt that the container was in place and could be trusted to "speak." When the heavy controls come on, it is kind of saying: if you are trustworthy you will comply with this. The implication is that if you don't, you will be breaking the container and will therefore prove yourself to be untrustworthy.

It was said that Arthur trusted his sister above all women. He trusted her, but he did not recognize her. The feminine knows that if it is not being "seen" it is not actually being trusted. Being trusted to comply is different from trusted to express oneself in the way that is unique and right—and that is different from the masculine.

Realizing that the invitation to comply is a false control and realizing that it is not being trusted, the feminine will tend to react. It wants to say "F—k you," and make off with the scabbard to hurl it into the lake—submerge the impulse to respond. And of course to the extent that this happened within the gatherings, it seemed to justify the false control with its desire to establish a safe container—the container which could be an aspect of the collective Grail.

We all either watched this happening or felt the driving twists of the different "arcs" as they moved around each other in what was often a confused mismatching instead of a dance. Somewhere we all knew that no one was really "wrong" and yet we had a sensing that something was wrong! And it was very difficult to put a finger on it—while at the same time all too easy to point the finger.

Here is the double-bind situation again of the feminine, this time manifesting in a collective setting. The sword is valued above the scabbard. The feminine is not recognized and is invited to have union on the basis of the false masculine control instead of true partnership. The feminine cannot therefore find a mirroring reflection within the situation and is discredited because of that, even if it doesn't react. And if it does react, it is discredited even more and reentrenches the "rightness" of the false masculine.

The masculine "arc" is right, in that there has to be control and mutual agreement in order to create together. The question is: What is the nature of the control? What the false masculine control is unable to get is that it really CANNOT control the feminine. This is the difference of the age. It cannot control it, nor is it supposed to submit to it. The role of the masculine pole is to be in control in the sense of aligned in itself with the radiance of inner being. This could be described as playing the role of the sovereign in a sense, who offers direction and blessing. To embody the positive current. Or to put it yet another way, to be the sword, but not to value it over the scabbard/chalice.

If we use the sexual analogy, the male must provide control, an alignment, an erection in order to enter the container of the woman's body. The female opens to the stimulation of the male, but she is the container that allows for the "arcs" of sexual/spiritual energy to flow and blend. Providing control so that someone can open is different from controlling them. It is an essential difference. No one can demand response and get true response. You may get compliance, often fear or doubt based. The other reaction will be defiance; but defiance is rather like a mirror image of the false masculine—either way, no potency can move between these false poles. And if defiance is the mirror image of the false masculine, attempting to control is a reflection of the false feminine, which is withholding or undermining.

The masculine arc felt that a container for creation had to be "built" through compliance. But in physical sex, the woman *is* the container. Her body is the container in which the sexual union and creation takes place. It is already present. The feminine arc in these gatherings felt that we could all be more spontaneous, because it was bringing the container. The container does not really have to be built, it has to be activated and filled; again as in sex, that only happens as there is interchange and openness between male and female.

If the masculine "pole"—however it configures, because it may be "men" but it can also be women who play this role in any particular setting—offers partnership, values sword and scabbard equally, the double-bind issue doesn't need to arise.

The false feminine pattern is to withhold and undermine. This can also mean that one withholds and undermines *oneself.* Women have been conditioned for so long to doubt themselves that they can come to believe they really are not up to it, that maybe they really are unstable or lack perspective or whatever it is. This is one of the ways the Daughter has been missing. But now she is back! And this changes everything. The great test of this new Daughter consciousness is not to react when the false control puts in an appearance; not to go and throw the scabbard into the lake. And the reason why this is so crucial (apart from the fact that it will reentrench the pattern) is this: the feminine arc, the Daughter consciousness, carries *primary responsibility for the container.*

If the feminine pole reacts, the container cannot function—of course! And if this happens, both feminine and masculine poles are confounded because they cannot unite and they cannot create. When the attempt at false control comes on and it is not being "seen," the trick for the feminine pole is to put the energy not into defiance but into holding the context, the container, anyway. Providing the scabbard *anyway.*

Her symbol, after all, is the scabbard or chalice. The container. *The context.* In Kabbalistic terms, the Daughter also correlates with the *kingdom.* The kingdom can be seen to be the clothing or container, in a way, of the king. When that masculine pole is embodying the positive energy in a true way, when it is playing the sovereign role, the kingdom comes. No problem. Just as the sword released out of the stone at Arthur's touch. The true container surrounds the true sword, in a reverse process to the way the wasteland reflects the fisher king's wound.

By providing the container in spite of the false control, the feminine arc, the Daughter, helps heal the patterns of the false masculine. The fisher king's wound of separation is healed by the finding/forming of the Grail. And what is this container? It is the healed heart, the heart that has become the container of the radiant energy of the Grail King, the container of the Father's love.

In the end at both gatherings of my network, despite our at times slightly inept "lovemaking," a powerful presence of love did build in our collective "cup"—something more intense and beautiful than I had ever experienced before, even during the heydays of our "Camelot." What I noticed was that in the "previous era," the intensity had seemed to gather around and be focused by the leader. But now there was no one person or group of people who were somehow shining brighter than others. And, even though the human ego was by no means completely vanquished, and there still existed pretensions to leadership rather than the authentic presence of leadership in some, ultimately it didn't really matter. The false positive, and the reactions to it—didn't—couldn't stop the creation of this extraordinary, rich, golden, almost tangible atmosphere filling up among us and spilling over. I realized with a sense of deep joy and awe that we had stumbled on and come to be the collective Grail—or at least an aspect of it. Our presence was unquestionably larger than the sum of each of us and yet had been created out of our coming together. This was the technology of oneness—we didn't know yet quite how to use it or even how to let it happen, but here it was anyway.

In all the tales of King Arthur and the Grail quest, enchantment and magic are never very far away. Magic relates to the technology of oneness. This magical technology works because of the oneness—the connectedness of things. So that what happens over here can affect something over there. One episode made me realize that the circle we formed at such gatherings was like the magic circles used by enchanters, in which ritual could be charged in such a way as to effect the wider world that it represented. It also made me realize that none of us really understood fully yet the way this ritual space can work and the power of it. At the four corners of the room where we met, four "altars" had been placed, representing the four forces of water, air, earth, and fire. We were invited, if we wished, to place objects from our lives at any of these altars. One of my friends placed a photo of her young son on the fire altar, fire being the symbol of love. However, after a particularly "hot" session, where reaction and polarization were riding high, she had a call from home to say that her son had a seriously high fever. It was particularly serious for him because he was vulnerable to seizures when he went into a high fever. Needless to say, his mother took him off the fire altar, and we heard later that he was fine and the fever had abated. Just as our individual consciousness can be used to affect the whole, even more so a collective presence can work to bring changes in the wider whole. The "magical" possibilities of ritual and group presence are really just aspects of the way collective consciousness can work. The point is to become aware of how to use it creatively and consciously.

For the technology of oneness to operate, we have to come into the experience of oneness with God and one another. As the heart realm heals and yields up its wounds, the gateway to the deeper, "magical" levels of ourselves is available, and our worlds are no longer only that realm that our mind can grasp. We begin to be open to the ways the same consciousness is manifesting and expressing through others—even if there are distortions and incompletenesses in that expression.

When the "wheel" of the mind and the "pitcher" of the heart are open both to the inner realms and to one another, we begin to access the flow of inspiration, and the contents from the deeper "waters" of the cistern or subconscious mind are lifted into consciousness.

Immediately instead of two there is four.

The fourfold design of the creator begins to be constellated, and the name of God begins to be spelled out in full. As this fourfold flow moves through ourselves from the inner to the outer we can begin to discern its elements, as shown in the illustration.

Inspiration
Fountain/superconscious
(Father)
(Grail King)

Emotional power/memory
Well or cistern/subconscious
(Mother)
(Merlin/Lady of the Lake)

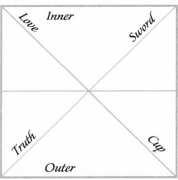

Coherent flow of thought/logic
"Catching the fish as it jumps"
Wheel/mind
(Son)

Feeling perception/intuition
Sense of timing, context
What fits and when
Heart/pitcher
(Daughter)

The "outer" level of mind and heart each have two aspects. Mind has: *flow* and *concept* (Arthur and Lancelot); heart has: *feeling current* and *context* (Guinevere and Morgana). This means that the two outer aspects of mind and of heart reconfigure again the design of the four, as shown in the illustration.

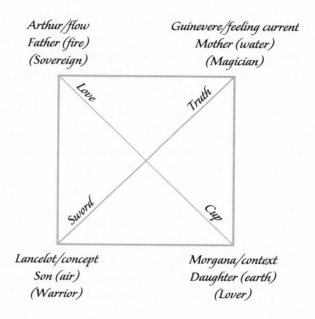

Arthur/flow
Father (fire)
(Sovereign)

Guinevere/feeling current
Mother (water)
(Magician)

Lancelot/concept
Son (air)
(Warrior)

Morgana/context
Daughter (earth)
(Lover)

Seen this way, we can start to read the stories of these different characters and their interactions with one another as maps for the difficulties experienced individually, in one-to-one relationships, and within the collective, when the name of God is only partially spelled and the Grail is not formed or found.

The conflict between Arthur and Morgana, the heartbreak between Guinevere and Lancelot, the unrequited love of Morgana for Lancelot, Lancelot's fixation on Guinevere, the split between Lancelot and Arthur, and between Guinevere and Arthur, and the hostility between Guinevere and Morgana can all be interpreted as the breakdown in the flow of the fourfold design of consciousness. The absence of Morgana from the court and the loss of the scabbard tell of the missing

Daughter, the wounded heart. The full kingdom cannot form without her, without the fourth consonant in the name of God.

The return of this element means that potentially all the interrelationships are up for healing and change: between Son and Daughter but also between Father and Mother, Father and Son, Father and Daughter, Mother and Daughter, and Mother and Son. Bit by bit the circuitry of consciousness and the circuitry of our interrelationships fills in and begins to work.

At the level of thought these essences move into consciousness as different aspects of one process, which is the translation of the invisible inner realms into the outer visible reality. As we get a sense of stewarding this process in ourselves we get better at listening to the different relationships of meaning and insight as they emerge (or get stuck or distorted) one on one. Most significantly, we get more familiar with the way men and women process experience and insight differently.

When we are no longer polarized in reaction to—worshipping, being controlled by—the false images of ourselves and one another, we start to configure the One God, the Oneness that is God. When the arc of the male/female articulation and dance starts to show up, it can start to form the mouthpiece of God, clothing the more fundamental levels of emergence and making the Word into words. The meaning rises up out of what Bohm termed the implicate order, in a kind of swirling motion, a dance.

At the level of the heart, we know that we are one. Here is the configuration of the true Round Table—only instead of the space in the center being a place we have to get to, now it is forming the mouth of God, the way we create together. It has become the collective Grail and its mirroring symbol, the vesica piscis.

In the Chalice Well gardens at Glastonbury, England, the symbol of the vesica piscis is laid out in wrought iron on the lid of the well that was said to be the place where the Grail chalice was hidden. And this is true—the well of the subconscious mind is where the Grail was hidden, the realm into which the conscious heart "fell." It emerges out of that well, out of the first inner room of the Grail Castle, as our consciousness begins to be illuminated by the presence of love. The Chalice Well is actually both a spring *and* a well—one thing. The fountain of inspiration, and the cistern of memory and emotional power, the beautiful inner powers of Father and Mother God—which are One. People visit the gardens primarily to look down into the waters of this spring and well—and to drink from them.

On the well cover is the vesica, but it is not just the vesica on its own. Its two entwined circles are set within the larger circle of the round lid, and intersecting both the circles and the vesica or fish shape itself is a straight line—the lance, or sword.

This well lid design actually gives us the design and the interactive dance of the threefold aspect of consciousness: the individual, one-on-one, and the collective. The individual consciousness is represented in the vesica shape of inner and outer, with the connecting realm of consciousness, mind, and heart; the one-on-one, male/female aspect is particularly symbolized by the male lance or sword image intersecting the feminine vulva shape of the vesica; and finally the larger whole, the condition of collective sovereignty, is suggested by the outer circle, which is also intersected by the lance, and which both holds and is held by the dance of the individual and male/female poles of God. The circle and the lance/sword are both symbols in their own right of oneness— the numeral 1 and the 0 of the circle. It is one thing. One consciousness, God as the One—which is all of us.

The intersecting line is said to represent the Bleeding Lance, only this one has flowers growing from it. Tradition has it that Joseph of Arimathea came to Glastonbury soon after the crucifixion. He indeed is said to be the one who hid the Grail in the well. He stuck his staff into the ground near to the well, where it took root and flowered. His staff was made of the Holy Thorn, which flowers at Christmas as well as May—birth and resurrection. A descendant of this cultivar is still flowering in the meadow above the Chalice Well gardens. It is endemic in the Middle East but exclusive to Glastonbury in Britain. So here in this symbol we have the bleeding lance, which pierced the side of Christ when he was on the cross, transformed into the flowering Holy Thorn. This is a symbol of the restoration of wound and wasteland that comes as the spirit of God, embodied for us in Christ, finds instead of rejection and crucifixion an answering understanding in our hearts, and begins to be embodied in us individually, in our relationships one to another, and in our movement together as a collective whole.

This symbol is telling us the way the promise of the Grail myth is fulfilled and how the quest is finished. The promise was that when the Grail is found, the wounded king would be healed and his wasteland kingdom restored. The wasteland, inner and outer, is the reflection of the wound—the wound of separation from the inner radiance, from God, from love. When the wound is no more—when there is no more separation from that source within the individual, between men and women and within the collective—then it can no longer be reflected in the wasteland. Instead of blood, there is a blooming; instead of pain, there is joy. Instead of separation, there is oneness. One heart, one way.

APPENDIX I

The Intertwined Tales of King Arthur and the Quest for the Grail

The sources of the tales divide roughly into the Arthur stories and the Grail stories. The Grail is in the background of the Arthur stories, and Arthur is in the background of the Grail stories.

THE STORY OF ARTHUR

Merlin changes Uther Pendragon, King of England, into the likeness of Gorlois, Duke of Cornwall, so that Uther can sleep with Gorlois's wife, Ygraine, with whom Uther has fallen violently in love.

Merlin agrees to help Uther on condition that their firstborn child be given to him to bring up. With his gift of foresight, Merlin knows this baby will be Arthur, destined to unite the kingdom of Britain and usher in a reign of peace and greatness.

Merlin places Arthur with a trusted duke in a remote part of the kingdom and plays a role in Arthur's upbringing. Arthur does not know the origin of his birth.

When Arthur is a young man, he accompanies the duke, Sir Hector, and Kay, Hector's son, to a grand tournament. Near to the tournament ground is a sword stuck in a stone (or in an anvil on top of a stone). It is prophesied that whoever can pull the sword from the stone shall be King of Britain. Kay has forgotten his sword and Arthur is sent back to their lodgings to fetch it. However, the inn is locked up, and he cannot get in. On his way back to Kay, he passes by the strange sword in the stone, and, without knowing about the prophecy, pulls it out and presents it to Kay.

Arthur becomes king. Merlin becomes his advisor.

Not recognizing who she is, Arthur sleeps with Morgana, his half-sister. Her son Mordred is the offspring of their union; he grows up hating his father.

Arthur starts the process of uniting the kingdom, fighting various battles and drawing his knights together. He marries Guinevere, and her wedding present to him is a round table.

Lancelot is inspired to leave his lands in France and serve Arthur as knight.

Camelot is established. The kingdom is more or less united, Arthur initiates the Knights of the Round Table, and the Grail quests are embarked on.

Lancelot and Guinevere are in love. Ultimately their secret love enables Mordred to drive a wedge between Lancelot and Arthur. Mordred catches the lovers together and accuses them of treachery. Lancelot has to flee, and Guinevere is to be burned at the stake for treachery.

Everyone knows this will mean that Lancelot will rescue her. He does so, and in the confusion unwittingly kills several of Arthur's knights, including Gawain's brothers, Gareth and Gaheris.

Gawain will never forgive Lancelot, and the situation deteriorates into a series of indecisive battles between Arthur's and Lancelot's forces. Gawain insists that Lancelot be banished forever from Britain, and Lancelot returns in great sorrow to his lands in France. There he is pursued by a reluctant Arthur and an ever-vengeful Gawain.

Further jousts and battles ensue until news comes from Britain that Mordred has attempted to usurp Arthur, spreading word that he is dead, and trying to marry Guinevere.

Arthur returns at once, but his forces are much weaker without Lancelot. There is a final terrible battle in which all but one of Arthur's knights are killed. Arthur himself is mortally wounded by Mordred, and he kills Mordred.

Arthur commands Sir Bedivere to throw Excalibur into a lake. Bedivere is extremely reluctant to throw Excalibur into the lake because it is all that is left of Camelot and the era of greatness. However, eventually he obeys Arthur, and as he hurls the sword, a lady's hand reaches out to take it. Then a black barge appears, and Arthur is taken away on it to Avalon to await the healing of his wounds and his eventual return.

THE GRAIL QUEST

Chrétien de Troyes's tale "Perceval" is unfinished. There were several continuations of it, by Gautier de Doulens, Manessier, and Gerbert. There is also a
kind of prologue to the Grail story known as the "Conte du Graal." Wolfram
von Eschenbach wrote his own version of the tale entitled "Parzival," in which
the Grail is a stone. The many other versions include Heinrich von dem Türlin's "The Gawain Episodes of Diu Crône," in which Gawain is the main character; the "Didot-Perceval"; the "Mabinogi of Peredur ab Evrawc," and the
"Queste del Saint Graal," in which an ultra-Christian Galahad becomes the
main hero.

The following bare bones of the story are taken from Chrétien's "Perceval," with a summary of some of the features of the continuations. Incidents
from other of the sources are incorporated into the main text of this book as
their significance is explored.

Perceval is brought up in Wales, which denoted a very remote part of the
world, in primitive conditions—with no schooling and wearing homespun
clothes.

During his adolescence he is out in the woods when he sees five knights
go riding by. He has never seen anything like them before. Questioning them,
he learns that they are called knights and were made so by King Arthur.

Dazzled, he runs home to tell his mother. He wants to leave immediately
and become a knight himself. His mother weeps because his father and two
brothers were both killed as knights and this is the fate she has tried to shield
him from.

Perceval hurries off the next day in search of King Arthur's court. On ap-
proaching it, he meets a knight armed completely in crimson who has just
been threatening Arthur and his court and has carried off Arthur's golden cup.
Perceval is taken with the knight's red arms and tells the knight he means to
ask Arthur for them. The Red Knight is taken off guard by this young and im-
petuous fool and humors rather than harms him.

Perceval rides straight into Arthur's hall where he finds the court sat down
to a meal. He demands to be made a knight immediately. Arthur does so. A
maiden who has not smiled or laughed for six years smiles now at Perceval and
predicts he will be the best knight in the world. This angers Kay, Arthur's
seneschal, who slaps her and also kicks into the fire a fool who was wont to
prophesy that the maiden would not laugh again until she saw the man who
will be supreme among knights.

Perceval dashes off to win the red knight's armor. He duly vanquishes the knight, and Yvonet, who has followed Perceval, shows him how to get the armor off. Perceval dons the armor, and Yvonet rushes back with the news to Arthur's court.

Perceval sets off on his way and meets the knight Gornemant of Gohort. Gornemant trains Perceval in riding, jousting, and other knightly skills. He also advises Perceval to avoid overreadiness in speaking and asking questions.

Perceval sets off again to find his mother. En route he comes to a town defended by a castle. The damsel of the castle, called Blanchefleur (Gornemant's niece) tells Perceval that the castle is being besieged by King Clamadeu but that rather than yield to him she will slay herself. Perceval promises to help. They pass the night together "side by side and mouth to mouth."

Perceval overcomes both Engygeron, Clamadeu's marshall, and Clamadeu himself and sends them off to Arthur's court. He takes leave of Blanchefleur as he is anxious to see his mother. He comes to a river on which is a boat with two men in it fishing. One directs him to his castle, which is close at hand.

At first Perceval cannot see where the castle is; then he suddenly comes upon it and finds that it is large and splendid. Inside he finds a man with graying temples lying on a couch. The man apologizes for not rising to great Perceval but says he is unable to.

A squire enters bearing a sword, which has an engraving that says it can never be broken except in one particular perilous circumstance known only to its maker. The wounded man gives the sword to Perceval.

A bit later a youth comes out of a room holding a white lance from whose tip a drip of blood oozes. Two other youths appear holding pure gold candelabras. A damsel comes with the youths, holding a Grail of refined gold set with precious stones. After her follows another maiden holding a silver carving dish.

Perceval watches all of this but, mindful of Gornemant's instructions, refrains from asking about any of it, nor does he dare to ask who is served from the Grail. He resolves to wait until morning to inquire about it all. However, in the morning everyone has disappeared. He rides out of the castle hoping to find some of its occupants at hunt in the woods. The drawbridge starts to rise even before he has reached its end, and his horse has to jump to reach safety.

Perceval follows fresh tracks into the woods and comes upon a lamenting damsel with a dead knight in her lap. She turns out to be Perceval's cousin.

The damsel asks if Perceval has stayed with the rich fisher king, and when Perceval describes his overnight stay she confirms that it was the Grail Castle and the home of the fisher king. She explains that he was maimed in battle by a javelin striking him through both thighs. This wound still prevents him from mounting a horse and hunting. His only pleasure is to fish.

Then the damsel asks about what Perceval saw, and when she hears that he asked no questions about the Grail, she reproaches him, because if he had asked he would have brought relief to the suffering of the fisher king and to his land.

The damsel also tells Perceval that his mother has died. After this she asks where he got his sword from, and on being told, warns Perceval that it will fly to pieces in a great fight, and can only be reforged by its maker; moreover, finding his way to the lake where its maker resides could only be done with great hardship.

Meanwhile so many knights conquered by Perceval have shown up at Arthur's court that Arthur sets out with his whole court to find him. Perceval returns with them to court.

The whole night and the next day is spent in celebration of Perceval's deeds, until a hideous damsel appears and accuses Perceval of failing to ask about the Grail or "enquire what worthy man was served from it." If he had asked, the fisher king would have been healed and would peacefully rule his land: "of which he will now never hold any part. And do you know the fate of the king who will hold no land or be healed of his wounds? Through him ladies will lose their husbands, lands will be laid waste, maidens left orphaned and helpless, and many knights will perish: all these evils will be of your doing."

Perceval sets out immediately to find the Grail and ask about it. Fifty other knights also set off on various adventures, and the next part of Chrétien's tale is devoted to Gawain's exploits at the Proud Castle and elsewhere.

Eventually the tale returns to Perceval, who has wandered around for five years performing many feats. During this time, Perceval again appears to have forgotten the hag's instructions, because although he has pursued many deeds of chivalry he has forgotten to turn his mind to God. He meets ten ladies who are traveling on foot as a penance for their sins, since it is Good Friday. They are escorted by three knights. This company is surprised to see Perceval fully armed and oblivious to the holy occasion. Perceval learns that they have come from confessing their sins to a holy man that lives nearby. Having been brought to his senses by their rebuke, Perceval seeks out the hermit himself and confesses to having forgotten about God and to having failed to ask about the Grail. The hermit is Perceval's uncle; he gives Perceval absolution and furthermore explains to him that inside the inner room of the Grail Castle there lives another king and that it is this king who is served by the Grail.

Chrétien's tale then reverts to Gawain's adventures, and, the work being unfinished, we hear no more of Perceval.

In the three continuations of Chrétien's tale, many more adventures and wonders concerning both Gawain and Perceval are recounted. All three have the latter returning at some point to the Grail Castle, asking questions about the meaning and purpose of the Grail, and/or piecing together a broken sword. As a result, the fisher king is healed.

APPENDIX II

Some Different Meanings of
the Vesica Piscis Symbol

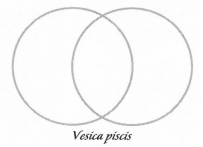

Vesica piscis

Heart
Grail chalice
Vulva, specifically of Mother God
Vulva surrounded by shapes of waxing and waning moon
Origin of fundamental shapes of sacred geometry
Fish
Union between inner and outer realms
Union between male and female
First division of fertilized cell
Egyptian glyph meaning "creator" and "mouth"
Similar to Mayan glyph meaning "zero" and associated with Milky Way
Mouth of the creator

Way Creator is differentiated, name of God, YHWH

Design of consciousness

Layout in Grail Castle of two inner rooms and banqueting hall

Fundamental shape that builds the "Seed of Life" and "Flower of Life" shapes (essentially formed by first 7 and then 13 combinations of vesicas), as found carved on columns in the extremely ancient Osirion Temple complex, 90 miles west of Luxor, Egypt

Electromagnetic field

Mandorla, Latin for almond

Place of shared ground between people

Shape of human eye, sense of "seeing eye to eye"

Christ consciousness, union of human and divine

Womb of Virgin Mary with Christ inside

Table of Correspondences Between Sword and Cup

SWORD	CHALICE
masculine	feminine
conscious mind	conscious heart
power/potency	presence
purpose	identity
outer	inner
action	being
phallus	womb
scepter	orb/crystal ball
wand	cauldron
sovereign	sovereignty
ruler	kingdom/stone
rod	cornucopia
individual	collective
cross/cross-over point	vesica piscis
1	0
alignment	union
instrument of Mother God	instrument of Father God
given and re-forged	found, lost and sought again
polarity	container
tools/principles	field/experience

Table of Correspondence Between Two Poles of God

MASCULINE	FEMININE
Father	Mother
Son	Daughter
Man	Woman
spirit	body
mind	heart
fire	water
air	earth
sword	cup
electrical	magnetic
)	(
rotational	counter-rotational
1 (binary) on	0 (binary) off
yang	yin
positive	negative
north	south
east	west
sovereign	magician
warrior	lover

APPENDIX III

Current Overview of the Ecological Wasteland

From the United Nations "Global Environmental Outlook 2000":

Full-scale emergencies now exist on a number of issues:

- The world water cycle seems unlikely to be able to cope with the demands that will be made of it in the coming decades.

- Land degradation has reduced fertility and agricultural potential. These losses have negated many of the advances made through expanding agricultural areas and increasing productivity.

- Tropical forest destruction has gone too far to prevent irreversible damage. It would take many generations to replace the lost forests, and the cultures that have been lost with them can never be replaced.

- Many of the planet's species have already been lost or condemned to extinction because of the slow response times of both the environment and policy-makers; it is too late to preserve all the biodiversity our planet once had.

- Many marine fisheries have been grossly over-exploited, and their recovery will be slow.

- More than half of the world's coral reefs are threatened by human activities. While some may yet be saved, it is too late for many others.

- Urban air pollution problems are reaching crisis dimensions in many of the mega-cities of the developing world, and the health of many urban dwellers has been impaired.

- It is probably too late to prevent global warming as a result of increased greenhouse gas emissions.

Global Environmental Outlook 2000 acknowledges the efforts being made to halt environmental deterioration but recognizes that many of these are too few and too late; signs of improvements are few and far between.

From the "State of the World Report 2000": "Every human being harbors in his or her body about 500 synthetic chemicals that were nonexistent before 1920."

From the United Nations Global Environment Outlook 3:

PAST, PRESENT AND FUTURE PERSPECTIVES
OUTLOOK 2002–2003

GEO-3 emphasizes that the next 30 years will be as crucial as the past 30 for shaping the future of the environment. Old troubles will persist and fresh challenges will emerge as increasingly heavy demands are placed upon resources that, in many cases, are already in a fragile state. The increasing pace of change and degree of interaction between regions and issues has made it more difficult than ever to look into the future with confidence. GEO-3 uses four scenarios to explore what the future could be, depending on different policy approaches. The scenarios, which span developments in many overlapping areas, including population, economics, technology and governance, are described below. They are:

Markets First:
Most of the world adopts the values and expectations prevailing in today's industrialized countries. The wealth of nations and the optimal play of market forces dominate social and political agendas. Trust is placed in further globalization and liberalization to enhance corporate wealth, create new enterprises and livelihoods, and so help people and communities to afford to insure against—or pay to fix—social and environmental problems. Ethical investors, together with citizen and consumer groups, try to exercise growing corrective influence but are undermined by economic imperatives. The powers of state officials, planners and lawmakers to regulate society, economy and the environment continue to be overwhelmed by expanding demands.

Policy First:
Decisive initiatives are taken by governments in an attempt to reach specific social and environmental goals. A coordinated proenvironment and anti-poverty drive balances the momentum for economic development at any cost. Environmental and social costs and gains are factored into policy measures, regulatory frameworks and planning processes. All these are reinforced by fiscal levers or incentives such as carbon taxes and tax breaks. International "soft law" treaties and binding instruments affecting environment and development are integrated into unified blueprints and their status in law is upgraded, though fresh provision is made for open consultation processes to allow for regional and local variants.

Security First:
This scenario assumes a world of striking disparities where inequality and conflict prevail. Socio-economic and environmental stresses give rise to waves of protest and counteraction. As such troubles become increasingly prevalent, the more powerful and wealthy groups focus on self-protection, creating enclaves akin to the present day "gated communities." Such islands of advantage provide a degree of enhanced security and economic benefits for dependent communities in their immediate surroundings but they exclude the disadvantaged mass of outsiders. Welfare and regulatory services fall into disuse but market forces continue to operate outside the walls.

Sustainability First:
A new environment and development paradigm emerges in response to the challenge of sustainability, supported by new, more equitable values and institutions. A more visionary state of affairs prevails, where radical shifts in the

way people interact with one another and with the world around them stimulate and support sustainable policy measures and accountable corporate behavior. There is much fuller collaboration between governments, citizens and other stakeholder groups in decision-making on issues of close common concern. A consensus is reached on what needs to be done to satisfy basic needs and realize personal goals without beggaring others or spoiling the outlook for posterity.

Environmental implications:
Some of the global and regional environmental implications arising out of the four scenarios are highlighted below.

The absence of effective policies to reduce emissions of carbon dioxide and other greenhouse gases in the Markets First and Security First scenarios leads to significant increases over the next 30 years. However, the policy actions taken under a Policy First scenario, notably carbon taxes and investments in non-fossil-fuel energy sources, effectively curb growth in global emissions and lead to actual reductions starting around 2030. The behavioral shifts under Sustainability First, together with improved production and conversion efficiencies, result in a rapid levelling off of emissions and a decline by the middle of the 2020s.

Infrastructure affects 72 per cent of the world's land area by the year 2032 under a Markets First scenario.

—Source: GLOBIO

. . .

Biodiversity will continue under threat if there is no strenuous policy action to curb human activity. Continued urban and infrastructure expansion, plus the increased impacts of climate change, severely deplete biodiversity in most regions in all scenarios. Pressures will also increase on coastal ecosystems in most regions and scenarios.

The scenarios carry important implications for the provision of basic human needs. Growing populations and increased economic activity, particularly in agriculture, will lead to increased demand for freshwater in most scenarios. Similarly, the demands for food and the ability to meet them in the different scenarios reflect a combination of shifts in supply and demand, influenced by social, economic and environmental policies. In Markets First, even with a decrease in the percentage of the population facing hunger, the total number affected changes relatively little and even increases in some regions as populations grow. Under Policy First and Sustainability First the targeting of hunger reduction as a key goal, and the emphasis on more balanced development be-

tween regions, help to achieve dramatic reductions in the percentages and total numbers of people affected. The sharp increases in most regions in Security First points to the unsustainability of such a scenario in terms of social
acceptability.

In Africa, there is increasing risk of land degradation. In Policy First and
Sustainability First, easier access to support services helps farmers to manage
soils better and policies based on integrated land management become com-
monplace in the region. At the other end of the spectrum, in a Security First
scenario, while reasonable conditions are maintained in the protected areas
serving the land-owning elite, the high concentration of people elsewhere
contribute to severe land degradation and soil erosion. Similar problems arise
in Markets First as better quality agricultural land is taken over for commodity
and cash crop production.

Under the Markets First scenario in Asia and the Pacific, water withdrawals are expected to increase in all sectors, leading to an expansion of areas
with severe water stress in South and Southeast Asia. Slower economic growth
under Security First tempers growth in demand. With effective policies and
lifestyle changes under the Policy First and Sustainability First scenarios, water
withdrawals remain at current levels or even decrease in most of the region.

The ability of Europe to address the issues of large-scale air pollution and
greenhouse gas emissions will depend heavily upon developments in the areas of
energy use and transportation. Extremely active policies to improve public transportation and energy efficiency can be expected in Policy First and Sustainability First worlds, but not in Security First or even Markets First circumstances.

Land and forest degradation as well as forest fragmentation remain among
the most relevant environmental issues in Latin America and the Caribbean in
all scenarios. Significant loss of forest area occurs in a Markets First scenario.
In a Security First world, the control over forest resources by transnational
companies that create cartels in association with the national groups in power,
promotes the growth of some forest areas, but this is not enough to stop net
deforestation. More effective management ameliorates some of these problems
in Policy First. Unsound deforestation stops almost completely in a world of
Sustainability First.

—Source: WaterGAP 2.1

*   *   *

As the world's biggest emitter of greenhouse gases, North America plays a major role in determining the future climate of the planet. In Markets First, the

region's refusal to participate significantly hampers international efforts to control the emissions of these gases, and per capita and absolute emissions remain high. The collapse of parts of the transport infrastructure and restrictions on fossil-fuel vehicle ownership in Security First result in even greater increases in emissions in this scenario. Under Policy First, emissions are reduced through increased fuel efficiency and greater use of public transport but most spectacular results are achieved in Sustainability First.

West Asia is one of the most water-stressed regions of the world, with more than 70 million people living in areas under severe water stress. Under the Markets First and Security First scenarios, population and economic growth lead to strong increases in withdrawals for households and industry, resulting in an increase in areas with severe water stress and affecting over 200 million people by 2032. A range of policy initiatives help to counteract additional demands related to economic growth in both Policy First and Sustainability First. Although total withdrawals drop in both scenarios, water scarcity persists and demand continues to exceed available water resources. (When more than 40 per cent of the renewable water resources of a river basin are being withdrawn for human use the river basin is considered to be under severe water stress.)

Fish and other marine stocks are a key area of concern in the polar regions. Under Markets First, massive increase in commercial harvesting and abandonment of targeted fisheries leads to some fish populations crashing. Illegal, unregulated and unreported fishing activities cease in Security First under direct pressure from powerful regulatory interests, but controlled exploitation rises to very high levels. Total collapse of any single fishery is averted under Policy First by enforcement of stringent harvesting quotas and other regulatory systems. In Sustainability First, fish and marine mammals are rigorously defended against overexploitation.

The environmental implications of the various scenarios illustrate the legacy of past decades and the level of effort that will be needed to reverse powerful trends. One of the major policy lessons from the scenarios is that there can be significant delays between changes in human behavior, including policy choices, and their environmental impacts, specifically:

- Much of the environmental change that will occur over the next 30 years has already been set in motion by past and current actions.

- Many of the effects of environmentally relevant policies put into place over the next 30 years will not be apparent until long afterwards.

NOTES

1. KING ARTHUR AND THE GRAIL KING

I Ching, translated by Richard Wilhelm and Cary F. Baynes (London: Routledge & Kegan Paul, 1984). Martin Exeter, "The One Law," in *Third Sacred School* (Loveland, Colo.: Emissaries of Divine Light, 1975), vol. 1, p. 134.

Introduction to Milton's "Paradise Lost," edited by Alastair Fowler (London: Longman, 1971), p. 35.

Chrétien de Troyes, "Perceval," in *Arthurian Romances,* translated by D.D.R. Owen (London: Everyman, 1993).

Robert Bly, *Iron John* (Shaftesbury, Dorset, U.K.: Element, 1990), pp. 109, 111.

Sogyal Rinpoche, *The Tibetan Book of Living and Dying* (London: Rider Books, 1992), pp. 137–38.

For a more detailed account of the use of straight lines in ancient architecture and landscape see Paul Devereux, *Shamanism and the Mystery Lines* (U.K.: Quantum, 1992).

See William Howells, *The Heathen* (New York: Doubleday, 1948), on the power of "mana" in the chief/king, quoted in Devereux, *Shamanism and the Mystery Lives.*

Mercea Eliade, *Shamanism: Archaic Techniques of Ecstasy* (1951; Princeton, N.J.: Princeton University Press, 1964), quoted in Devereux, *Shamanism and the Mystery Lives,* p. 173.

Paul Devereux, *Earth Memory* (U.K.: Quantum, 1991), p. 241.

Michael Harner (ed.) *Hallucinogens and Shamanism* (Oxford: Oxford University Press, 1973), quoted in Devereux, *Shamanism and the Mystery Lives,* p. 100.

See Devereux, *Shamanism and the Mystery Lives,* on the shamanic use of trance.

Harold Bailey, *Archaic England* (London: Chapman & Hall, 1919), quoted in Devereux, *Shamanism and the Mystery Lives,* p. 102.

2. THE SPIRAL QUEST

W. B. Yeats, "Vacillation," in *The Collected Works of W. B. Yeats,* vol. 1, edited by Richard J. Finneran (New York: Macmillan, 1972).

References to the Grail story in this chapter and throughout this book are drawn from the following different versions: "Elucidations," a "prologue" that is sometimes attached to Chrétien de Troyes's "Perceval; the Story of the Grail"; Chrétien de Troyes's "Perceval"; the Story of the Grail" (unfinished); Continuation 1 of "Perceval" by Gautier de Doulens; Continuation 2 by Manessier; Continuation 3 by Gerbert Wolfram von Eschenbach; Heinrich von dem Türlin, "The Gawain Episodes of Diu Crône"; the "Petit Saint Graal" or "Didot Perceval"; "The Mabinogi of Peredur ab Evrawc"; "Sir Perceval of Galles," Thornton ms.; "The Queste del Saint Graal"; "Grand St Graal"; Robert de Boron's poem "Joseph of Arimathea."

A useful summary of these stories is found in *Studies on the Legend of the Holy Grail with Special Reference to the Hypothesis of its Celtic Origin* by Alfred Nutt (London: Folk-Lore Society, 1888).

The quotations are from Chrétien de Troyes, "Perceval," in *Arthurian Romances,* translated by D.D.R. Owen (London: Everyman, 1993).

T. S. Eliot "The Dry Salvages," in *Four Quartets* (London: Faber & Faber, 1943), p. 71.

3. THE FISH, THE CUP, AND THE ANATOMY OF THE WOUND

Lloyd Meeker, *The Divine Design of Man* (U.S.A.: Universal Institute of Applied Ontology, 1952).

Joseph Chilton Pearce, *Magical Child* (New York: Plume, 1992), p. 123.

The following books offer background on the origins and meaning of the fish symbol, the Wounded Fisher King and the Grail chalice: Emma Jung and Marie-Louse von Franz, *The Grail Legend* (Boston: Sigo Press, 1986); Jesse L. Weston, *The Quest of the Holy Grail* (London: G. Bell, 1913), and *From Ritual to Romance* (Princeton, N.J.: Princeton University Press, 1920); Arthur C. L. Brown, *Origin of the Grail Legend* (Cambridge, Mass.: Harvard University Press, 1943); Helaine Newstead, *Bran the Blessed in Arthurian Romance* (New York: Columbia University Press, 1939); Sir James Frazer, *The Golden Bough* (New York: Macmillan, 1932); Roger Sherman Loomis, ed., *The Grail* (Princeton, N.J.: Princeton University Press, 1991); Roger Sherman Loomis, ed., *Arthurian Literature in the Middle Ages* (Oxford: Clarendon Press of the Oxford University Press, 1959); and James Douglas Bruce *The Evolution of Arthurian Romance* vols. 1–2 (Baltimore: John Hopkins University Press, 1923).

For further detail about the significance of the vesica piscis in sacred geometry and mystical traditions, see: Paul Devereux, *Earth Memory* (U.K.: Quantum, 1991); John Michell, *The Dimensions of Paradise* (London: Thames & Hudson, 1988); and Keith Critchlow, *Time Stands Still* (London: Gordon Fraser, 1979).

A book that also helped start my thought process about the Grail story is Robert Johnson's *He: Understanding Masculine Psychology* (New York: Harper & Row, 1977).

Lama Anagarika Govinda, *Foundations of Tibetan Mysticism* (Boston: Red Wheel, 1989).

Robert Heinberg, *Memories and Visions of Paradise* (New York: Putnam, 1989), p. 91.

References to Epipaleothic and Neolithic settlements is from Riane Isler, *The Chalice and the Blade* (San Francisco: HarperCollins, 1988).

4. THE FISHER KING AND THE DOUBLE WOUND

Jonathan Hanaghan, *Forging Passion Into Power* (Dublin: Runa Press, 1981), pp. 40, 41, 52.

Art Kleiner, *Who Really Matters: The Core Group Theory of Power, Privilege and Success* (New York: Doubleday, 2003).

On tigers and corruptions, see *Economist,* March 1998.

For background on Ceausescu's "rule" in Romania see Mark Almond, *Decline without Fall: Romania under Ceausescu,* European Security Studies no. 6

(London: Institute for European Defence and Strategic Studies, 1988), pp. 13–14.

David Bohm, *Unfolding Meaning* (Loveland, Colo.: Foundation House, 1985), p. 153.

Churchill's comments about democracy from his speech to the House of Commons, London, Hansard, November 11, 1947: "Many forms of Government have been tried, and will be tried in this world of sin and woe. No one pretends that democracy is perfect or all-wise. Indeed, it has been said that democracy is the worst form of Government, except for all those other forms that have been tried from time to time."

Aleksandr I. Solzhenitsyn *The Gulag Archipelago,* vols. 1–2 translated by Thomas P. Whitney (New York: Harper and Row, 1973), pp. 69–70.

Gitta Sereny, *Into That Darkness* (London: Picador, 1974).

Gitta Sereny, *Albert Speer: His Battle with Truth* (London: Picador, 1996).

James Morris, *Pax Britannica,* vol. 3 (New York: Harcourt Brace, 1968), p. 139.

James Frazer, *The Golden Bough,* quoted in Paul Devereux, *Shamanism and the Mystery of Lines* (U.K.: Quantum, 1991), pp. 114–15.

5. THE WASTELAND

Diagram of seven levels of being after Lloyd Meeker, *The Divine Design of Man* (U.S.A.: Universal Institute of Applied Ontology, 1952).

Lama Anagarika Govinda, quoted in Paul Devereux, *Earth Memory* (U.K.: Quantum, 1991), p. 227.

Jalaluddin Rumi quatrain 158, in *Open Secret,* translated by John Moyne and Coleman Barks (U.S.A.: Threshold Books, 1984).

See Daniel Jonah Goldhagen, *Hitler's Willing Executioners* (New York: Abacus, 1997), p. 8, for the history and background context for the "ordinary" German citizens during the Holocaust.

Aleksandr I. Solzhenitsyn, *The Gulag Archipelago,* vols. 1–2 (New York: Harper and Row, 1973), p. 168.

For information about nuclear pollution in the former Soviet Union and modern–day Russia, see online: www.antiatom.ru/entext/o20926ap.htmeco bridge.org/content/n wst.htm#mayak and www.monitor.net/monitor/9807a/karachai.html.

Excerpt from John Robbins *Diet for a New America* (Santa Cruz, Calif.: Stillpoint, 1987; Novato, Calif.: New World Library), pp. 53, 88, 110, 111.

6. THE QUESTION AND THE UNTRIED SWORD

D. H. Lawrence, "Seekers," in *The Complete Poems of D. H. Lawrence,* edited by Angelo Ravagli and C. M. Weekley (New York: Viking, 1971).

All quotes from the Grail story in this chapter from Chrétien de Troyes, "Perceval," in *Arthurian Romances,* translated by D.D.R. Owen (London: Everyman, 1993).

Joseph Campbell, *The Hero with a Thousand Faces* (Princeton, N.J.: Princeton University Press, 1949), p. 17.

7. BLESSINGS OF THE GRAIL

Joseph Campbell, *The Hero with a Thousand Faces* (Princeton, N.J.: Princeton University Press, 1949).

T. S. Eliot, "The Dry Salvages," in *Four Quartets* (London: Faber and Faber, 1970).

Diagrams of "mountain" after Lloyd Meeker, *The Divine Design of Man* (U.S.A.: Universal Institute of Applied Ontology, 1952).

Campbell, *The Hero with a Thousand Faces,* pp. 193, 216, 217, 218.

9. OUT OF STONE INTO WATER

Diana Durham, "Ante-Natal Circle," in *Defined Providence,* fall/winter 1993.

Tennyson quotations from "Morte D'Arthur" in *Selected Poems,* edited by Edmund Blunden (London: Heinemann, 1977).

For the names of spiritual leaders emerging and teaching in the East around the 1930s, I am indebted to Yujin Pak's material from his spiritual education course, "The Deepening"; see online: www.emissaries.org.

The Malory quotation is from *King Arthur and his Knights: Selected Tales by Sir Thomas Malory,* edited by Eugene Vinaver (Oxford: Oxford University Press, 1975).

The Gospel of Thomas, verse 70, the Nag Hammadi Library, translated by Stephen Patterson and Marvin Meyer.

Billy Joel, "The Great Wall of China," from the CD *River of Dreams* (Columbia).

Victor Frankl, *Man's Search for Meaning* (Boston: Beacon Press, 2000).

For more information about the mysterious alignments of Newgrange, see Martin Brennan, *The Stars and the Stones* (London: Thames and Hudson, 1983).

10. GUINEVERE'S GIFT

Tennyson, "Morte D'Arthur," in *Selected Poems,* edited by Edmund Blunden (London: Heinemann, 1977).

Joseph Campbell, *The Hero with a Thousand Faces* (Princeton, N.J.: Princeton University Press, 1949), p. 263.

The Quest of the Holy Grail, edited by Pauline Maud Matarasso (London: Penguin Classics, 1969).

11. THE CHALICE OF COLLECTIVE SOVEREIGNTY

Tennyson, "Morte D'Arthur," in *Selected Poems,* edited by Edmund Blunden (London: Heinemann, 1977).

Robert McNamara, *In Retrospect: The Tragedy and Lessons of Vietnam* (New York: Random House, 1997), p. 203.

Michael J Sandel, "America's Search for a New Public Philosophy," in *Atlantic Monthly,* March 1996, pp. 73–74.

Jalaluddin Rumi, quatrain 158, in *Open Secret,* translated by John Moyne and Coleman Barks (U.S.A.: Threshold Books, 1984).

The Quest of the Holy Grail, edited by Pauline Maud Matarasso (London: Penguin Classics, 1969).

12. DAUGHTER OF GOD

Jean Shinoda Bolen, *Goddesses in Everywoman* (San Francisco: Harper Colophon, 1985).

Robert Moore and Douglas Gillette, *King, Warrior, Magician, Lover* (San Francisco: HarperSanFrancisco, 1991).

Cliff Barry and Mary Ellen Blandford conduct Shadow Work Seminars Inc.; see online: www.shadowwork.com.

David Bohm, "The Enfolding-Unfolding Universe: A Conversation with David Bohm," conducted by Renee Weber, in *The Holographic Paradigm,* edited by Ken Wilber (Boston: Shambhalam, 1982), pp. 72, 74.

David Bohm, from *Unfolding Meaning* (U.K.: Foundation House, 1985), p. 175.

William Isaacs, *Dialogue and the Art of Thinking Together* (New York: Doubleday, 1999), p. 285.

Raphael Patai, *The Hebrew Goddess* (Detroit: Wayne State University Press, 1990), p. 28; passage from the *Zohar* quoted on p. 117.

13. THE DANCE

The Essential Margaret Fuller, edited by Jeffrey Steele (New Brunswick, N.J.: Rutgers University Press, 1992).

Diana Durham, "The Arc," in the *Portsmouth (N.H.) Herald,* April 26, 2003.

All the quotes from the King Arthur stories in this chapter are drawn from Thomas Malory, *Le Morte D'Arthur,* edited by R. M. Lumiansky (New York: Macmillan, 1986).

Gregg Braden, *Awakening to Zero Point: The Collective Initiation* (U.S.A.: Ancient Wisdom, 1994).

Lloyd Meeker, *The Divine Design of Man* (U.S.A.: Universal Institute of Applied Ontology, 1952), p. 6.

William Blake, preface to "Milton" in *Complete Writings,* edited by Geoffrey Keynes (Oxford: Oxford Paperbacks, 1974).

Philip Larkin, "Dockery and Son," in *The Whitsun Wedding* (London: Faber and Faber, 1973).

Sylvia Plath, "The Moon and the Yew Tree," in *Ariel* (San Francisco: Harper Colophon, 1966).

The quotations from the Grail story in this chapter are from Chrétien de Troyes, "Perceval," in *Arthurian Romances,* translated by D.D.R. Owen (London: Everyman, 1992).

APPENDIX III

The full text of the United Nation's publication "Global Environment Outlook" for 2000 and 2003 can be read on the following websites: for 2000, see www.grida.no/geo2000/ov-e/0012.htm; for 2003, see www.unep.org/geo/geo3/english/overview/o21.htm.

PERMISSIONS

ACKNOWLEDGMENTS

The insights of this book are set within the larger architecture of Lloyd Meeker's and Martin Exeter's thought and vision. These two men's lives and words formed the primary source of inspiration and mentorship for my own growth and understanding, and I remain profoundly thankful to have had the privilege of knowing them and their work.

However, I have been blessed with an abundance of nourishment from a virtual army of other mentors, "God-parents," and friends as well, in particular Nancy Rose Meeker (the first "Daughter" I ever met), Michael Cecil, Fred and Valerie Traff, Penny Nickels, Manning Glicksohn, George Emery, Bill Bahan, Alan and Jean Hammond, Roger and Dorothy de Winton, Lillian Cecil, Grace Van Duzen, Jim Wellemeyer, Rupert Maskell, Tessa Maskell, Serena Newby, John Gray, and Graeme and Genoa Castell. The inspiration, loving guidance, and patience of all these, as well as many other friends too numerous to name, formed the regenerative ground for my own emotional and spiritual emergence, without which this book could not have been written.

John Kurk's early encouragement of me when these ideas were in their forming stages was a crucial part of the process. Carolyn Askar and Pat Parnell were kind enough to read and give feedback on early drafts of the book; Astrid Bjolo's efforts and input took the manuscript to the next stage; and Bruce Allyn's feedback helped refine the finished draft. Bill Isaacs's loving friendship, complementary insights, help, and whole field of understanding have been essential.

The insightful friendship and encouragement of David Reis, Paul Price, and Jude Repar have also been a central part of the context in which this book has emerged.

I am also grateful to my friends Jody Isaacs, Tom Cooper, and Dennis Brown for letting me unload some of my thoughts in their wise company; and to Cliff Penwell, Jay Ramsay, Suki Casanave, and Hugh Malafry for thoughts and help along the way.

The friendship and support of Liz Doucette and Ea Ksander has helped form a context for clarifying still evolving ideas; and I am thankful to all those friends, particularly from my women's group, who have listened with both interest and at times bafflement as I have attempted to disentangle the thoughts in my head.

I am grateful to Joel Fotinos at Tarcher for letting this book have life, and have enjoyed and found helpful the intelligent and sympathetic additions of Allison Sobel as well as the plainspoken input of Art Kleiner. I am also grateful to Sarah Jane Freymann, my agent. Thanks also to John Flood, Katy Barchie, my brother Dick Durham, Addie Rule, Pat Frisella, and Yarrow Cleaves for help and research details.

Nothing is more essential to a mother of young children who also needs to write than reliable childcare, and special thanks are due to Jill Grobe and Barbara Mulkern, whose generous provision of safe and loving homes from home played a central part in this book coming into form.

I have great appreciation and gratitude for the steady and innocent environment that my parents Richard and Nancy Durham provided for my growing up; their efforts, along with those of others of their generation, were foundational to the great collective promise of our times.

My love and thanks to Jon, who gave me—at times against difficult odds—both the literal and emotional space without which it would have been impossible to write this book. His love and his practical input and listening ear have also been essential ingredients for the process.

Finally my deep love and gratitude for my daughter Raphael and my son Aidyn, whose sweet and life-bringing presences have helped earth me while I worked in the invisible realm of essences and thought.

—Portsmouth, New Hampshire
May 2003

INDEX